Explaining the Unexplained

Unexplained

Stephen Ellis

iUniverse, Inc.
Bloomington

iUniverse books may be ordered through booksellers or by contacting:

iUniverse
1663 Liberty Drive
Bloomington, IN 47403
www.iuniverse.com
1-800-Authors (1-800-288-4677)

Because of the dynamic nature of the Internet, any web addresses or links contained in this book may have changed since publication and may no longer be valid. The views expressed in this work are solely those of the author and do not necessarily reflect the views of the publisher, and the publisher hereby disclaims any responsibility for them.

Any people depicted in stock imagery provided by Thinkstock are models, and such images are being used for illustrative purposes only.

Certain stock imagery © Thinkstock.

ISBN: 978-1-4502-9806-3 (sc)
ISBN: 978-1-4502-9805-6 (hc)
ISBN: 978-1-4502-9804-9 (ebook)

Printed in the United States of America

Library of Congress Control Number: 2011903059

iUniverse rev. date: 09/22/2011

TABLE OF CONTENTS

PROLOGUE

Sometime around 1979, I had occasion to move to San Francisco to do some work. Inasmuch as I was going to be there for at least six months, rather than check into a hotel room for that length of time, I rented a furnished apartment in a large complex on Dolores Street in the Mission District. The apartment was small, but it had a living room, a bedroom and a kitchen, a lot of amenities…and it was furnished.

The first night I was there, I awakened feeling extremely uncomfortable. It was about 2 AM. I opened my eyes, and in the corner of my bedroom I saw a girl standing with her arms folded in front of her looking directly at me. I saw her with such clarity that I could tell she was a blonde girl with shoulder-length hair in a kind of pageboy hairdo, and she was wearing a beige pantsuit. She was somewhere between the ages of twenty and twenty five and quite attractive. It's somewhat amazing that in a darkened room I could see her that clearly, but, obviously, I did.

Not that I normally object to finding a pretty girl in my bedroom, it was both startling and somewhat frightening to see a stranger in my bedroom at 2 AM. I immediately asked her who she was and what did she want. She said nothing but continued to look at me.

I turned away for less than a second and switched on the lamp on my night stand…and she was gone! I searched the apartment thoroughly and found no trace of anyone.

After shaking my head a few times to be certain I was awake, I assumed that, being in a strange place, perhaps I had awakened in a semi-sleeping state while still dreaming or some such thing. I have occasionally had a dream that lingered as I slowly awakened. I thought this was the case and, in any event, I wrote it completely off my mind.

Now let's fast-forward: In San Francisco, there are probably no more than five or ten days a year when the skies are clear and the weather is warm and friendly. Almost three weeks after the experience in my bedroom, San Francisco had such a day, and just about everyone in the entire apartment complex was out by the rarely used swimming pool. It was a Sunday, so like just about everyone else in the complex, I had to take advantage of a day like that. I donned my swim trunks and joined the crowd of apartment residents at the poolside. I was going to bask in the sun and soak up some rays.

This being San Francisco, a young, somewhat effeminate, man named Derek started to talk to me. I'm not gay, but then neither am I homophobic. We started talking and, inasmuch as I did not have many friends in the Bay Area, it was nice having someone to talk with. It was obvious that Derek was one of the gay body-builders I'd heard so much about.

I commented on his excellent physique, and he must've taken it as a sign of encouragement, because he excused himself, ran back to his apartment, and returned with a stack of photographs he had posed for on another fine day by the poolside. They were pictures of himself flexing his muscles. Derek insisted that I look at them. As he went through them one at a time, I suddenly bolted upright and cried "stop"! There, in the background of a photo of Derek were two girls just walking by...but one of them was the girl I had seen in my bedroom. She was wearing a bikini swimsuit and not a beige pantsuit, but there was no doubt, whatsoever. It was the same girl.

I asked my astonished new friend, "Who's that girl?" and pointed to her.

He looked at me and said "That's Leanne Polski, she used to live in your apartment."

My next question was automatic: "Where is she now?"

The expression on Derek's face grew dark. "Didn't they tell you when you rented the apartment?.....She was murdered by her boyfriend in that apartment a few weeks before you moved in."

So...what was it that I saw that first night? Is that what they call a ghost?

Before going into the explanation of what it was that I saw and whether it was a "dream" or a "ghost", the incident had a remarkable affect on my life: I immediately started to go to the library and research what I could find on "ghosts". The internet had not yet become the super-highway of information it is now. What I found was a ton of unsubstantiated material that apparently was written by people with vivid imaginations.

It's not that there was not some excellent material…there was some good reading. But at least 90% of it was fiscally-inspired trash and "cult" material. Almost all of the available material about ghosts and life-after-death were written by people with their own agendas offering to communicate with the dead for a fee or join a group of believers…for a fee, etc. The thing that piqued my interest was that many of the tales and/or so-called explanations of ghosts or life-after-death were intertwined with stories concerning mind-body separation, reincarnation, psychic phenomena, mediums, people who claimed to be able to talk with the dead, etc. None of what I read really explained any of these paranormal things in terms that I could understand or even approach in a logical way.

Then and there I decided the time had come for someone to look at these things through eyes that were not controlled by a church, a cult or some money-making organization. I felt that if I examined these things objectively, I might be able to find some logical explanations or, at least apply some common sense to them.

My very nature is such that I have never feared the unknown. Perhaps I could begin to blaze a trail that would lead others to understanding of some of life's mysteries.

That's what this book is about: things we hear about and read about for which we have had no genuine or rational explanation. As my research revealed, much of the so-called "paranormal" has logical explanations backed by strong empirical and circumstantial evidence.

It is understood that no amount of evidence will alter the thinking of some people. My father always used to say, "If you do not believe something, no amount of proof will convince you. If you do believe something, no proof is necessary."

Chapter 1

Questions all Around Us

Ever ask yourself, "Is there really a God?" Ever wonder about flying saucers and UFOs...or think, perhaps, that the Air Force may be suppressing information to the public? Ever wonder if you've ever lived before ...or maybe wonder what really happens when you die? What about these TV psychics and people who claim to be able to talk to the dead? Are they for real? How did we get to be living on a little ball in the middle of deep space? Have so-called "faith healers" actually cured incurable diseases without medicine?

Our world is replete with unexplained things: Millions of questions are asked every day about such things as religion, ghosts, UFOs, paranormal phenomena, our very place in the cosmos, etc. The answers we're often given to many of these questions may sound reasonable at first glance, but when you start to look at them closely, the term "reasonable" no longer applies. In fact, some of the answers we get to our questions defy our common sense, but we accept those answers because we have no place else to go...no place to even look.

It's normal to question things about subjects such as the creation of the world, or our place in the cosmos. As teen-agers, didn't we all search the sky at night and ask ourselves questions about the beginnings of the Earth or whether there is life on other planets somewhere in our cosmos? Most of our parents and teachers gave us simple answers. But as we matured, some of those answers began to sound pretty far out and just didn't hold water. We ask questions about God and religion and we get answers that aren't answers at all: "God moves in mysterious ways." It would be easy to go on and on, but the fact is that we are being fed a lot of so-called information and answers that don't make sense. The thing that makes the situation even more difficult is that the information we are being fed comes from the people who profess to be experts.

It's only natural to want to believe people who purportedly have the educational and work background in specific subjects when we seek answers to our questions: That's why we ask the physician about medical things; we ask the attorney about legal matters; we ask astronomers and NASA scientists about our cosmos; we ask our priest, cleric or rabbi about God and religion; etc. We tend to accept their answers as being true... until common sense makes us realize that a lot of what the experts have said is just not logical. In order to get better answers, we must take what the experts have told us and then start thinking for ourselves. If you really want answers that make sense and can be backed-up, we have to look at areas in which there are no experts.

I will be the first to admit that minds, far more highly trained than my own, have tried to offer plausible explanations of happenings that we don't understand, usually under the guise of being scientifically correct. But, as our knowledge of physics, astronomy, medicine, and in fact all fields that we loosely call the sciences, has expanded, we have begun to realize that no science is exact nor can it be relied upon as much as we might like it to be.

WHAT SCIENCE DOESN'T KNOW

The fields that we refer to as the sciences are, in large part, not scientific at all. They are merely theories. Some scientists put their endorsement on it and we are supposed to accept it as scientific fact. I'm not challenging things like chemistry or biology and other sciences that can be tested and proven in a lab. I'm talking about the so-called scientific theories that come out of astronomy, medicine, nutrition and physics. Physics, more than any other science, pretends to be the most exacting of the sciences.

Even the theories of physics have been forced to change as physics expands into areas physicists didn't even know existed slightly more than fifty years ago: Things like nuclear physics, quantum mechanics and astrophysics, to name just a few.

There are many times during my lifetime and most readers' lifetimes that science has "changed its mind" from one dogmatic opinion and come up with what they feel is a better, dogmatic opinion…only to change their minds again a few years later.

Probably the most simple examples of science changing its mind can be found in the food we eat: Just think back to how many times "science" has told us that certain foods are "good for us" or "bad for us"…then done a complete reversal. It was not that long ago when scientists told us that tomatoes were a poisonous fruit. More recently we were told that white sugar will kill us…that we should use sugar substitutes. Then we were told that the sugar substitute, saccharine, causes cancer. Then we were told not to eat eggs (one of nature's most perfect foods) because the yolk is pure cholesterol. Then we were told to eat lots of fish…then not to eat fish because it's loaded with mercury. I'm certain you can think of several more without my help. Right now, the current fad in medicine is cholesterol… HDL (good cholesterol) and LDL (bad cholesterol). A few years ago, most medical journals universally published reports that all cholesterol was bad for you and your heart.

Science certainly has its place. Medical science has helped most people live longer and better lives. But it is a very big mistake for us to accept science as offering the definitive answers. Even the term "scientific" connotes accuracy. To most people, something scientific is generally accepted as representing facts and accuracy; something not to be challenged. Actually, nothing could be further from the truth. I could fill this entire book with "scientific" inaccuracies. There are answers out there, and not all of them are scientific.

The term "paranormal" immediately implies the exact opposite of "scientific"; something that lives only in theories and in people's imaginations. In the past fifty years, some of the world's finest scientists (including Albert Einstein) have recognized that some paranormal things may have a sound scientific basis and offer answers to questions that have puzzled science for years.

Scientists can tell you a lot about your physical body; how it functions and how it will react under specified conditions. When your body stops working, science says that you are dead. But is that all there is to life? Your physical body? What about all those thoughts of love…of dreams of visiting strange new places…or being able to solve a problem you are anticipating. Obviously, these things are not contained in the physical body…so, by logical deduction, they must emanate from someplace outside of the body.

Skeptics are always calling for "scientific proof" of anything we call paranormal. But the fact is that there is no scientific proof of anything except things that repeatedly get the same results in lab tests. Show me any scientific proof that explains why we live on a little ball in the middle of nothingness that keeps rotating and revolving about a star at the same rate year after year. What science offers as "proof" are simply theories that sound logical.

As someone who had decided to take on the task of explaining the unexplained, I conducted a non-scientific search for the truth about paranormal phenomena using common sense and logic. Logical answers to questions science has been unable to answer, or about which science has given us unreasonable answers. I'm certain there will be many readers who will disagree with me for trying to use simple logic or common sense to challenge our noble institutions of science. But, if coming up with a theory or two that offers reasonable answers to questions that have plagued humanity since man was created, then I plead "guilty". There is no hard, scientific, evidence for the theories set forth in this book, but then, there is really no hard, scientific, evidence to support some of science's favorite theories, either. There is, however, very strong circumstantial or empirical evidence to support the content of this book.

You may not agree with what I've written in this book because it is original thought. Albert Einstein once said, "For every human who has an original or different thought, there will be a hundred people who will try to destroy that thought and the person from whom the thought originated".

SCIENTIFIC AND EMPIRICAL PROOF

In a court trial, the best evidence is called forensic evidence. Things that can be proven in the lab; the "scientific proof". When forensic evidence is unavailable, both the prosecution and the defense will use what is called "circumstantial" or "empirical" evidence. If the circumstantial evidence is strong enough, the case becomes believable. When the circumstantial evidence provides logical or reasonable answers to "unanswerable" questions…and makes sense…then no matter how far-out those answers may initially seem…serious consideration must be given to them. Both judges and juries routinely convict and/or acquit people based on circumstantial or empirical evidence.

This book will provide answers…logical answers to a thousand unanswerable questions, inexplicable happenings, etc. Not only will the circumstantial evidence be strong, but we will find the evidence opens the doors to a lot of things that science has failed to explain. Many of the world's mysteries will fall neatly into place.

When we were children, and our mother told us that the stork brought us, we believed it. As we got a little older we realized that the "stork theory" didn't hold water. Soon we learned that we came from our mother's stomachs, and a little later we learned how we got there.

Getting a little more complex, when we were very young, most parents taught us about God and made us say our prayers at night. As we got a little older we were imbued with religious training. As we matured, we began to question some of the things in the Bible: How could Noah get two of every living creature into one ark? What kind of a giant fish could swallow Jonah whole and then, a few days later, spew him out still in one piece? Perhaps we began to wonder why God let our dear Aunt Heather die when she was so young and always so good to everyone. Maybe some of us began to question the very existence of an omnipotent God.

1. In the first instance above, we learned about birth and the answers were complete. They made sense and they followed the physical laws by which we live. In the second instance, however, the answers we received were incomplete and created even more questions. Perhaps our religious training was so forceful that we were told we must "believe" the Bible because it is the word of God and if we didn't believe it, unquestioningly, it would make us a "bad" person. To a child that threat can be a very powerful force. Many adults have never outgrown that fear of being thought of as a "bad" person and devote their entire lives to some religion and a God they have no proof exists.

This book is not about religion. Religious beliefs are something that must be explored because, like many of science's theories, we are asked to accept facts without scientific or even empirical proof of any kind. Religion is a very powerful force throughout the world, and it influences the lives of billions of people. Therefore, it is important that we view religion carefully as a part of this book to understand it, to learn how to live with it and to see if there is any real truth to it.

There is a chapter, towards the end of this book that talks about the Bibles, because they are important: In seeking answers, it was important to first find the origins of the books that have become an integrated part of our society and guided so many people's lives. The Bible, especially the Old Testament, is about as much of recorded history as we have of life before 400 BC.

Were Adam and Eve really the first people on Earth? Did Ezekiel actually see some visitors from outer space? Is the Old Testament just a collection of unrelated stories or is there a thread of consistency contained in them that can be followed? The Old Testament leaves a myriad of questions about our past and our creation unanswered...unless, of course, you accept the "God created the world in six days" theory as a precise and satisfactory answer to all questions regarding creation. In that case, you won't want to waste your time reading this book, because your mind is sheltered in a certain way, and far be it from me to attempt to enlighten you.

Similarly, we must view the New Testament, the Koran and the Book of Mormon in light of the historical facts that surround them. No attempt will be made to preach, but the little-known facts about their origins will be set forth as historians have recorded and you can draw your own conclusions.

HISTORY'S STORY

Truly ancient history does not exist. We have no history to refer to except the Bible in its many forms and the admittedly colored scraps of information from the Greek Hellenic period (about 400 BC). The Bible refers to a beginning of the world that started about 5500 years ago, and we have strong evidence that man has been here on Earth for hundreds of millions of years. Are we "bad" people if we believe that man has been around longer than the Bible tells us?

Actually, any written history of man only goes back about 2400 years to the Greek Hellenic period, and most of the early Greek writings were not historical, but were embellished tales of heroic events such as were written in the Iliad and the Odyssey.

Sometimes I will refer to "the many forms" of the Bible, because there are over 100 different versions of the Bible in circulation today, each one claiming to be the word of God. Obviously, they can't all be the complete truth, because they vary on so many important points. It is not likely that the omnipotent God referred to in each of those biblical texts would openly contradict Himself. Yet, if we look at some of the Biblical stories closely, we may find some interesting stories worthy of note and analysis.

Does a careful reading of the first chapter of Ezekiel describe some visitors from outer space? It is possible! We'll talk more about it in Chapter 5.

What about the giant fish that spewed Jonah up? Was it really a fish? Think about it: Assuming the tale of Jonah had some basis in reality, how would someone five thousand years ago describe a surfacing submarine or other submergible vehicle? A giant fish?

What about Adam and Eve? Were they really the first people on Earth…or, perhaps, were they the first of a different humanoid-type species on Earth? The Book of Genesis tells us that the only people on Earth were Adam, Eve and their two sons, Cain and Able. Cain killed Able…and then went to the land of Canaan where he found a wife. Does that sound reasonable?

Of course, the stories read to us in Sunday School have been greatly enhanced from the truth and altered over the years. Still, since these stories have endured thousands of years, it makes one wonder if somewhere, behind the biblical stories, were the actual incidents upon which the Biblical tales were based. A review of some of these tales became essential.

This book will attempt, in a very simplified and factual manner, to find the answers…or, if the answers have been buried in millenniums of dust, to clues and concepts that may lead us to logical conclusions. Maybe some readers will find this book reinforcing their religious beliefs. We live in a strange, unexplained world, and a lot of the smattering we have of recorded history can be interpreted in many ways. If the facts, as revealed in this book, support your own beliefs, more power to you.

Nor is this book support for Atheism or Agnosticism. As was said earlier, if you want to believe something is true, no proof is necessary. I have no quarrel with people who are Agnostic, Atheist, Deist, Hindu, Buddhist or any accepted religion….but after looking at history's version of how these religions got started, it is possible that some readers may become quite upset.

In seeking to explain the unexplained we must also consider the argument about Evolution versus Intelligent Design. Followers of Darwin's Theory of Evolution will swear that absolutely everything evolved naturally. Still, it stands to reason that since we are the only planet in our solar system that has shown any signs of sustainable life, that someone or something made it happen. If you want to call it a Deity or God, fine. But as we go through the logical sequence of events, we may discover that if there is/ was a Deity or God that had a hand in creating this world He may not be the kind of God that our Bibles have written about.

So, let's make this first assumption: We didn't just pop up from nowhere. Whether you believe in Evolution or in Intelligent Design, there had to be someone or something that started the first speck that has now become our universe. The belief that some mysterious Deity is the source of everything is accepted by most people because they don't have any reasonable, alternative answers.

Answers to all questions exist, but the limited capabilities of our minds and our brains have not been able to fathom them…perhaps not even recognize them when we see them. Yet history, for what there is of it, has left traces of a trail that can be followed…and the path leads to some very surprising conclusions.

CREATION

Let's try a simple scenario: For just one brief moment, let's assume that there was a "power", a "creator", a "Diety" or "whatever" that created this world. Let's also assume that whoever or whatever created our world had a plan to create an absolutely "perfect" world. The world is not yet perfect although, believe it or not, the world is proceeding in the right direction (surely, it would take an extraordinarily naïve person to believe that man today is not a far superior creature to the man of Neanderthal times). Let's further imagine that this creator wanted to plan and control the development of this world so that it could, over hundreds of millions or even billions of Earth years, eventually, be made "perfect".

"If" the preceding paragraph were true, the first problem we would encounter would be that in order for a creator to observe the progress of his new world, he/she/it would have to be somewhere that time was measured very differently than it is here on Earth. Assuming it has taken the Earth hundreds of millions (or billions) of years to develop, and assuming a creator was observing it, that means that the creator would have to live for that full length of time, or he could not observe it or do anything to improve it in any manner. So, either the creator must have an awfully long life span, or, alternatively, and more reasonably, that creator must live in a world where one year to the creator was equal to hundreds of millions of our years so he could live long enough to observe (and possibly influence) the progress of his new world. Certainly, it has taken eons of time here on Earth, to gradually improve the world, its people and its other living creatures using the technique we have come to know as "survival of the fittest".

Maybe the two preceding paragraphs are a bit much to visualize. But, if you can accept them as being possible, then the scenario of our world's creation in Chapter 14 should be simple to follow.

Do the above assumptions make any real sense? Maybe not, as yet. But as we delve more deeply into the mysteries of the world that science has failed to explain adequately, perhaps a lot of the things that now seems far out will fall neatly into place and make more and more sense.

As thinking human beings, we must ask ourselves: Why has our scientific research failed to provide us with good, logical answers to many common questions...such as "What really happened to the dinosaurs?" Many millions of years ago, they ruled the Earth. The popular scientific theory of an unexplained, major cataclysm that just "happened" and the dinosaurs were all killed off...except for a few crocodiles seems to lack credulity. Science has offered nothing more than theory. No forensic or empirical evidence to support it

My scenario about someone or something wanting to create a perfect world, like science's theory about the dinosaurs, has no forensic or empirical evidence to support it. But if a scenario I will describe in Chapter 14 makes more sense and actually "fits" better than the scientific theory, why shouldn't it be considered? Scientists will write-off my scenario as nonsense while supporting their own, far less reasonable, theories.

A simple example: Many scientists have alleged that the dinosaurs were killed off by the last Ice Age. O.K. At first glance, it sounds plausible. But what is an "Ice Age"? How did it happen? Science tells us (with a straight face) that the ice from the poles reached out to the temperate areas and killed all the reptilian life that needed heat and moisture to live...and then retreated back to the poles. Why? How? What caused it and what physical laws did it follow?

It makes a lot more sense to me that when the Earth's poles became too heavy with ice, the Earth started to go out of balance. To maintain its balance, the axis of our planet tilted! The logical result of the tilting is that the Polar Regions became the more temperate or equatorial regions of the Earth, and the warmer regions of the Earth became the Polar Regions. Naturally, once the weight stabilized, the new equatorial regions being closer to the sun, started warming up, and the ice retreated back to the new poles. It's just a theory and a simple variation on what science would have us believe, but not only is it more plausible, it makes logical sense.

Can the axis of the Earth change? Can the polar regions move? What would happen if they did?

Of course the axis of the Earth can change. If one part of the Earth becomes too heavy with ice, the spinning Earth will shift to balance the weight in order that the Earth continue to spin at the same rate of speed. And clearly the poles can move. Ask any sailor or pilot. The magnetic poles move a little every year. I read recently that the magnetic North and South Poles have moved hundreds of miles in the past several years. Does that mean we're going to have another Ice Age? What would happen to the people living on Earth if we had another Ice Age or if the Earth's axis shifted?

If the axis of the Earth changed suddenly, the oceans would rise hundreds or thousands of feet. The feelings of gravity would probably be temporarily lost or shifted as the Earth adjusted, etc. It would be a major cataclysm. But if the change in the tilt of the Earth's axis is slow, it would happen almost unnoticeably as the equatorial regions became colder and the polar regions became warmer. Is this what's happening now? Is this what we refer to as global warming? Or is global warming just another scientific theory that will be exploded?

There are lots of unfounded theories that science has asked us to accept unquestioningly. I find the "Big Bang" theory of creation to be terribly flawed, and I do not accept the scientific explanation that the oil we pump from the Earth is made up of decomposed dinosaurs. Oil is in sub-surface pools. Science would have us believe that the dinosaurs lived and died in small pockets and not spread throughout the world. Come on!

Science is always demanding "proof". Yet, for all of the back-up documentation and material some scientific theories have, you might as well read a science-fiction novel. Some of the science-fiction stories contain better and more plausible explanations than science offers us.

AN IMPERFECT WORLD

If we assume that there was a creator of sorts, seeking to create a perfect world, a good question might be, "Why isn't the world more perfect?" Although the Earth has been around for hundreds of millions (if not billions) of years (if we accept science's theory) there has never been a period of more than 100 years when there were not some wars or significant battles going on somewhere. In fact, if there were some sort of extra-terrestrial beings in UFOs looking at us, they would probably view the Earth as an extremely "warring" planet. Maybe interesting to observe, but hardly a place you'd want to visit.

Maybe, if there was a creator, his job just isn't done yet. Certainly the world is not a perfect place nor have its creatures achieved a level of Nirvana. Far from it! There are still enormous blocks of people throughout the world that have not progressed very far above the Neanderthal stage (witness the religious fanatics in Africa and the Middle East), and many, many centuries of refinement are necessary before the world as we know it can even approach becoming a "perfect" world as may have been envisioned by an assumed creator(s).

At least, in the more modern world, we can say that people are more intelligent now than they were in the past. Even the most intelligent people make mistakes. In fact, the only people who don't make mistakes are people who don't do anything.

I used the term "most intelligent people", and must apologize and digress for a moment, because I, too, have fallen victim to the facade scientists would have us believe: Are some people really more intelligent than others? Why? This is one of many questions which scientists are much too quick to answer.

The answer to the above question is one of those things that seems obvious on the surface. But let's look at it more closely: Of course some people appear more intelligent than others using the scales we use to measure intelligence! Certainly IQ or SAT scores can vary markedly from individual to individual, and scientists will tell us that these are accurate measures of human intelligence.

But do these standardized tests really test intelligence? Each of us has a brain. The IQ Tests that science claims to measure intelligence actually measures only the power of the brain to reason mathematically and to comprehend what is read. These tests do not measure many of the hundreds of other things of which the brain is capable. People who have never graduated high school may become world business leaders, or be able to write beautiful music, or capture the colors of the world in their imagination in paintings…or simply be a loving and nurturing parent or teacher to children. Everything we try to measure, like intelligence, we try and measure to the scientific standard. This is one of the most misleading things we do here on Earth and it tends to diminish public respect for the creative aspects of which we are capable.

Why do some people appear more intelligent than others? Again, it's because of the facade science has imbued in our heads: We believe someone using ten-letter-words in his or her normal speech is more intelligent than someone with speech problems. Each of us is limited by the capacity of our brain, but our brains may be more conducive to learning some things rather than others. We tend to give far more intelligence credit to people with greater academic and mathematical capacity than we do to others with more common sense or artistic capabilities. That's because we allow the influence of science to tell us what is and what is not "smart". Some people have greater brain capacity in specialized areas than do others, and so we call those people "gifted". What science does not consider is that the "gift" some people have is not measurable on their tests. Each person on Earth has something to offer other people.

The class distinctions created by the world of science gives rise to problems that go much deeper than simple outward appearance. Of course, most people that science has measured and labeled as "highly intelligent" tend to be deceived by the glitter of their own test scores. Most commonly, such people try to use what they believe is their own superiority as a tool for personal gain. Instead of trying to share their gifts and improve the world around them, they use their (measured by IQ tests) superior intelligence and abilities as food for their ego. They often become very wealthy people, or set themselves up as demagogues, frequently preaching a religion and a lifestyle that they, themselves, do not practice. They make themselves idols of the opposite sex and seekers of physical pleasures and material assets which, in fact, have very little meaning in the overall view of the world and its people. Is this a characteristic of the humanoids that inhabit a warring planet?

O.K. The perfect world has not, as yet, been achieved. There are still many problems of inequality, prejudice, etc. As man has become more sophisticated, material things, personal wealth and power have become the goals rather than the tools to achieve higher, more qualitative, goals.

A very wise psychiatrist named David Viscott once said to me that when he was young, he set his goal as having a million dollars in the bank. When he had achieved that goal, he looked back and reflected on what a stupid goal that was. When he attained it, it really brought little or no real satisfaction or comfort. Most goals that we set for ourselves are like that:

Often, many young men will set a goal of sexual conquest with some beautiful female creature. But if they achieve that goal, it really becomes an "empty" achievement. Sure, it may feel great to see that beautiful girl lying in bed next to you, but how meaningful is it in the overall perspective of your life? By the next day, it may still offer you the pride of accomplishment, but within a month or a year it has become meaningless.

So, we live in an imperfect world; one I believe someone, some power or some force is trying to perfect …and probably will in many lifetimes past yours or mine. No one can really address the future, but this book can take a hard look at our poorly documented past and how it brings us up, quite logically, to our documented present.

As you will see, this book offers answers… sometime multiple answers … sometimes questions that only you can answer for yourself. Sometimes the answers may have a lot of personal meaning for you…and other answers may be passed-off by you as pure baloney. Each of us has certain talents that can help this world. You know more about your personal talents than anyone else. Hopefully, this book will inspire you to find ways of using your personal talent and ability to help make this world a better place to live. When you accept the fact that you can make a difference, it already makes a difference.

Now let's start taking a closer look at some of the things science can't explain. Let's start to explain the unexplained.

Chapter 2

Extra Sensory Perception (ESP)

All human beings have five senses of which we are aware. The senses are sight, sound taste, touch and smell. This is not to suggest that some of us may not have damaged senses such as hearing problems or the need to wear glasses. The fact is that all of us have those five senses; some to a greater degree than others: My wife's sense of smell is so keen that she can name the brand of perfume being worn by a woman across the room.

Whether any or all of the five senses are highly developed or somewhat dull is not important. The fact we have those five senses distinguishes us as an animal here on Earth.

There are other things that are constantly going on around us that, generally, we can't perceive. First and foremost among them is "thought". People can very seldom tell what other people are thinking.

Another thing we can't normally perceive are "memories" of others. Even if you are not thinking about them, your memories go a long way in making up the complex animal that is "you". The difference between perceiving someone's thoughts and their memories is evident: Thoughts are currently in their mind. Memories are not.

Then, too, most people cannot detect the energy that is in the air and surrounds each of us.

These are just a few of the things that we, normally, cannot detect with our five senses.

But, make no mistake about it, there are some people who can sense these things. If you doubt this, read on:

THE SIXTH SENSE

As mortals living on this little ball in the middle of nowhere called Earth, science has acknowledged that we have only five senses. If we cannot see something, hear it, taste it, touch it or smell it, science leads us to believe it simply does not exist. We can't see, taste, touch, smell or hear the air…but it's definitely there. Maybe we can feel it when it accelerates, or smell it when there is smoke or something else in it but, generally, the air we breathe is not something within our five senses. Yet, nothing would exist without it.

Hundreds, if not thousands, of books have been written about a "sixth" sense. One which enables us to see, smell, taste, hear or touch something that others cannot. The so-called sixth-sense has been attributed to people who can, ostensibly, communicate with the dead; can read the minds of others; can forecast events to come; can sense a myriad of things that we normal people cannot seem to do. Because we are talking about an extra "sense", this has come to be known as extra sensory perception (ESP).

Actually, ESP can be divided into many subdivisions: Mental telepathy, precognition, communication with the dead, thought transference; mind/body separation, etc. If we are going to look at ESP objectively, we must first start with a "show me" or "prove it" attitude. We should not make the assumption that the things perceived by people with a "sixth sense" are, in fact, real until the evidence becomes so strong that it cannot be denied: That there are some people who can read the minds of others; that there are people who have experienced their mind separating from their body, etc.

Without strong evidence (not scientific proof) that these experiences are real, we have no place to go: we must conclude that all ESP is a fraud. But as we start researching, we will find there is a mountain of evidence and historical records indicating that it is not a fraud. So let's investigate it together with a positive outlook.

Some ESP topics, such as communication with the dead, have been so overburdened with vast amounts of faking, pretense, and plain B.S., that it becomes difficult to discern whether the parties alleging the ability to communicate with the dead are, in fact, telling the truth, putting on a show, or just deluding themselves.

When someone in your family dies, it's natural to want to communicate with them for guidance, for reassurance of love and many other things. If you have spent your life sharing things with someone else, when they die, there is a void. So a lot of people try to talk to or communicate with their dead loved ones.

There's a lot of money to be made by those claiming the ability to act as a medium and communicate with the dead. And, since communication with dead loved ones is a strong desire for many people, there will be some people who, for a price, will claim to be able to put you in touch with the dearly departed.

It seems that there are a lot of people who are willing to pay significant sums of money to talk with a dearly departed child or spouse, and wherever there are people willing to spend the money, there will be many people willing to take that money. Some of the most ornate and elaborate acts in the world have been created to support the pretense of talking to or communicating with the dead. Séances were and are excellent businesses for the alleged "mediums"…but almost all (if not all) are as phony as a three-dollar bill. The performances of most so-called mediums are really performances by unscrupulous actors and magicians using luminescent props and cold-reading techniques to convince a hopeful, unwary person that they are, in fact, communicating with the dead.

At this point, we should spend a moment to mention Harry Houdini and his efforts to communicate with the dead. Harry Houdini was an escape artist and a magician. Actually, he was more of a magician's magician and an icon or legend in the world of magic. To this very date, there are shrines built to him and vast numbers of books written about him. Houdini was convinced that people did not really die…only their bodies died. Therefore, he assumed, there must be a way to communicate with that portion of the deceased that did not die.

In those days, he referred to it as communicating with the spirits of the dead. Houdini never claimed to have that ability himself, but during the 1920s there was a lot of publicity given to séances conducted by famous mediums such as Edgar Casey.

Houdini believed that most (or all) of these mediums were fakes, but just on the chance that one of them may be genuine, he offered a reward of $10,000 cash (in a day and age when that $10,000 would be equivalent to at least $250,000 today) to any medium or other person who could genuinely prove the ability to communicate with the spirits of the dead. Of course, "proving" communication with the dead might be a little difficult, so Houdini said that if he, as a magician, could not duplicate their performances and so-called communications with the dead, he would consider it "proven".

There were numerous attempts to earn that $10,000, but of those who tried to collect the reward, none succeeded. There was not one single person, group or medium that could do anything that Houdini could not duplicate with props and magical paraphernalia. No one ever claimed the prize.

Just before he died, Houdini told his wife, "If there's a way to communicate with you from the grave, I will do it!" As a result, for more than fifty years, on the anniversary of his death, a séance was held wherein his widow and a Medium tried to communicate with Houdini…without success.

The above having been said, it may surprise you to learn that I believe that many people have communicated with the dead, or rather the "spirit" or aura of the dead.

I'm a strong believer in "numbers": There are more than a hundred thousand claims of people (not seeking a reward or financial gain) who believe (and in many cases have documented) communication with the dead. Granted that most claims are probably just "wishful thinking", but there are such vast numbers of people who have claimed this with no apparent axe to grind, that serious consideration must be given to the concept. When thousands of people, unrelated and unknown to each other, say the same or a similar thing happened, it becomes evident that something did happen. What that "something" is will be gone into in this book.

To the best of my knowledge, I have never been able to personally communicate with a dead person, or their spirit…either on the receiving or on the sending end. I can't look at a corpse and garner any information other than that the person is dead and/or that the mortician did a nice job. But there are people who can, or at least claim to have received information from the dead; information about things that the living could have no possible way of knowing.

These are not people who allege to have a sixth sense, but are ordinary people like you and me! The fact that these people make no claim to having any special power, gives them more credence in my eyes.

Here is one case that I am familiar with, first-hand:

I knew a girl (only eighteen years old at the time) whose mother and father were killed together in an automobile crash while vacationing in Europe. The night following their unfortunate demise, the girl told me that when she went to bed, she suddenly woke up and saw her father standing by her bed in her darkened room. He spoke to her just as if he was actually in the room and instructed her to get a pencil and paper and to write-down what he told her, but once she turned on her desk light, not to turn around until he had finished speaking. For some reason (she said) she wasn't frightened at all, and did what her father told her to do. He proceeded to give her a list of secret bank accounts he had (some in foreign countries), and in what name(s) they were held and, in a few cases, a password or number to access them. He gave her the location of two safe deposit boxes she knew nothing about and he told her where to find the keys. She finished writing and looked up…and her father was gone. Suffice it to say that she didn't sleep for the rest of the night. She studied the things her father had told her to write down.

I asked her if she wasn't frightened…or at least surprised to see her father whom she knew had just been killed. Her response was that it was like a dream, and she wasn't really certain she was awake. She felt surrounded by his love and felt no fear whatsoever.

The next morning, she telephoned her father's attorney who had been a close friend of the family for many years. The attorney said he knew nothing about any of these supposedly secret accounts or safe deposit boxes, and that she must've had a dream. Because he was like a second father to her, he said if she would give him all the information, he would check it out. The information she had written down all proved accurate!

How do we explain this? Did she just create a big lie to impress me? Did she just stumble across a list of his secret bank accounts and think they came to her in a dream? Was there actually some form of communication between her and her dead father? The truth is that we'll never know for certain. Even if we did know that there were spirit communications, we could never prove it. Being rational, all we really know is that she came up with a list of bank accounts and documents in her own handwriting, (that she swears she didn't know about), for which there are few, if any, rational explanations.

What we do know (and will go into in much greater detail later) is that almost all claims of psychic experiences concerning communication with the dead, occur either during or immediately following a deep sleep.

In my opinion, this girl was incapable of telling a big lie. I had known her and her family for many years, and I would have serious doubt that she would say or do anything just to impress someone.

The important thing to note was that she claimed to have communicated with one, specific dead person. She made no claim to being able to communicate, in general, with dead people. Interestingly enough, most of the verifiable cases of communication with the dead have been one person communicating with one specific person only. That person may be a husband, a wife, a child, a parent, a lover…usually someone very close. When I use the term "verifiable", I use it with extreme caution. None of the incidents I have researched concerning communication with the dead or the spirits of the dead is "verifiable" in a scientific sense. But many of them are so bizarre in nature (including one that I will discuss in the chapter on "ghosts") that they simply defy any rational explanation. When all rational answers have been eliminated, whatever remains, must be considered as true…no matter how far-out the remainder seems.

So, then is that a "sixth sense"? Maybe! Later in the book, we will go into possible explanations of this phenomenon, but for the time being, let's look at this as being an example of a sixth sense:

Virtually all people have some form of "sixth sense". How many times have you had a déjà vu experience where you have the feeling that you've been somewhere before (although you haven't), or you have the feeling that you know, when talking to someone for the first time, that you've had the same conversation…with the same person…before? We all possess a form of this "sixth sense", especially when we are under inordinately strong emotional stress. When the stress dissipates, so, normally, does the sixth sense. But this does not mean that we all have psychic powers per the accepted definition of the term. The difference between a normal, average, person and a psychic person is that the average person has very rare occasions when his or her "sixth sense" kicks-in. In a true psychic, it kicks-in quite frequently.

THE TRUE PSYCHIC

The true psychic really defies definition because there are so many variables that go into making a person a "true psychic". For the moment, we will refer to people who have frequent "sixth sense" visions as "psychics".

Please do not confuse a genuine psychic with the garden variety of commercial psychics advertised on radio, television and on store fronts. These people are almost always complete frauds. Naturally, the frauds are the ones who usually proclaim the loudest that they are truly genuine psychics. Since anyone with any degree of rational, common sense knows they are frauds, their protests have the peripheral affect of tending to destroy the credibility of the few genuine psychics. And, yes, genuine psychics do exist. I had the great pleasure of knowing one, and we will talk about him momentarily.

Can a true psychic actually communicate with dead people? I've heard of such instances, but like Houdini, it's never been demonstrated convincingly to me. Can a true psychic actually read someone's mind? I've heard of many such instances from sources I deem reliable. Can a true psychic accurately pull details of your past from some object like your keys or cigarette lighter? Again, I've heard of such instances, but in this case, I've seen it happen and been totally astonished...dealing with a psychic named Peter Hurkos, who was a genuine psychic. (More about Hurkos later.)

If, in fact, a genuine psychic has ever communicated with the dead; if, in fact, a psychic has ever, accurately, read someone's mind; if, in fact, a psychic has ever had a single instance where he pulled details of a person's life from an inanimate object like keys...then these are things for which science has no explanation. As I've said before, there *are* answers out there, but most of them will not be found in scientific textbooks.

Let's start using some common sense and logic: If a psychic can discern information not readily available to other people, then (1) that information must be out there, somewhere, for the psychic to be able to get it and (2) whatever source it is that is offering this information to the psychic must be considered a genuine source of information, even if most people cannot perceive it. What this really means is that the information garnered by the psychic must exist somewhere, but you and I can't see it, hear it, touch it, taste it or smell it. But the true psychic has an extra sense, a sixth sense, which can somehow perceive it.

As mentioned previously, all of us have that extra sense which pops in and out of our minds at random: How many times have you been thinking about a person whom you haven't seen in years…and a few seconds later the telephone rings and it is that person? How many times have you looked into someone's eyes for the first time and felt you know that person…or cannot trust them…or feel a special warmth emanating from them? The really scary thing about this is that most of the time you're right!

We already know that, to a limited extent each of us has that sixth sense ability. But what really makes a psychic a psychic is that he can control…or can seemingly control …his perceptions to a significantly greater extent than the average person.

I know a female lawyer from Oklahoma who was looking for an apartment to rent. When she walked into an apartment with her mother and her real estate broker, she inexplicably began to choke. She went outside where her breathing became normal. She did not know how to explain what had happened, but stated that the atmosphere had seemed filled with death. Unknown to her, her mother, or her real estate broker…someone had died a violent death in that apartment only a few weeks earlier.

Some of us have better control of our sixth sense than others but, again, not nearly enough to be called a true psychic. My daughter, Debbie (also a lawyer) will meet people with whom I am contemplating doing some business: she will warn me to stay away from certain people and encourage me to do business with others. She has never been wrong!

To try and understand what it is that makes some people have a sixth sense that seems to work regularly rather than sporadically, we have to look at the mind versus the brain. They are, unquestionably, not one and the same. The mind being a super-fast, invisible, thing that feeds the brain, and the brain being the body's computer. The brain is a truly amazing computer. As computers go, it is hundreds of times faster than the fastest computers we have on Earth. It has a memory capacity thousands of times greater than any PC, and it is designed so that if one part of it breaks down, there is another part ready to stand in for the broken part. It is an incredibly sensitive machine. Even a few bars of a song can set it in motion.

With all that our brain can do, it still is very limited: The brain it is so sensitive, the maker of our bodies put a myriad of buffers around our brain to protect it. These buffers, however, play a very strange role: They limit a lot of what the brain can perceive. Let me give you a wild example:

When we bite into an apple, our five senses get to work: We can see the apple, we can taste the apple, we can smell the apple, touch it, and we can hear the sound of the crunch as we bite into it. Now let's use our imagination again:

Let's imagine that an apple is a living thing: It comes from a living tree and is, effectively, the child of that tree. Let's imagine that the apple has feelings, and is screaming with pain when we bite into it…but we cannot hear that scream because the sound the apple makes is blocked in our brain by the buffers.

Could it be? Of course it could. Is it true? Probably not…at least I hope not because I enjoy eating apples. But the buffers do exist…and just what they buffer away from our senses is anyone's guess…even an apple's. But it is clear the buffers keep many things from entering our brains: There are sounds we cannot hear, things we cannot see, touch, smell or taste. Sometimes when we go someplace, we get a "feeling"…but there is nothing that our brain can perceive…and it is the brain, not the mind, that controls the functions of the body and its five senses.

These buffers are very important to the functioning of our computer/brain. Break one of the buffers and the computer may be permanently damaged. There are occasions when we believe a buffer has been broken and the human has survived with little or no apparent damage. This may give us a big clue as to what the sixth sense really is.

THE STRANGE CASE OF PETER HURKOS

The story of Peter Hurkos, the psychic, is one of the strangest (but completely true) stories you are ever likely to hear. My first introduction to Peter Hurkos was through his wife who, like me, was a stamp collector. I met her in a small Hollywood stamp collector's shop, and thought she was very attractive, so I flirted slightly with her. I had no idea at that time that her husband was one of the most famous psychics in the world. She told me that she was having a few friends over to her house that evening, and she'd like me to come over. I said fine!

When I got there, I met her husband, Peter, who spoke with a thick Dutch accent. The first thing he did was ask me to give him my car keys…just for a moment or two. I was a little apprehensive, but I did. He held my keys in his closed fist and shut his eyes. Then he proceeded to ask me if I had made up my mind about the new job offer that had just been presented to me.

I said "No, I haven't decided yet."

Then he asked me if my brother had fully recovered from the automobile accident that nearly took off his head.

I didn't respond.

Then he told me that I always felt very close to my brother. Did I still remember when I was about six years old how my brother had pulled me from the railroad tracks when a train was coming?

I couldn't answer. I was speechless.

Then Hurkos wanted to know if my mother, despite her age, still danced professionally. Then he asked me if I had made up my mind about asking my wife for a divorce.

He told me several other things…in all, he took less than two or three minutes…and I was drenched with perspiration! My knees were wobbly and weak.

Hundreds of thoughts went through my head trying to figure-out where he got all that information. That was stuff that nobody knew… except maybe my brother who lived 3,000 miles away. When I had fully recovered (which took most of the evening) and I saw him do the same thing with two other guests, I made a mental note to find out what I could about Peter Hurkos. The public library had several books about him (the Internet did not yet exist).

What I found out was this: *Hurkos was a young man during World War II and, when Germany occupied the Netherlands, Hurkos became a member of the Dutch underground, doing what he could to upset the Nazi occupation of the Netherlands. He blew up railroad yards, sabotaged incoming German ships, etc. One night, the Germans were laying in wait for him and his fellow members of the Dutch underground. The Germans captured or killed most of his buddies. Somehow, Hurkos managed to escape the trap and tried to get away by running across the rooftops in Rotterdam with the German troops in hot pursuit.*

Fate suddenly stepped in: Hurkos slipped and fell…and landed on his head. By all rights, the fall should have killed him, but it didn't. Hurkos woke up in a hospital about one week later with two German guards and an interrogation officer by his bedside. The German officer started to question him and recorded both questions and responses on what was then a new type of recording device called a wire recorder.

The responses Hurkos gave to the questions appeared completely nonsensical, and in listening to the wire transcription later, the German officer felt certain that Hurkos' brain had been damaged and he would be of little use to German Intelligence. Hurkos' responses to the questions seemed not to be responses at all.

As he listened to the transcription for a second time, the German Intelligence officer noted a very strange thing: by placing Hurkos' responses one question back, every response was both rational and made sense. In other words, it seemed that Hurkos was responding to each question <u>before</u> it was asked.

The German officer immediately told his superiors, and Hurkos was whisked from the hospital and placed in a special isolation ward where other German doctors could examine him. What they found was that Hurkos had many unusual abilities. Among them, he could hold some inanimate object belonging to a complete stranger in his hands, and from that inanimate object, he could tell who the owner was and some things about the owner.

Then came D-Day, and the Americans and British invaded Europe. Hurkos was supposed to be sent to Germany so their scientists could examine him more thoroughly, but the invading US and British troops were of more immediate concern to the Germans. Before the Germans had much of a chance to do anything with Hurkos, Hurkos managed to escape and reach the U.S. troops. The US Army had no knowledge of Hurkos' unusual abilities.

Looking for a way to earn a living in postwar Holland, Hurkos decided to capitalize on his newly discovered talent, and became an entertainer as a psychic. He created an act of "phony" psychic stunts for entertainment. On occasion, while performing some of his "entertainment" acts, he would suddenly change his demeanor and start demonstrating real psychic powers. Without being prodded, he would tell some members of his audience things that it would have been impossible for Hurkos to know. Not the "general" statements or "cold readings" used by entertainment psychics, but graphic details of strangers' lives. More and more, Hurkos started minimizing the entertainment aspects of his performances and started to hone his true psychic skills. Hurkos began to build a reputation as a genuine psychic.

Hurkos' talent wasn't always entertaining. On a few occasions, he was demonstrating his increasingly sharp psychic abilities to fellow Dutchmen when the objects belonging to them, placed in Hurkos' hands, revealed to Hurkos that they had been Nazi collaborators…war criminals now living with different names; their appearances had been changed; etc. Hurkos was responsible for breaking through the disguises of several Nazi war criminals that had changed their identities and moved to the Netherlands from Germany.

As a result, Hurkos' reputation burgeoned. He became a hero among his fellow Dutchmen and one of the best-known and most respected psychics in the world.

Hurkos' reputation as a genuine psychic began to assume massive proportions. When a seven year old girl was missing in Amsterdam and the police had no clues as to what happened to her, the girl's parents suggested Hurkos be contacted. Because the Amsterdam police felt that time was of the utmost importance, Hurkos was asked to help the Amsterdam police to try and find the girl.

The following is documented: *Hurkos, tried to pick up some extra sensory trace of the missing girl by first touching and holding some of her clothing, dolls and other things she handled often. Then he proceeded to walk around the neighborhood where the girl played; through the streets of Amsterdam across many of the literally hundreds of bridges over the small canals for which Amsterdam is famous. On one bridge he stopped and stared at the water. Then, very sadly, he told the entourage of police walking with him that he felt her body was buried in the water but would appear there the following morning. Needless to say, every Dutch newspaper (and many from neighboring countries) was there at that bridge when, the following morning, the little girl's body bobbed to the surface. At the autopsy it was determined that she had fallen into the canal and gotten stuck in the mud and weeds. When the current freed her body, it bobbed to the surface. Hurkos became an international celebrity.*

How did Hurkos know? How was he able to predict with complete accuracy an event that would happen the following day? How was he able to do many of the things for which he became famous?

Subsequently, I had several lengthy visits with Hurkos and discussed some of his better-known successes…and how sometimes he could see images like a television screen and sometimes he could not feel any images at all.

Here is what I concluded: That fall from the rooftops in Rotterdam damaged one of his brain's buffers. Remarkably, it did not kill him or damage his brain sufficiently to make it stop working, but it opened up a new vista for him: Because that buffer was not there , his mind was allowed to perceive things others could not perceive. He had developed another sense…a sixth sense, if you will…which made him sensitive to the thoughts of others. Like every part of the body that is injured, the body tries to repair itself. Frequently, the body replaces what had been good tissue with scar tissue. It is my belief that it is this scar tissue that sometimes blocks Hurkos from getting images.

Andrija Puharich, MD, a noted physician and researcher of ESP was so impressed by the stories about Hurkos that he invited Hurkos to the USA in 1956 to study what seemed to be Hurkos' unique psychic abilities under laboratory conditions. Hurkos was studied at Dr. Puharich's Glen Cove, Maine, medical research laboratory under what Dr. Puharich considered to be very tightly controlled conditions. The results convinced Dr. Puharich that Hurkos' psychic abilities were far greater than any he had ever tested (before or thereafter) . . . a remarkable 90% accuracy. After two and-one-half years of testing Hurkos, Dr. Puharich said, *"I am convinced that Peter Hurkos, is the greatest of anyone I have ever tested as a psychic. His abilities are so far reaching, that he hasn't even scratched the surface of what he can do with his abilities and mind."*

Hurkos subsequently gained worldwide acceptance as a psychic detective, working on cases involving missing airplanes, persons, and murder victims. Some of his most illustrious cases were "The Stone of Scone" [London, England], "The Boston Strangler Multiple Murders" [Boston, Massachusetts], "The Missing Thai Silk King, Jim Thompson" [Asia/Thailand], "The Ann Arbor Co-Ed Murders" [Ann Arbor, Michigan], and "The Sharon Tate Murders" [Los Angeles, California]. In each case Hurkos was credited for finding and/or identifying the culprits.

Virtually every newspaper in the world has done stories on Hurkos, and Hurkos has received testimonials and awards of recognition from several prominent figures including U.S. Presidents Johnson and Reagan.

Hurkos, now deceased, believed that inanimate things that stay close to the body or are handled frequently are surrounded by parts of a person's natural aura. How is that possible? I'm not at all certain, but since the mind works so much faster than the brain, perhaps some of the mind's thoughts are implanted in things close to the person; things that he touches and handles a lot...like keys, wallets, favorite toys.

Hurkos told me that his forte was psychometrics, the ability to see past-present-future associations by touching objects. He said, *"I see pictures in my mind like a television screen. When I touch something, I can then tell what I see."*

O.K....that's a possible explanation as to how Hurkos was able to tell intimate things about me from my keys. But how did he know where to find the dead girl's body?

My multi-year association with Hurkos gave me one of the most important clues about ESP: the mind and the brain are two completely separate things! For centuries, scientists have always believed that the mind is a part of the brain…although thousands of experiments have failed to locate the part of the brain that contains the mind.

Actually, the mind could be located anywhere. All we really know is that we hear our own voice inside our head telling us what our mind is thinking. But that's to be expected: even if our mind was located in some external thing, it would have to feed our brain and be interpreted into language that our brain would understand. It is our brain that has been taught the language(s) we speak…so any thoughts we have would come through our brain.

If the mind cannot be located in the brain, where is it?

Every human being is surrounded by a mysterious electromagnetic aura. This aura can be photographed using infra-red photography and it has some amazing characteristics. No two people's auras look alike. Your aura is as distinctive as your face and body although there are no such distinguishing features as a face and body to an aura. What is this aura? Where did it come from? What is its purpose?

As we go on in this book, the evidence will clearly demonstrate that your aura contains your mind. It's like the keyboard of a computer. It feeds the brain…and the brain is your body's computer. By definition, your aura emanates from a different dimension: You can't see it, hear it, taste it, touch it or smell it. Therefore it belongs in a different dimension than anything that happens in normal living. Some people may question the "hearing" part, but what we hear is not our mind/aura, but rather we hear our own voice as interpreted by our brain. More about this later.

Think about it! If the mind was located in the brain, when people suffer brain injuries in an accident, in football, boxing, from cerebral palsy, etc., it would affect the mind. Almost all people with injured brains can think as clearly and as lucidly as people with uninjured brains. The brain may not allow the physical body to respond or move as the mind wants it to, but the mind is generally as clear and thoughtful as ever.

Accepting the fact that the mind/aura and the brain are two different things will open the doors to a lot of explanations about things we call paranormal. For starters, when we die, we know the brain dies, too. But the mind/aura? Does that die, too? There is a lot of evidence to support a case that it does not!

OUR MYSTERIOUS AURA

Our science, primitive as it may be, has learned to detect that there is an electric or electromagnetic field or aura that exists (mostly around the head) and surrounds the human body during lifetime. This aura has been photographed with special, infra-red cameras. They have given this aura all sorts of names, but clearly it is something about which we know little. One amazing thing, as has been photographed with infra-red video cameras, is that as someone dies, this aura does not. The heart and brain may be completely dead, but the aura remains. In fact, it remains near the body for a while then, as aura photography has shown, moves around and seems to leave the room where the dead body lies in state. Or, more accurately, it simply moves-off to someplace the cameras cannot follow.

Religious people may start calling this aura the "immortal soul", but even if the term fits, it creates problems to those who think logically: Using the term "immortal soul" tends to become a simplistic, religious explanation that helps to block a realistic, rational explanation of what may be happening.

There is a growing tendency among the scholarly who seek answers beyond the scientific gibberish, that this aura may actually be the location of what we call our "mind". If so, there are a lot of answers that fall into place quite nicely.

We should have been able, by now, to recognize the possibility that the mind is not, necessarily, a part of the body. It could very well be an outside force that feeds the brain as much information as the brain can compute. I believe it is a force that seems to stay with one body at a time.

Identifying the existence of an aura that we all seem to have is one thing; what its purpose is and how it works is quite another:

A natural question that should be pursued is, "Is our mind something that is a separate entity unto itself, or is it a part of the brain that helps the brain to develop?" All studies I have researched lead me to the conclusion that the mind tries to feed the brain as much as the brain can compute. Again, it's like the example stated earlier: the brain is the body's computer, and the mind is at the keyboard.

A simple example: You get sick and come down with a fever. The brain reacts and sends white blood cells to fight the invading virus. An example of the brain controlling the physical. The mind tells the brain that the white blood cells are not strong enough and tells body to phone the doctor or get the proper medication into the body to help the blood cells do their work.

The brain controls the reactions of the body to pain, pleasure, motion and activity. But it is the mind that directs the thoughts in your head. Thinking is not a physical process. It takes place without any bodily movement being involved. We know the brain can be taught to recognize symbols and mold them into words and sentences. But it is the mind that gives meaning to these sentences.

We assume that children are born with a mind...but the brain is so formative that there is not much information it can accept. As the child grows older, the brain can accept more information from the mind. Inasmuch as children's brains grow at different rates, it can explain why some children appear much more intelligent than others; why some seek rebelliousness against their parents' guidance at earlier ages than others. It can also explain why, as children mature, they can become totally different people than their parents, with totally different sets of values.

Going one step further, the mind, in the course of feeding the brain as much as the brain can compute, may find certain areas of the brain less resistant to information than other areas and thus, more receptive to certain things. Accordingly, a musical prodigy child may not be able to spell "house", but can play Beethoven's Sonata in C sharp on the piano. The concept of the aura being the mind, if true, would explain a myriad of contradictions in the accepted scientific theories concerning the mind and brain.

Now let's go even another step further: When the brain is not yet fully formed and able to filter thoughts from the mind, the mind may put memories into the brain that defy scientific explanation: There are numerous cases of children having memories of a previous life that seem to dissipate as the brain matures. Almost all recollections of a previous life (discussed in the chapter on reincarnation) are either from young children or from people who have been hypnotized and regressed back to their childhood. Apparently, as the brain matures and fills itself with the very act of living, these memories become deeply buried.

This immediately raises the questions of "What is the aura?" "Where did it come from?" "What happens to it when the body dies?" "Have we really lived before?" The answers to these questions have left a clear, evidentiary trail we will look at later in this book.

Think that the idea of having lived before is pretty far out? This may account for what the mind really is; where your aura came from and where it goes when you die; what a déjà vu experience really is; how you can feel that you know someone you've never seen before, and a myriad of other unanswerable questions. Again, I'm not stating that this is actually so; only that "if" it was so, it would go a long way towards explaining some of our unexplained phenomena.

One of the questions that the theory creates is, "Since the "auras" must have a lot of memories, why aren't we born with memories?" Or, "Why, when we get older, don't we remember things that this thought aura or mind must have learned from millions of years of experience?" Both good questions with one very simple answer:

Please forgive my being repetitious: The brain is physical. It is the body's computer. It cannot accept input beyond its capacity to receive. When a child is born, the brain is almost worthless. It can tell the body when it is uncomfortable or when it needs food. But beyond that, nothing! As the body matures, the brain matures. It can accept more input. And, if you will notice, as the brain matures, people become individuals with thoughts of their own. A child does what it is told to do. An adolescent has thoughts of its own, and often does the opposite of what its parents instruct. A completely mature individual may be nothing, whatsoever, like his/her parents. The brain has matured…to its extremely limited capacity. It can become smart enough to ask questions, but, except in very few cases, rarely seems to get smart enough to know the answers…even though the aura is probably trying to feed those answers to the limited capacity of a person's brain/computer.

What happens to this electromagnetic aura when we die? I'm not certain, but I believe the aura actually has several options: It can go back from whence it came; It can stick around to watch after those who are still on Earth acting as a spirit guide; it can attach itself to a person or a place where it feels a degree of comfort; It can attach itself to a newborn and live another life here on Earth as the aura of a different person or, when there is a newborn in the family, it may very well attach itself to the newborn. How common it is that children born shortly following the death of a family member take on many of the characteristics of the decedent. If the aura was comfortable with one family, it may want to stay there.

Is that what is called Reincarnation?

It is possible, isn't it? This is not the proper time to discuss reincarnation or whether the concept has merit. I've devoted an entire chapter to the subject. Read it and draw your own conclusions.

If the mind or aura doesn't die, what's to stop it from finding another newborn to attach itself to? Not only could that help to explain some of the déjà vu or past-life experiences we have, it could also give some credence to the religious belief of an "immortal soul".

Where and how did the concept of an "immortal soul" originate?

Surprisingly, it did not originate in the Bible (New or Old Testaments). In fact, the Bible never mentions an immortal soul. Teachings of most religions, including Christianity, Judaism, Islam and Buddhism all not only preach the existence of an immortal soul, but since the soul, ostensibly, does not die, what happens to it when the body dies? It has to go someplace. Thus was created the story of Heaven and Hell to provide a place for the immortal soul to go.

Actually, we have the Greeks to thank for the theory of an immortal soul. A philosopher of no less stature than Plato himself taught his students that every person has an immortal soul which stays with the body during the body's lifetime, and when the body dies, moves on. This immortal soul contains the memories of the body it left. So, if you follow Plato's thinking through, the concept of meeting a loved one in an afterlife, is not really so far-fetched.

Whether we call it an immortal soul, a mind or an aura, is really unimprtant. What is important is that we recognize the evidence that there is an electro-magnetic field surrounding the body that does not die when the body dies. If we also recognize that there is a significant probability that the aura is the true location of our mind…then we have taken a giant step towards the understanding of many of life's mysteries.

Where did this aura originate? Inasmuch as we cannot see it, feel it, touch it, hear it or taste it, it becomes reasonable to assume that our aura is from another dimension: a world we cannot, as humans, perceive except in our minds. If this is so, it means that worlds in other dimensions do, in fact, exist.[1] Whether they are populated by people such as us (probable) or by space-like creatures (improbable) is really inconsequential. The fact is that there are other worlds, in other dimensions that not only exist, but are communicating with us by teaching the brain as much as the brain can absorb. A true psychic is one whose "aura is more sensitive to other "auras" around him and is able, on some level, to communicate with other auras.

Psychically sensitive people will get images from other auras while they are awake, while they sleep, while they are watching TV or "whenever". These messages may not be clear unless the psychic is concentrating on a particular person or object. By holding onto my keys, Hurkos was probably able to become sensitive to my aura and pulled things from my memory banks in my brain; things that I was not consciously thinking about.

When Hurkos was being questioned by the German Intelligence officer, the officer probably had a list of questions to ask as well as a wire recorder to record Hurkos' responses. The officer was probably thinking

---

1   Physicists and astronomers are now tending to agree. The latest "Super String Theory" is highly indicative of other dimensions we cannot sense.

ahead or preparing to ask the next question while waiting for Hurkos to respond. Hurkos' sensitivity picked-up the question that was being thought of rather than the one being asked.

It may still sound somewhat confusing, but it will become even more clear as we go on. Certainly, it would explain the how Peter Hurkos was able to do the unimaginable.

MENTAL TELEPATHY & DÉJÀ VU

Many will say that what a psychic does is merely a form of mental telepathy. Actually, there are many differences and many similarities. A true psychic picks up on the "auras" of other people. Those "auras" may be surrounding inanimate objects like a set of keys, a cigarette case... Mental telepathy is more the ability of one person to read another person's thoughts without touching that person or something very close to that person. Again, I am not referring to stunts performed by magicians who make people believe their mind was read by the magician. Take my word for it, any mental telepathy done for public consumption is 99% trickery. I don't say 100%, because although I have lived with magic and magicians most of my life, there are still a few (very few) whose "mental" acts have me fooled.

True mental telepathy is a form of ESP where one person can tell what another's current thoughts are. This is what happened when Hurkos was being interrogated by the German Intelligence officer. Later, of course, Hurkos was far more sensitive to picking up a person's aura rather than their current thoughts. Perhaps as Hurkos' injured brain healed, changes in its sensitivity took place.

Very few people have the ability to read "current" thoughts. Clearly, there are innumerable instances of this happening although not with any apparent consistency. The numbers of testimonials to "current" thought transmission (often referred to as telepathic communication) are, again, far too vast to simply deny without serious investigation. Even at Duke University's psychic-testing lab, there several hundred confirmed cases of thought transference. This is far from meeting the standards of scientific proof, but it is strong circumstantial evidence.

Telepathic communication is most often noted in identical twins. Many twins have shown that they can communicate with each other without speech…and sometimes, before developing speech in an accepted language, they develop a private language all their own. I believe this is most likely true when the buffers in the two brains are so similar that they can bypass each other. Of course, as the children grow older and their thought processes begin to get clogged by external events, the buffers in the brain begin to take on individual characteristics and the ability to communicate telepathically diminishes. Just think about it: How many times have you spoken with twins where one twin starts a sentence and the other finishes it? Obviously, both "auras" were on the same wavelength.

But telepathy also exists between many people who are not related:

I had an experience many years ago. I was walking east along 50th Street in New York City between Seventh and Sixth Avenues. As on any business day, the street was packed with people going to and from their business, shoppers, sightseers, etc. For some reason, I happened to think about a girl I hadn't seen in months. In my thoughts she was wearing a yellow, flowered, dress. The vision left my mind almost as quickly as it entered. Until, about fifteen or thirty seconds later, I reached the corner of 50th Street and Sixth Avenue, and, walking north on 6th Avenue approaching 50th Street was that girl…wearing that particular dress. It was a little startling and I asked her if she had been on 50th Street…She said "No".

Can I prove to someone that it actually happened? No. Has it ever happened again? No. But it did happen that once. And, if it happened once, there must be some explanation as to why it happened. Inasmuch as I am not a believer in coincidence, I've come up with no better explanation than to say our "auras", although measurably attached to our bodies, have the ability to separate from our bodies and move about freely. Perhaps she was thinking of me at that very moment or perhaps, because I was concentrating on my walk and not thinking about anything in particular, my aura wandered over to Sixth Avenue, saw the girl and came back to me with an image of her. Certainly, I have no way to be sure. But anything that happens must have a reason for its happening, and the free-floating aura idea is consistent with everything else in this book.

This brings me to a very important point: Unlike our bodies which are confined to one spot...even when we move...our "auras"...or perhaps portions of our auras... are free-floating, and can move about at will. Distances mean nothing to "auras" because nothing travels faster than thought.

Examples of this happen to most of us: We're sitting at home, just relaxing when, for reasons unknown, you happen to think of someone you haven't seen for a long time. Just then the telephone rings and it is the person you were thinking about. The term "déjà vu" is most commonly applied to situations like this. The numbers of people who have experienced this type of telepathy is most significant. There are many millions of claims by people to having had experiences like this. There are probably hundreds of millions more people who have the experience, but because they don't understand it, say nothing about it. Many people claim to have these experiences regularly.

The biggest problem with mental telepathy incidents is that they cannot be proven. We have no way of knowing whether the person relating the incident is lying, perhaps just exaggerating a little...or whether it actually happened the way it was described. You would think that a person would turn to science to find out the "why" and the "how" of such experiences, but as we already know, getting answers that make sense is difficult. Déjà vu experiences cannot be tested in any scientific manner, because the recipient of the déjà vu experience never knows when or "if" it's going to happen again. What makes it increasingly difficult to prove is because it is never easy to discern whether or not you have had a genuine déjà vu experience or whether something you had reason to anticipate, just happened. Then, too, most déjà vu experiences happen in your sleep...and for good reason, as we will see.

To some degree, almost all of us are psychic. I've had other experiences that loosely fall into the category of déjà vu: Going to a strange place and feeling that I've been there before...even to the extent of knowing where certain businesses are located; meeting someone for the very first time and having the feeling that I've known that person before; having a conversation with someone and feeling strongly that I've had that conversation with the same person before.

Having a feeling or premonition about something is not really the same as experiencing a psychic event such as my visualizing the girl in the yellow dress, although both are forms of ESP.

A very intelligent Los Angeles radio commentator named Michael Jackson (not the pop singer), when interviewing an ostensible psychic was asked if he had not looked at some stranger and had the feeling that they had met before. Jackson caustically replied "Not when I was visiting Pakistan!"

At first glance, Jackson's comment would seem to have merit and be a strong argument against the déjà vu concept. But if you think about it, there is an excellent reason for this: Logically, the déjà vu experience is one aura communicating with another aura (as much as the brain will allow). In this "communication", familiar things...possibly even past lives...play a large role. But if the "auras" are functioning in totally different languages, it would be virtually impossible for historical data or anything else to be communicated. Your mind or aura speaks to your brain in the language you understand; like a voice inside your head. It would be ludicrous for an English-speaking person to think in Urdu (the principal language of Pakistan). Therefore it would become exceedingly difficult for your aura to find compatibility with or communicate with the aura of a person who thinks in Urdu. If we think it through, it follows that anyone we meet who gives us that déjà vu feeling is thinking in the same language as we do. It's not that your aura may not be able to speak or understand Urdu...but when it is with you, it thinks and speaks in the language you understand. An aura thinking and speaking Urdu (or any other foreign language) would, understandably, not be readily be picked up by a mind or aura that thinks in English. While déjà vu "feelings" are almost impossible to test scientifically, science has been trying for many years to ascertain the validity or non-validity of mental telepathy.

The best that science can do is to test simple mental telepathy using its own definition of what it is. This may or may not have any bearing on what true telepathy is, and the means many scientific labs have chosen to test telepathy are totally devoid of merit: Recognizing that something like telepathy is, at best, extremely difficult to prove, science set about to create certain standards of testing. Their options were few, so they said if someone passes their test, it was telepathy...if it doesn't pass their tests, it wasn't.

The criteria used to test ESP as set by scientists at Stanford University (where they have been testing ESP for many years) are virtually impossible for anyone having psychic ability to pass: One test is to take a set of cards (5 or 6 cards) each with a different symbol (usually geometric) on their face, and place them face down. The "telepathic" individual being tested is then to try and identify each of the symbols on the cards.

The prime reason for this being a foolish means of testing is that there are no thoughts for the telepath to read or be sensitive to! The cards are placed, face down, in a random order...so how is the telepath supposed to be able to read them? I tried it several times and I averaged one out of five correct. Yet, I know I have certain psychic sensitivities such as the incident in New York on 50th Street or the experience I had in San Francisco (in the Preface to this book and in section entitled "Ghosts").

The telepathy test results change markedly when the cards are placed so that the tester can see the faces of the cards while the individual being tested cannot see them. With thoughts from which to gain impressions, many telepaths have had consecutive readings where all cards were read perfectly although concealed from the telepath's view. But, inasmuch as the testing scientists feel there might be some secret way of sending a signal to the telepath, or the so-called telepath being in cahoots with the tester, or some small mirror being concealed... scientists at Stanford will not allow it and discount this kind of test completely.

Other science-approved tests include placing the telepath being tested into locked lead-lined room with a power field (usually electromagnetic) surrounding the room, and seeing if he can determine the objects (again, often the same type of cards) on the faces of cards.

If, in fact, telepathy is the reading of one aura by another, getting through a lead-lined room may be possible, but since the aura is believed to be a type of electromagnetism, it would be highly unlikely that one form of electricity could pass through another without being disturbed. Again, the scientific test is doomed to failure. On this basis, most scientists will deny the existence of any paranormal or ESP happenings.

To a limited extent, I cannot blame science for being so rigid and careful in their testing, because the numbers of frauds alleging the powers of ESP are very high, and some of the frauds are remarkably clever and can be quite convincing.

I was introduced to a man several friends said was a genuine psychic. He, willingly, allowed me to test him: I took five cards, each with a different geometric symbol and asked him to identify them. He asked to study the cards first, which he did. Then he asked me to mix the cards and hand them to him face-down. He identified each one several times in a row, and I thought I had found a genuine psychic...until I re-examined the cards, and noticed that he had used his fingernail to put slight dents in the edge of each card. One dent was for a triangle, two dents for a square, three for a circle, etc. Using the same cards, it was easy to identify each geometric symbol by running my fingers over the edge of the card. Just another clever fraud.

There is still another problem when it comes to testing someone for genuine psychic ability: Even the genuine psychics are not consistent. There may be some days when their psychic abilities shine, and there may be other days when they can't read the meter in a taxicab. Then, too, most psychics can be 100% right with some people, and they simply cannot read others.

If scientists, instead of being rigid in what they will accept and what they won't, would look beyond their own noses for a moment, it would be readily understandable as to why scientific experiments fail in the area of proving psychic events.[2] No one, to my knowledge...or that I have read about... has been able to control their own psychic abilities. Even Peter

---

2   It should be noted that both the CIA and the Stanford University studies on psychic phenomena gave strong indication that psychic ability and precognition exist based on probability. But neither study was able to conclusively state that any psychic ability resides within people in any controllable form. Duke University has been studying psychic phenomena since 1927. They will often have a subject who displays very strong psychic abilities only to see those abilities disappear upon re-test.

Hurkos, who had uncanny accuracy in many of his witnessed and famous psychic predictions and readings, could not control it. At times he had it… and at times he didn't. And he didn't know why.

It would be reasonable to suppose that access to your own aura is difficult. How can you use your own mind to send messages to your own mind. It would be like trying to talk while some else is talking because when you think, your mind is active. It can't think things and be fed things at the same time. That's why most ESP experiences occur when you are sleeping and the aura can feed you and not have your mind clogged up with other things.

I firmly believe each of us can communicate with our own aura. We simply have to talk to the aura…not "think" thoughts to our aura, but talk, aloud, to it. I strongly suggest, if you don't want people to think you are "nuts" that you do so in private and not in public places. The fact is that if you talk to your aura it will listen…and you may be greatly surprised at what it can do for you.

There are many books available on so-called "spirit guides" and "Indian Guides". Each of us does have a spirit guide: Your own aura! Tell your aura what you would like it to do for you…and if the request is reasonable and feasible, it will probably do it for you. But don't ask it to do anything "physical", because its power is purely mental.

Trying to communicate with the aura of another person may have several limiting factors: Access to another's aura may be possible only when weather conditions are right; the moon is in the right phase, etc. Even if the other person's aura is sensitive enough to receive your "aura's" communication, the brain of the other person may not be able to compute it and/or act upon it.

Perhaps the damaged buffers in the brain of Hurkos gave him a greater number of windows through which he could communicate, but certainly not an open door.

One brief side note: I have often been amazed by the numbers of people who have accepted my theories concerning the human aura who have asked me, "What about pets?" "Do animals have an aura? ""If I die, my aura may be able to contact some of my dearly departed loved ones. But how about my pet dog that was like a child to me when I was alive?"

The answer to this is slightly complex: Do animals have thoughts? The answer is "Yes", but to an extremely limited extent. Animals can feel excitement, fear, love (not like human love) and other basic feelings. They do not have the capability to analyze those feelings...or to think about them. If an animal has been domesticated and lives in an area where it can be surrounded by the "auras" of humans, the answer is possibly a very doubtful "yes".

Dogs and other pets do not have a language with which to communicate. Perhaps they can send signals of hunger or pain or sorrow...but, clearly, they do not have any language. If they do not have a language, they cannot think. I have seen my dog's paws moving while it slept, as if they're running. So, even without communication, some dogs can dream. But whatever those dreams are, it is doubtful that they involve "thought".

The conclusion that must be reached is that household pets are surrounded by the language of the household and, to a very limited extent can recognize certain words, phrases and even spoken language.

The explanation for this is that, in your home, your aura moves about freely.

It would be expected that, on occasion, your aura would try and feed the brains of your pets. It would speak to them in the language you use... which would also be the only language that your pets would find familiar and that they may understand slightly. Thus, when the pet sleeps, thoughts that emanated from your aura might enter their brain and cause them to dream.

It logically follows that your aura will carry the memories of the brains it has entered and, when you die and become your aura, your aura will be carrying the memories of your pets, too, and you may sense their presence, even after death.

On the other hand, wild animals that have never lived with "auras", are most unlikely to ever dream or live any kind of life beyond their basic instincts. When they die, so does everything about them.

CHAPTER 3

Mind/Body Separation

The concept that each of us has an individual electromagnetic aura that is physically separate and distinct from our body, but yet is mysteriously connected to it, is strongly backed by the evidence of infra-red photography. Assuming that the cameras do not lie, it also provides a very rational explanation for another phenomenon: mind/body separation. Most people have heard about this, but few of us have experienced it. This seemingly strange, but often documented, occurrence is called "astral projection". For purposes of this book the terms "mind" and aura are interchangeable.

Astral projection is when, for reasons we have not pinned-down, a person's aura leaves the body and wanders about. The body can be in a sleep mode or, more commonly, in an artificially induced sleep (more about this later). One of the strangest parts of this phenomenon is that although the eyes are closed on the physical body, the aura seems to be able to see and hear. We are all well aware that our sight comes from our very physical optic nerve and eyes and our hearing from our ears and vibrating ear drum. Yet, the evidence is overwhelming that, during mind/body separation, the separated mind/aura can both see and hear. The other worldly senses of touch, taste and smell seem to absent. Those who have described astral projection say that all they feel is a warm, comfortable feeling. But they do see and hear things that would be impossible to see and hear in a normal, unseparated, state.

As examples of this, I have met several people who regularly practice astral projection and they tell me they have visited other cities, other countries, etc. and observed places they have never been. They have visited people they know who live far away and listened to conversations that were later verified. Time and distance appear to have little meaning while astrally projected.

I've also met several people who have experienced mind/body separation on an "occasional" basis; people who would not know how to astrally project at will. These are the people who provide what I deem to be irrefutable empirical evidence because they are not trying to "impress" others. There have been many occasions when people who have "incidentally" astrally projected have communicated with me and asked for guidance and understanding of their astral projection experience.

The setting for incidental astral projection is most often a doctor's office or a hospital when the body is under some sort of anesthesia. Perhaps the unnatural sleep that is induced on the subject helps the brain to sleep, and when the brain is sleeping, the "aura' is most active. When the brain goes to sleep or goes into what we might call a "rest" mode, the aura may feel free to separate from the body to which it has become attached.

Among those with whom I've spoken, this type of thing seems to happen when a person is being operated on. The body may be on the operating table, but the mind leaves the body and travels around. Often it listens to the conversations the surgeons may be having…or for the more adventuresome, the mind leaves that operating room and visits another site; perhaps the operating room next door. The aura may listen to the conversations of doctors and nurses not in the same room. In more extreme cases, the aura leaves the body and travels elsewhere…to other cities…to other countries, all in less than a few seconds. Most people who experience astral projection on a regular basis like to make mental notes of the places they have gone and the people they have seen. The recollections these astral travelers have when they return to their bodies and awake are almost 100% accurate. Again, when the mind seems to astrally project, things are observed (and even noted) that the person experiencing astral projection could have no possible way of knowing.

Once a person has astrally projected (usually by surprise while under an anesthetic) it seems to get easier and easier for that person to astrally project again. There are many people who claim to be able to astrally project at will. They put themselves into somewhat of a hypnotic trance and their mind/aura travels to places in the world they have never seen.

SCIENTIFIC PROOF?

There is one very famous case of astral projection, with a man named Sasha K. Sasha often boasted that he could control his mind/body separation. So a group of skeptical scientists from NYU (New York University) agreed to participate in a "test". Another group of skeptical scientists from the University of California (Berkeley) went to a house belonging to one of them in San Francisco. In the living room of that house, they set up a table. On that table, they opened a mutually agreed upon book and circled one of the words on the open page and left the book and page open and readily available to anyone to see. The challenge was for Sasha to astrally project himself from New York to that apartment in San Francisco, identify the circled word and bring it back with him to New York while his actions were observed by the group from NYU. Sasha would be given the address of the home in San Francisco and nothing else. Sasha said he was willing to try this.

On cue, Sasha put himself into a trance. One of the scientists, a physician, examined Sasha and commented that his body was functioning properly, but he did not react to any of several things the physician did to stimulate the man. Sasha was, apparently, in a state of sleep, strongly resembling a coma. In a matter of a few minutes, Sasha opened his eyes and appeared to come back to life. Sasha then, correctly, named the word in the San Francisco book.

Is this scientific proof? Certainly it would seem so. However, it's necessary to go back to the last lines in the prologue of this book: "If you don't believe something, no amount of proof will convince you. If you believe something, no proof is necessary.

The scientists both in San Francisco and New York agreed that what they saw was an absolute impossibility. Since it was an impossibility, they dismissed it and agreed that there had to be some sort of trickery involved; that someone among the scientists knew the word in advance and fed it to Sasha, before the experiment started hoping to capitalize on the anticipated publicity.

Even though the scientists dismissed it as a hoax, it did make a few lines in the New York Post. Not headlines…just a small item on one of the inside pages.

None of the so-called astral projection phenomena are strongly documented in a scientific sense, nor are they provable. Like almost all psychic happenings, they are virtually impossible to prove scientifically, although there are thousands of testimonials by those who have experienced it and have identified specific places, incidents and events that they should have no possible way of knowing about from the location of their physical form. But testimonials are not scientific proof: Science debunks virtually all psychic phenomena because they can't really test it. And, that which they cannot prove to their scientific satisfaction, under controlled conditions is simply cast aside as the ravings of maniacs, publicity seekers or poor, hapless, writers like me.

In a way, I can't blame them. It is true that many supposedly psychic events are trickery by people seeking money or publicity...or both. Perhaps the result of misguided beliefs. But, even if ninety percent of those claiming psychic experiences are pure baloney, that means that ten percent are genuine.

Simple arithmetic tells us that if there have been a million cases of astral projection reported, and only ten percent are genuine, that means that a hundred thousand reportings are genuine. That's a lot of mind/body separation experiences to simply write-off as science fiction.

When I first started investigating psychic phenomena, I was as much a skeptic as any scientist. But there's an old axiom: "If one person tells you that you are drunk, you may or may not be...but if ten people tell you that you are drunk, there's an excellent chance that you are drunk." It is the weight of numbers that convinced me to start exploring the so-called psychic world. How could so many millions of people who have experienced similar things be discarded as so much rubbish?

In truth, you cannot simply ignore the part of the world that we cannot see...or rather, can see only on rare occasions...without giving it serious thought. We can't see the air we breathe...but we can feel it and see the reaction of many things to it. So it is that we cannot see psychic phenomena, but almost all of us have felt it and seen the reaction of others and ourselves to it.

JOE'S STORY

Personally, I have never experienced astral projection, but I have a friend named Joe W. who has: Joe is a mortgage broker living in the San Francisco Bay area of California. Joe is a very normal person in appearance, and comes across as a humble but financially successful person. Joe is well-respected and an exceptionally intelligent man. It's because of his intelligence that he has become a highly inquisitive person and tried to find answers to a lot of so-called unanswerable questions. Like so many others seeking the truth that science would not provide, he sought answers in the Church of Scientology and several other cult groups. Joe never stayed with them for very long because Joe always wound up disappointed. These groups promised answers that were never delivered.

In the many years I have known him, he has always been 100% honest. I knew him quite well over the course of many years, and I never heard him tell a lie, even when a lie may have been a choice of better discretion.

Joe told me that when he went for dental surgery, the dentist put him under nitrous oxide (laughing gas) to minimize the pain of the procedure. It's called "laughing gas" because as you go under and as you awaken, you seem to laugh. But, in truth, it knocks you out and puts you to sleep. Joe told me that while he was under, he felt his mind rise to the top of the room and looked down at himself. He watched the dentist and nurse's procedures on his mouth with great interest, and listened to some of the things they were saying. A little frightened, at first, Joe soon became almost euphoric at his newly-found ability; he decided to let his mind have a "look-around". He absolutely controlled the movement of his mind or aura and allowed it to wander into the waiting room and listened to a conversation between a mother and her son. He told me he then allowed his mind to rise up through the ceiling into another office directly above the room where the surgery was taking place. Joe told me he had the feeling he could leave the building and travel anywhere…but he was too frightened and unsure of how far he could push things, so he went back down to where the surgery was taking place and returned to his own body.

When he awakened from the anesthesia, he jotted down notes of what he had heard his dental surgeon and nurse say, and what he had heard the mother and son in the waiting room say. His notes proved to be 100% accurate. He also took a trip up one floor in the medical building and looked inside the office directly above his dental surgeon' office. He said it looked slightly different than when he saw it when he was under anesthesia, but, unquestionably, it was the same place. Joe looked at me and said, "I'm not afraid to die now…because I know that when I do, my mind is going to separate from my body and I will be very happy."

While I have never experienced astral projection or mind/body separation, I think Joe may be right! There is extremely powerful empirical evidence that the aura around the body of a dead person does not die…it simply moves-on.

Again, a fascinating aspect of Joe's story is that he was able to both see and hear when his mind wandered to the ceiling of the room, into the waiting room and even the office above. Inasmuch as Joe's truthfulness is above reproach, I have to believe that he was able to see and hear although his brain and body were on the operating table or dentist's chair. We think of it being necessary for the eyes to do the seeing and the ears to do the hearing. But apparently, your mind/aura has other ways of seeing and hearing.

Did he dream the whole thing? If so, how did he know the details about the conversation between a mother and her son in the waiting room or the appearance of the office above?

If Joe's story is accurate, it means that our minds/auras/thoughts have visual and hearing abilities of their own. This would explain how, when I was walking along 50th Street in New York and I got the image of a former girlfriend in a yellow, flowered dress...my aura had to be able to see that girl and reflect the image into my brain. When I carefully reviewed the events of that day, the girl and her yellow dress did look slightly different than when I saw her on 6th Avenue. The differences were minor...but there were differences.

I concluded that we, as people see through our eyes and hear through our ears. But our aura uses something different with which to see and hear. This might also go a long way towards explaining why it is that the images we see in our dreams can be highly detailed...but even extremely familiar faces and places look slightly distorted.

Try a simple experiment: When you are waking up in the morning... just before you open your eyes, try and picture your bedroom in your mind. Certainly, you should be familiar, in intricate detail, as to what your bedroom looks like. But, I'd be willing to bet that when you open your eyes and see your bedroom the way it is...it will be different than you visualized it just prior to opening your eyes.

This is because although your mind/aura can see, it does not use the same optic nerves, lenses, etc. that the eyes in your body do. That's why, when you dream about things...even very familiar things or people, they appear to be slightly distorted from the way you see them when your eyes are open. They are, unquestionably, recognizable… but your mind/aura sees things slightly differently.

It would also make sense, then, that after we die and our brain is completely dead, through our mind/aura we will still be able to see and hear things. This gains further support from people I have spoken to who have experienced astral projection and who document their mind's travels with the details of an eyewitness account.

The problem, again, is how do we prove these things actually happen? There are many pretenders who claim to be able to separate their mind and body at will and offer to demonstrate it for money. Maybe some of them can actually do it, but the likelihood is that they cannot. The numbers of phony psychics probably outnumbers those having genuine psychic abilities by a thousand to one…or more.

Most people who call themselves para-psychologists are also phonies: people who prey upon the hopes and beliefs of others for the sole purpose of fattening their own bank accounts. Most wouldn't know the truth if it slapped them in the face. It would not be fair to group all parapsychologists under one umbrella any more than it would be to treat any group of people as being the same. I'm certain there are some who genuinely believe in their work. It's just that caution is highly recommended before you part with any of your hard-earned dollars to them.

The world in which we live is filled with paradox: Everyone wants to live a long life, but no one wants to grow old. Many people are afraid of dying because death is an unknown. Is it simply the end of everything? Or, perhaps is it the beginning? Or a continuation? Millions of people believe in the concept of a Heaven and Hell because they want to believe that life is eternal; when their body dies, their spirit is going to go someplace. Others believe that if they sacrifice their life here on Earth, they will go to a great hereafter. Almost all religions preach that if you follow their teachings, you will be rewarded in the afterlife. The philosophy of most people preaching orthodox religions seems to be "Go ahead…promise them everlasting life…they'll never know it if you're wrong."

I, for one, am totally convinced that there is an afterlife. What that afterlife actually is I will not know until my time has come. But astral-projection gives me a very strong clue. The mind/aura does not die. It is free to move about. It can see…it can hear…it is free to contact and communicate with other auras…although it does not seem to have too much success contacting living brains…except its own…and even then, only on occasion.

Following that thought through, it would not only seem possible, but even probable that you will again communicate with your dead father or friends as the free-moving mind/auras communicate. But what happens when the mind/aura seeks another body to surround? As the déjà vu and astral projections have shown, the "auras" still communicate. The "auras" may not always be able to penetrate the waking brain sufficiently to convey precise messages…but then, there are those "feelings", aren't there?

There are some people who tell me they are able to perform mind/body separation frequently and do so as often as possible. I have been told of people who do it to relax. Although I cannot attest to having met any people who have demonstrated this for me, what they have told me seems to concur with everything else in this book: Those people will lie back on a chaise or a sofa and meditate, or listen to sound recordings of waves coming into shore, or birds chirping in the wilderness. They say that only when their mind and body are completely relaxed can the astral projection take place.

Two methods that seem to be a favorite of many people who astrally project are self-hypnosis and meditation. There are no better ways known to man that will completely relax the body and the brain than the use of meditation and/or self-hypnosis. People who practice this, even if there is no mind/body separation, tell me that they feel "at one" with the world. I think a more knowledgeable way of phrasing that is that they become one with their mind/aura.

Chapter 4

Ghosts

Ghosts are an unusual topic: Almost everything else in this book deals with unexplained things that can happen during your lifetime. Common sense, logic and a peek into what I term "other dimensions" can explain most paranormal things.

The first question that must be answered is "Are there really such things as ghosts or should they be confined to movies and Stephen King novels?" If there are such things, what are they?

Webster's Dictionary defines a ghost as "a disembodied soul; especially: the soul of a dead person believed to be an inhabitant of the unseen world or to appear to the living in bodily likeness". Personally, I believe that ghosts are the auras of dead people who may not recognize that they are dead, or who are aware they are dead and are trying to say something to the living.

Inasmuch as auras are composed of electromagnetic energy, it is safe to say that if ghosts exist, they are composed of electromagnetic energy. I have rarely heard of the ghost of someone who did not die in an unexpected manner. People who were murdered (such as the girl in San Francisco) or died in an accident (the father of the girl with the bank-account numbers) are examples of a continuing existence after death.

From what I have been able to garner, when people die, their aura goes to a special place where (a) they can remain for a while or (b) where they wait to be re-born. If someone refuses to recognize that they are dead, neither of the above options would be selected. I've read numerous tales of haunted houses where ghosts remain because they still believed they lived-in and owned that house.

Ghost chaser organizations have often said that will go into an ostensibly haunted house; locate a room in which their instrumentation detects a "presence"; and loudly explain to that "presence" that he/she no longer lives there nor still owns the house. Very often the ghost or haunting will disappear forever.

I'm not suggesting that these could not have been "staged" events; it's just that there have been a lot of them, and the weight of numbers always impresses me. Especially when they are done by people who do not get paid for their ghost chasing.

The definition that ghosts are the auras of people who refuse to accept the fact that they are dead may have seemed like so-much gobbledygook when you were in high school or college. Isn't it amazing, or coincidental, that the definition seems to fit what we've been discussing in this book, almost to the letter? As I've said before, I do not believe in coincidence.

One of the most unusual things about ghosts is that they allow themselves to be seen and, occasionally, heard. Sometimes not really seen, but their presence is almost always "felt". As we get into what ghosts actually are…the auras or energy of dead people…we should try to remember that auras cannot be sensed by any of our five senses and, therefore, are not of our dimension. Then how is it that…sometimes…ghosts can be seen or appear in photos?

This brings up another question: Why or how is it that ghosts sometimes appear on photos when nothing was seen at the time the photo was taken? Is there something about cameras that can detect images our eyes can't see? If so, this might help explain the spate of UFO photos that have appeared with increasing intensity as digital photography gets more popular. Most seemingly genuine pictures of ghosts and UFOs are objects that were not visible when the photo was taken. Of course we must remember that photo shops work best with digital photography, so we must rely on the integrity of the photographer.

Ghost stories, particularly those that seem to be real or create the feeling of reality have always been a favorite for kids…of all ages. But, if you try to convince someone that you've really seen a ghost, they will probably think you've been smoking something strange. If you took the time to read the Prologue of this book, I told about a true ghost story that actually happened to me when I was in San Francisco. I spoke of the appearance of a young (early twenties) girl in my new apartment and of her disappearance when I turned on the night lamp next to my bed.

Weeks later I learned that the very same girl had been murdered in that apartment a few weeks before I moved in. The question is and was: What did I see? Is that what they call a ghost?

Perhaps, as Peter Hurkos often said, inanimate objects can bear memories. Was the memory of that horrific event where she was murdered imbued in the apartment walls? If so, why didn't the ghost ever appear again?

Perhaps the aura of that girl decided to stay around not really convinced that her body was dead. Because I was asleep, maybe my aura sensed her presence and woke me up.

What I'm trying to get across is that the topic of "ghosts" is not, necessarily a simple one.

Inasmuch as I try to be rational, even about the most irrational things, I thought of the possibility of the inanimate walls bearing a memory because of the traumatic event which had taken place there. Believe me, I gave it a lot of thought…but it was not until years later that I began to realize what it was that I had seen…and why:

Remember the aura that doesn't die? Leanne Polski 's aura was very much alive, but still somewhat in shock from the sudden, unexpected death of its computer/brain. The aura, remained in that apartment and tried to communicate with me. But, since my brain was not nearly sophisticated enough to comprehend its communications, it tried to create a visual image for me to see. It did…and I did. Then, realizing that there would be no return of Leanne, the aura left the room and went somewhere else… perhaps it went back to its own dimension to await the birth of a new computer/brain…perhaps it went to visit some loved ones.

An interesting part of my research indicates that ghosts seem to prefer hanging around houses where they once lived, or places where they once worked. I've seen an occasional photo of a ghost in the outdoors and certainly there are many claims of ghosts appearing on lonely stretches of road…but generally, they seem to prefer places with which they are familiar: places where they felt a degree of comfort when they were living. "Outdoor" ghosts seems to prefer to remain where they met untimely and unexpected deaths…and have not fully recognized the fact that they are dead.

In a large way, the theory of the aura I've been expounding in this book goes a long way toward explaining what ghosts really are. Ghosts that have been seen (and many have been seen) are almost always the result of some traumatic and unexpected end to the human life represented.

A natural question to ask is why do some ghosts remain around so long? When the computer/brain the aura has adopted dies, why doesn't it just return to the dimension from which the aura came? There are ghosts that, supposedly, have been around for hundreds of years. Some of the haunted castles in England or in the Transylvania Mountains of Romania have been alleged to be around for several hundred years.

Actually, I think we've partially covered that: Remember, the aura is only a thought process, and the time differential between its home dimension and ours is vast. It may take the person controlling the thought aura a day or two to realize that their computer/brain has come to an abrupt, unexpected end…but that day or two may represent hundreds of Earth years.

Then, too, there is the possibility that the aura, finally recognizing that their body is dead, may try to travel around to seek out loved ones; even visit places they wanted to visit during their lifetime, but never did. Maybe the aura wants to search around to find another body to attach to. There can be hundreds of reasons, many beyond our comprehension as to why the aura sticks around.

There are so many ghost stories that can be explained by the thought aura. The girl whose father died and was awaked in the middle of the night by her father's ghost…who told her the location of several secret safe deposit boxes and bank accounts she and her attorney had not known about. This time, the aura was so closely related to the girl that the aura was not only able to create an image, but communicate, as well. While this is quite rare, there are many such cases on record.

Like everything else that falls into the category of being paranormal, ghosts cannot be proven scientifically. But there are so many millions of people who claim to have seen them or felt them…or even communicated with them, that we must search for answers beyond science.

SPEAKING WITH THE DEAD

Assuming there are such things as ghosts, is there any known way we can communicate with them?

One man, John Edwards, is a most interesting person: He has made millions claiming that he can speak with the dead. Does he really?

Most doubtful!

My tendency is to believe that when anyone commercializes on an allegedly psychic or paranormal talent, that talent is more of a performance art than an actual psychic ability. Let's look at the pros and cons for just a moment:

Edwards, on live television, has said things of such specificity that have raised my eyebrows in surprise. I remember him talking to a telephone caller on the Larry King Show (CNN). The caller was a lady who wanted to know about her dead brother. Edwards said he was getting the image of a dead dog, did she have a dog that died recently? The lady said "yes". Edwards then asked, "Was his name Max"? The answer was "yes".

Was this John Edwards communicating with a dead dog? Even the thought of this, to me, is absurd. Much more likely, the caller was a "plant". Someone that Edwards had told, in advance, to call into the Larry King show.

On the con side, Edwards guesses a lot and is an expert at what is called a "cold reading". He starts with a name; if that doesn't ring a bell, he goes to the first letter in that name. He plays his listeners very well, and Edwards is an extraordinarily talented person. He is a showman, and there are some serious dollars at stake if he is ever proven to be a fraud. I have been told by people who have attended the taping of his television show that he has numerous "plants" in his audience and that he has a staff of "screeners" who find out as much about audience members before he goes on the air. As if that isn't enough, I've been informed by people he's selected to talk to their dead loved ones that he will have the video tape cut and spliced before it goes on the air so that even in places where he makes a bad guess, the cut will show the audience member nodding his head in agreement.

I'm not calling Edwards a "fraud", but he has a long way to go before he convinces me that anything he does is for real.

Notwithstanding the foregoing, it does seem that Edwards may have some psychic abilities in the area of mental telepathy: the ability to pick up on the thoughts of people he speaks with. But this type of psychic ability would need to put both parties in the same room or in some reasonable form of proximity. It simply does not make sense that he can do it via telephone.

Granted that thought waves travel faster than anything else, the thought waves have to know where to go to bring the thoughts of a person from one end of a telephone line, probably going through fifty or so switching stations, to the other end of the line. Via satellite, there would be little difference as the thought wave would have to find which of 25,000 electrical impulses per millisecond from the satellite is going to the CNN studio. It is so highly improbable that a "reading" can be done over telephone lines that I give it no credence at all. On the Larry King Show, Edwards did all of his "readings" for people who called-in. As entertaining as it was, to me it was not convincing. And, if you've ever called a live television or radio show, you know that there is a "screener" who will put through those calls he feels will make the TV show the most entertaining.

Another famous medium who allegedly talks with the dead is James Van Paagh. I've seen Van Paagh perform and although I strongly admire him as a showman, I was duly unimpressed with his ability to talk to the dead. Again, because of my own background, I was quickly able to recognize what I felt was a "cold reading" technique Van Paagh was using.

COLD READING

To give you an idea as to how a cold-reading works, I'm going to set a typical one down on paper. What I will write may differ from a showman's routine by a few words and phrases, but will say, in essence, the same thing that most of the showmen will say. Just picture yourself meeting a so-called psychic or medium for the very first time. He looks at the palm of your hand…or into a crystal ball. Then he gazes into your eyes and says:

"I can see you have a great need for other people to like and admire you. You have a tendency to be critical of yourself. You have a great deal of unused capacity which you have not turned to your advantage. While you have some personality weaknesses, you are generally able to compensate for them. Your sexual adjustment has presented some problems for you. Disciplined and self-controlled outside, you tend to be worrisome and insecure inside. At times you have serious doubts as to whether you have made the right decision or done the right thing. You prefer a certain amount of change and variety and become dissatisfied when hemmed in by restrictions and limitations. You pride yourself as an independent thinker and do not accept others' statements without satisfactory proof. You have found it unwise to be too frank in revealing yourself to others. At times you are extroverted, affable, and sociable, while at other times you are introverted, wary, reserved. Some of your aspirations tend to be pretty unrealistic. Security is one of your major goals in life."

Wasn't he talking about **you**? Read the words again carefully because it is very doubtful you will not think it describes you. It is composed of many non-specific statements that sound like someone is seeing into your innermost thoughts. Remember, this was not written about you:

That's how cold readings work: Statements that apply to more than 90% of people are used by psychic frauds and astrologists, etc. as if these thoughts emanated from a psychic source. Note that while the report sounds specific, it really has said nothing specific about you.

Magician mentalists or fraudulent Psychics performing cold readings will often add general or semi-specific statements to try and deceive people: "There was, in childhood, a close brush with death "by you or someone close to you." "There were trials and many changes, the loss of someone close, and an illness or "bad accident." "You have a streak of stubbornness that is sometimes difficult to control." There are usually forecasts of financial gain, perhaps having to do with real estate or "property changing hands.

Or, commonly, the cold reader will tell a woman that she is making a mistake right now trying to reason her way to a decision — she should rely on her intuition and hunches: "If you do, the right course will always be presented to you, and that includes the little problem that's puzzling you right now." For a young man, he hears the ringing of a bell — or is it a ring "such as might be worn on the finger? I leave the answer to you."

For another woman, the cold reader sees "blue sky — or blue water?... And somewhere, far in the distance, I hear a voice calling, "Yes, I am here." I see good fortune in your future."

People well-practiced the cold reading techniques will also pick-up the subtle reactions of the person being read. A customer's slight nod of the head or a raised eyebrow may tell the cold reader that he/she is on the right track or, conversely, that an earlier statement needs to be smoothed-over or covered-up. An expert cold reader can convince almost anyone not familiar with cold reading techniques that they have Psychic/Medium abilities and powers; that they are revealing facts about the customer they should have no way of knowing.

CHARACTERISTICS OF GHOSTS

Aside from the entertainment aspect and people who make their living convincing you that they can talk with dead, there is an overwhelming amount of evidence that ghosts do exist: They are not the "ectoplasm" as shown in the movies, but they are there.

To the best of my information and research there have been millions of ghost sightings and/or experiences throughout the world. Now I'm not talking about Edgar Casey or John Edwards or anyone who makes their living writing about or talking to ghosts. I'm talking about average people who have no extraordinary connection with religion, or who would have no reason to lie about their experiences except, possibly, to assuage their own feelings of insecurity.

Granted that imagination may play a large role in many of the reports of ghosts: Most reports of haunted houses and ghosts are unusual sounds or happenings that could find another, more rational, explanation under careful scrutiny. Very few reports of ghosts are like whatever I saw in San Francisco. That having been said, I have read hundreds of reports of ghosts or haunting that defy more rational explanations. Most people who claim to have seen ghosts say that they saw shadows that moved…they felt chills….objects seem to have moved from place to place.

It's interesting to note that in all the hundreds of tales I've been told about ghosts, there has not been one single instance of a ghost harming anyone. Yet, most people are as frightened as can be of ghosts. I know a lot of people who are too frightened to walk in a cemetery at night.

For the most part, ghosts seem to be camera-shy although I have seen any number of photos that seem to challenge that statement. First of all, I give no credibility to photos of ghosts where the ghost seems to have posed for the camera. I view such photos as being patently false. But I have seen photos of people, of groups and of scenery where a human figure has seemingly appeared in the finished picture that wasn't there when the photo was taken. The problem with all such photos is that you are at the mercy of the honesty and integrity of the photographer. Adobe Photoshop on your computer can make anything you want appear on a finished photo. Still, there are several photos I have seen that I believe to be real because there appears to be no reason for the addition of the ghostly figure.

A lot of people have asked me: "If there is an afterlife and I do see my father (or mother), will I even recognize him (her)? Will he be a young man…an old man…? That question is simple to answer: Your aura will see another aura as you best remembered that person, and they will see your aura as they best remembered you. If they thought of you as a young, strapping man, that's how they will see you. If they thought of you in a nursing home, then that's how they will see you. You will always see yourself as a young, vital person, because that's how your mind/aura thinks about you. How many times have I looked into a mirror and wondered who that old man is…my mind still thinks I'm young, and will always think I'm young. The way you remember someone is how he or she will appear to you in an afterlife.

A VISIT TO A HAUNTED CASTLE

Again, let's put the children's stories aside and look at the hard facts: There are more than 100 castles in England alone that are "guaranteed" haunted. According to the books I've read, around the world, ghosts seems to take different forms…some are invisible, some are very viewable. Some appear to have very indefinite shapes, and others look as real as you or I do.

Have you ever been to a haunted house? I have. I went to a castle outside of London that my tour guide guaranteed me was haunted. Admittedly,

I didn't see any ghosts although I did hear a lot of strange sounds. But, it would be so easy in our high-tech world to create strange sounds apparently out of nowhere, that I really felt very cynical about them. There were, literally, thousands of places in that castle where tiny speakers could be hidden. I was genuinely unimpressed and was thinking, "What a waste of good money." Until…

The mid-afternoon temperature on the day I visited the castle was in the high seventies. Inside the castle, the air was a little more damp and slightly moldy, but the temperature was still quite comfortable. We went through several rooms in the castle, but no ghosts. Then, we entered a large, completely empty, room that had been a bedchamber.

We walked into a large room made of stone (as was the entire castle) where my guide simply said, "This room contains a cold spot." He led me to a point near the middle of the room and told me to pass my hand through a certain area.

As I passed my hand through what seemed like empty space, there was a spot, perhaps six or eight inches wide, where the temperature suddenly dropped from about seventy to about zero (Fahrenheit). As my hand completed passing through the spot, the temperature returned to normal. There was nothing visible in that area of the room that separated the cold spot from the rest of the room. I walked around the spot and tried it from several different angles. It was consistent. I carefully examined the ceiling and the stone floor. It was like a six-inch wide laser beam of coldness that went from the ceiling to the floor. I tried standing directly in it, but it was far too cold for me to remain there for more than a few seconds.

There was no way it could have been a draft, because a draft would have dissipated into the rest of the room and not remained in a cylindrical form. It could not have been a forceful cold wind because there was no particular movement of any wind in the room or in that cylindrical spot. So what caused it and what was it?

Of course, I asked my guide, and he glibly told me it was a "cold spot". I asked him what a "cold spot" was, and he told me it was a spot that always stays cold. I asked him what could have caused it, and he told me the castle was haunted. Very informative!

All the way back to London, I puzzled over this. I picked up a booklet that (ostensibly) told the history of the castle. To me, the booklet seemed more like a poor-man's version of a Stephen King novel than anything else. Nothing that could explain what that cold spot actually was.

As I pondered over it, the word "portal" came to mind. Could that cold spot actually be a portal of sorts? If so…to or from where?

PORTALS TO OTHER DIMENSIONS

At this point, I must step aside from ghosts for a few minutes and explain one more detail which is essential to the understanding of the explanations in this book: Throughout this book I have used the term "dimensions", but I haven't really explained what they are or what their importance is to us. I think my mentioning a "portal" means it's time we took a closer look at dimensions because they do help to explain many paranormal things:

I apologize to all my readers because this small section on portals and other dimensions is exceedingly difficult to understand: We live in a dimension that remains, basically, unchanged throughout our lives. The Earth, the country we live in, our home, our friends, etc. Everything that we can test scientifically belongs in this one dimension including, without limitation, our five senses of taste, smell, sight, sound and touch. But what if there are other dimensions which are too large or too small for us to see? Or maybe dimensions that are blocked by the buffers around our brains? Other dimensions of time and space…kind of like the old Rod Serling's "Twilight Zone", although maybe not with the same Hollywood type of dramatic flair.

The latest theory of our creation from the elite world-wide scientific community of physicists and astronomers, is called the Super String Theory. This theory, in part, suggests that the dimensions of our universe are separated by a fabric of time and space. And, like all fabrics moving in slightly different directions, that fabric may have developed cracks or portals through which someone or something from one dimension can visit another dimension.

According to the Super String Theory, there is strong evidence there are at least nine other dimensions of space and one of time. The problem is that we can determine, scientifically, that they "must be there", but since we can't see them, feel them, etc. we have no way of knowing what they are or where they are. Rocket scientists can actually measure the drain of the gravitational forces from our world into other worlds, but that's as far as science can go right now. So, while we know other dimensions exist, we know nothing about them.

We look into outer space: the distances and times are so vast that we simply cannot comprehend them. Distances are measured in terms of the numbers of years it would take a beam of light to go from the Earth to some other star visible only through a telescope. The speed of light (as measured here on Earth) is 186,000 miles per second (like 9 trips around our Equator in one second). The distance that a light beam would travel at 186,000 miles per second, in one full year, is called a "light year".

Some of the stars in our sky are millions of light years away from us… and that's just the stars we can see. Those beyond our limited ability to see may be billions or trillions of light years away from the Earth. Those worlds are too far away in time and space to even be considered a part of our dimension. They move at different speeds, in different directions and in a manner that our scientific minds fail to understand. It would be virtually impossible to communicate with them because a simple message broadcast into the vastness of space might take trillions of years to get to another star.

Then, we look into the microscopic world, there are trillions and trillions of particles moving so rapidly (as measured in our dimension) that if we could communicate with those tiny particles, they would also be in a different dimension because if we tried to get a message to one of these microscopic worlds, it might take trillions of years in that microscopic world for our message to reach there.

But there does seem to be a way for one world to reach another… certainly not scientifically…but through what I call "breaking the dimension barrier". Logically, this can only be done through cracks in the time-space fabric…or through the use of wormholes or portals. Like the "portals" in the Harry Potter novels that move someone instantly from one place to another, I believe a portal or a wormhole can move a person or an object from one dimension to another.

There is no rational explanation for the cold spot I felt in the haunted castle I visited, but I think it may be a portal or a key to a portal to some other world. We have samples of other worlds being able to enter our world, so why can't the reverse be true? That cold spot needs to be studied by minds more analytical than mine. It may have a lot to do with such things as ghosts, auras, UFOs, etc.

Where did our auras originate? Are they aliens from another planet? Are they visitors from another dimension? At this time, we don't know, but the concept of their being visitors from another dimension is starting to get some scientific support with the String Theory. Certainly they do not live as we do on Earth. As in the scenario in Chapter 14 about a super scientist on a super world somehow getting his thoughts accelerated to communicate with a microscopic world, it is very likely that our auras had to originate in another dimension. That's why there is limited communication with them and why, under most circumstances, we can't see them even if we sense their presence. If they were of our dimension, we could see them, feel them, etc.

How does someone from another dimension visit us…or how do we visit that other dimension? I don't have the answer (yet) to either question, but I am confident that there is a way. Certainly we know they have found a way for them to visit us.

Let's assume that this superior world of which I will speak about in Chapter 14 is real. How did they get from their dimension to ours? The only logical answer is that when conditions are right, they can visit us and return from whence they came…through a portal or wormhole of sorts. O.K., let's assume it's possible. If they can come into our dimension…can the reverse be true as well?

Using the same Einstein theories concerning space and time which state that it's possible for us to travel into the future, but we cannot go backwards in time, so it is that a superior world may be able to visit us, but we cannot visit that superior world. Remember, a few seconds on that superior world would be like hundreds of years on our world, and our bodies are designed for life on this world, not on another. We should, however, allow for the possibility that new technology that may be developed on Earth over the next million or so years, may give us the ability to transport from dimension to dimension. But right now, it's beyond our realm of thinking.

Back to ghosts: I have never been to a séance that was convincing. I've had people try to convince me that Ouija Boards were really spirit communication, that spirit force lifted a table of the floor, etc. It was entertaining, but not convincing. If, in fact, the aura of a person remains alive and can communicate with other auras, it would not have any physical powers. If, in fact, the auras emanate from another dimension, they cannot do physical harm…or good…to someone in our dimension. About the best they could do is communicate with each other to give people warnings or premonitions …or perhaps even help convince people to act in a certain way. But don't let them scare you. They can't hurt you. What may be even more important is that if you are ever able to communicate with a ghost, he or she may be of great help to you, because its aura may be able to give your brain some information that it can compute.

ORBS

No chapter on ghosts can be complete with a look at what are called "orbs".

The mystery of orbs has only been around for the past ten or so years. They may have been around since the beginnings of time, but their presence was first noted and written about ten years ago, and they seem to making an exponentially high increase in appearance in the past few years.

Orbs are round or semi-round balls or sphere-like objects that made their way into photographs and were initially thought to be imperfections on film. When they also started to appear in digital photography, scientists started to look at them more closely. Until recently, orbs seemed to confine themselves to photographs, but more recently they have been seen in homes, in open-air spaces and they are a puzzlement that deserves a closer look.

Scientists, in their fruitless attempts to give everything a label, have stated they believe the orbs to be balls of energy that have, somehow become displaced.

There are lots of problems with that scientific theory. First of all energy can't be seen. Orbs can. Maybe the scientific theory had some merit when orbs only seemed to appear in photographs, but there is one house in Perth, Australia, where they not only can be seen, they move about at their own free will without the aid of sunlight, wind or anything else. I've seen videos of them and a lot of still photography. There was another video of orbs that (supposedly) took place in a Florida home, but to me, that video is suspect.

I've spoken to experts who have looked at the Australian videos and attest to the fact that they have not been photo-shopped.

We know very little about these orbs. I've seen some still photos of them wherein it appears that some of the orbs have human-like faces although lighting and camera may have accidentally created what appears to be faces and are actually the orbs in motion.

Of course, when anything new appears on the paranormal scene, there are reports of people who claim to have had "encounters" with them. I don't know enough about the people who have made such claims to call them "phonies" or "liars", but when someone says that their three dogs were turned into pools of water when they attacked some orbs, a lot of red lights start flashing in my head. I try to be reasonable about all things, but I find such claims belong together with the claims of people who allege they were kidnapped and subjected to medical examination aboard a UFO. It's simply not reasonable to call such reports credible.

Another theory I have heard concerning orbs is that they are extra terrestrial life forms trying to find a home here on Earth. While this is still quite far-out for me to accept, I have to rationally acknowledge that we do not know what they are, they do seem to move about freely, although not with any apparent thought pattern behind their movement, and their numbers seem to be increasing. They do have a tendency to stay in particular areas: You are not likely to see any orbs around New York City, since they do seem to prefer rural, more desolate areas. At this juncture, I am not particularly concerned with them because other than a claim that their dogs were "liquefied", I have never heard anything that would make me think of them as being harmful in any way.

A couple of interesting notes: Most paranormal skeptics say that orbs are a) dust on the camera's lens, (b) dust or particles in the air or (c) droplets of moisture in the air. It's difficult to buy any of these explanations. It would be far too coincidental for all cameras to have moisture or dust on their lenses…and the motion of these orbs in videos could not come from dust or moisture. Infra-red photography has shown us that the orbs have a coating of energy about them. Photos have been taken of them with both film and digital cameras.

Some paranormal buffs have said that they believe orbs to be the same type of energy in our auras, that they are portals to a different dimension and that they are increasing in number and frequency.

At the present time, I can only say that they exist. Time and study will reveal their true nature.

One interesting theory is that we, as humans, expect other life forms to be in our image or in the images of animals here on Earth. Let's put our egos aside and recognize the possibility that other life forms may exist, and orbs may be another life form. If so, the life form would be on such a different plane as to obviate any possibility of communication…at least as far as we understand communication in today's world.

The only thought I have is what I've said earlier: I believe that there are cracks in the time/space fabric of our world. I have often said that I believe there is a good chance that this is where UFOs come from and where they return to. I believe it is possible that these orbs are a life form of sorts that have simply slipped through a crack in our space/time dimension. I note that they pass through solid Earthly objects as would a ghost, and this tends to support the possibility of their being from another dimension.

I'm not saying that this is so, only that it is an unexplored possibility.

Chapter 5

UFOs

It may seem more than just a little strange to bring in a topic such as UFOs and flying saucers into a book about the paranormal, but UFOs are integrated into everything else in this book in many ways that bear no semblance to the popular concepts about them. Actually, UFOs should be looked at seriously although it is difficult to do so when the subject has been so battered, bantered about and made into a joke by people seeking their fifteen minutes of fame, fortune and publicity.

At the outset I would like to state that I am not a UFO "freak" and I do not belong to any UFO societies.

Recently, there has been a plethora of UFO reports together with photographs that seem to be genuine. When I say a photograph is "genuine", I have no way of knowing whether it is the product of computer graphics or an actual photograph. But when I see a photograph where something else is the object of the photo and there appears to be a little speck in the sky…and that speck is blown-up to show some sort of flying object..then I take out my magnifying glass and study the object. Some photos I have seen do appear to be genuine.

The extremely significant number of recent UFO sightings…and the addition of UFOs to virtually every paranormal society's agenda means that they should be discussed in a book explaining unexplained things.

Do you believe in flying saucers? That's really kind of a silly question although it is one I have been asked frequently. I do believe they exist! With more than two million recorded sightings, are we going to call all of those people liars or fools? How about the fleet of them that appeared in northern Brazil on May 19, 1986? Is every villager lying about what they saw? Is the Brazilian army and Intelligence who also saw them making it all up? Doubtful!

Additionally, there have been enough sightings by people for whom I have the greatest respect so that, to me, there is little question about their existence.

There have also been a number of clams by people that they were kidnapped, taken hostage and medically examined by aliens from UFOs. I won't question that some people may actually believe that they were kidnapped by strange creatures on flying saucers. My position is that allegations such as that should not be taken seriously unless and until the claimants have a little something more than their stories.

They may be telling the truth, but I have to take the position that to me they do not sound believable. None of them have ever offered even a shred of forensic or empirical evidence to back their stories up.

Then, too, the numbers of people making claims of having been kidnapped by aliens are relatively small so I am not brought into the position of becoming convinced due to the weight of numbers.

Did a UFO really crash in Rosewell, New Mexico in 1947?

My initial reaction to this story was one of total disbelief. However, as numbers of military officers who (a) were there immediately following the alleged crash or (b) took some of the alleged debris to the infamous Area 51 in Nevada, questions began to arise in my mind:

Are these all people seeking their fifteen minutes of fame? Are these all people who are trying to write a book and hope that their perjured testimony will help to sell it?

I felt a closer examination of ostensible UFO crashes should be undertaken. I got some surprising results:

Just about everyone has heard of the supposed UFO crash near Roswell, New Mexico in 1947. The U.S. military said it was a weather balloon although most of the actual witnesses say it was something completely different. The problems surrounding the Roswell crash are (a) that there is no consistency in the information released about it and (b) so many UFOlogists have expanded, elaborated and written-up so called facts concerning Roswell that have no bearing on the truth.

So let's look at some of the other reported UFO crashes that have not received nearly as much publicity: Oh yes…there have been several UFO crashes that have been witnessed and photographed. All remains have been taken away and sent to labs for examination…and kept secret.

Let's look at a few of them:

The first UFO crash that was recorded was in Aurora, Texas in 1897 (there were many before this one, but they were not recorded). There were several witnesses and newspaper items about the crash of a huge flying object near Aurora…six years before the Wright Brothers made the first, famous, flight at Kitty Hawk. Remnants of the metallic, crashed object in Aurora were dumped down a deep well by the superstitious residents who may have thought that God was raining down fire and brimstone upon them. That deep well, although now buried in a five-foot cube of concrete still emits strong radiation. For those who think it might have been a meteor, meteors contain very minimal radiation.

There was another crash in Aztec, Mexico in 1948. Witnesses said there were no remains other than a giant hole in the ground. But there were numerous witnesses who claim to have seen a disc-like object crash.

In 1953, there was another UFO crash in Arizona. There were a lot of witnesses who saw this saucer-shaped object crash. But not one word from our government about it.

In 1962, there was a UFO crash just north of Las Vegas adjacent to the Nellis Air Force Base.

Although there were more than a hundred Airmen who witnessed the crash, the government and military have been completely silent about it.

In 1967, more than five hundred residents of Nova Scotia saw a huge round object crash into the sea at Shag Harbor.

In 1969, there was a famous crash in Sverdolovsky, Russia. There are videos available about Russian troops and scientists examining the crashed disc-shaped object. This was witnessed by many. Some details have just been declassified by Russian authorities.

In 1974 in Lladro, Wales, there was a giant UFO crash. US military and scientists were invited to join the British in examining the wreckage. Not one word about the crash until the Brits recently declassified some information about it.

In 1974, there was a UFO crash in the Mexican State of Chihauhua; about thirty miles south of Texas. There are any number of photos and videos of the wreckage. Claims of alien bodies in the wreckage have been made, but no genuine proof offered.

On August 28, 1991 there was a crash of a UFO that Russian authorities claim measured approximately 600 meters long. The crash took place in the Shaitan Mazar region in the Tien Sham Mountains of Kyrgyzstan (near the border with China). To this date, Russian military and scientists have not been able to get too close to the wreckage because the radiation is so strong that even our radiation-protective suits have not been able to fully protect the scientists and military who want to examine it. The only photos of this crash were taken from high-flying aircraft and have been kept as classified documents.

So why do most people still deny UFOs exist?

I believe that one of the reasons is that there have been so many published tales that are obviously false. Another is that there are a significant number of perverted people who will make models, throw them in the air and photograph them.

I have a lot of difficulty understanding the kind of perverted mind it takes to create artificial photographs of UFOs in order to convince other people that what is not so is really so. There have been thousands of documents touting the existence of saucers or, even worse, doctoring up motion picture and video tapes for the sole purpose of trying to deceive people. There's enough merit to the visual claims of over two million people without trying to build a science-fiction tale around it and using some computer photo-workshop to make the photos seem genuine.

At the end of this chapter, there is a brief description on how I usually spot the fake pictures.

It's possible I may have seen a UFO when I was about eleven years old…but I didn't know what it was until many years later when I read an eyewitnesses account of someone who claimed to have seen a flying saucer.

The similarity to what I had seen was so striking, that I think, perhaps, I can add my name to the growing list of millions who have seen UFOs.

What happened was this: When I was a kid, my family were "snowbirds". Residents of New York who would winter in Florida. Naturally, I went to school in Florida, and my family (mother and brother) rented an apartment from September to June in Miami Beach.

The apartment we had faced to the west (towards Biscayne Bay), although it was still a few blocks from the Bay. One morning, about 6:00AM, I got up because I was feeling uncomfortable. I went from my bedroom to the living room and looked out of the window. The sun seemed larger and brighter than ever before, so I stepped out of my front door onto a balcony and looked again. It was the brightest and largest sun I had ever seen. So much so, that I ran to get my older brother to show it to him. I woke him up and we both went into the living room…only the "sun" was gone. I told him what I had seen, and he thought I was "nuts". He explained to me that the sun rises in the east, and our living room window and balcony face west.

So what did I see? I didn't see something skipping along in the sky, but what I saw was not only real, it was so intense that I can visualize it to this day. It was only after many years, when reading some credible description of "UFOs" that I realized this may have been what I saw.

I have read a lot of stories and supposed eyewitness accounts of flying saucers, and I have discarded most of them as pure rubbish. But some have impressed me as being quite sincere:

One very sincere report was the account of a U. S. Navy Lt. Commander who was the Officer on Duty aboard a naval vessel somewhere off the coast of Peru or northern Chile. It was about 6:00 AM when he observed three round, disc-like UFOs, very bright, moving through the sky in a manner that no known aircraft could move: turning at right angles, moving in rapid spurts and then hovering. At no time did he feel they were aggressive or a danger to himself or his ship. He immediately called the ship's captain, but by the time the captain got to the deck, the objects had disappeared. Several other men who had been on deck had seen the same thing. The

Commander wrote a detailed account of his observations and sent them to his base commanding officer and to the Air Force's Project Blue Book.

This could have been passed-off as "just another sighting", but to me, one exceptionally interesting aspect of his very detailed observations was "how" they appeared and vanished from the sky. His description said that it was similar to watching a cartoon in which the character turns sideways so that all you can see is a thin line, then the line shrinks to nothingness and disappears. His statement said he observed this three or four times. Likewise, the appearance of these disc-like objects was in much the same way: a dot would appear in the sky; the dot would become elongated into a line, and when the line turned, it was an extremely bright round object.

How can this be possible? To the extent of my limited knowledge, there are two distinct possibilities: Either the objects moved so fast that the human eye could not perceive their motion...or, the objects came from and went back through a crack in the dimensional fabric to another dimension.

Inasmuch as I am a firm believer in "dimensions", I choose the latter explanation. What are these dimensions or where are they? Are they a part of our Earth or are they from another world...another galaxy? Or, as the physicists working on the Super String Theory have alleged, are they from a parallel universe that our senses will not allow us to see? At the present time, all we can do is guess. But I think we are coming closer to an explanation.

WHERE THEY ORIGINATE

Let's use some old fashioned "common sense": Whatever they are, they must be real. They've been seen by more than two million people. If they actually "pop-in-and-out" of our skies as was observed by the Naval Commander, then we must ask ourselves where they came from and where they are going. Among the very few logical answers available is that they came from and went back to someplace we cannot perceive. In several ways this may fit my description of another dimension. The question is how do they enter our dimension. The only reasonable answer is through a portal in time and space called a crack in the time-space fabric. There is another possible way: through a wormhole in space. Astronomers have only recently discovered these things and while they don't know much about them, Super String Theory Physicists suggest they may be a way into another dimension.

Another theory is that these UFOs come from someplace far closer to us than our galaxy: Our Moon! I have been reviewing a lot of written material, some of it by our own astronauts, that suggest that our 1969 visit to the surface of the moon was not the first visit to the moon by intelligent beings. While almost three-quarters of our planet Earth is still unexplored (more about this later), the fact is that we have explored less than one hundredth of one percent of the surface of the Moon. The Apollo 14 photographs of the Moon, taken from a height of approximately 100 miles above the Moon's surface, strongly suggest that there may be some intelligently-made structures on the Moon.

From 100 miles up, even the large cities on the Earth are not discernable except that enlargements of photos taken from that height can see the rectangular patterns of cities on the Earth's surface. Although no cities or large communities have ever been detected on the surface of the moon, there are, clearly, some rectangular objects and some perfectly shaped objects indicative of structures that were built by intelligent creatures rather than being "chance" creations of nature. There are some interesting enlargements of moon-surface photos on the Internet that show these objects. Of course, as expected, the camera resolution is too poor to definitely distinguish them as being natural or man-made.

Then, too, it is worthy of note that our most recent effort of blowing a hole on the surface of the Moon has revealed (a) the presence of water on the Moon and (b) a labyrinth of tunnels beneath the surface of the Moon. The presence of water also means that there is oxygen and hydrogen on the Moon.

I'm not stating or even suggesting that there are communities of intelligent beings living on or beneath the Moon's surface: But, as imaginative as that concept may seem, to me it is far more reasonable to believe that UFOs are Moon-based rather than that they have traversed the vastness of space to visit our planet.

Then, too, there are now videos on the Internet that purport to show Earth-size round objects circling our Sun only thousands of miles from the Sun's surface. We can't see them because of the Sun's brightness, but our Hubble Telescope recognizes that "something" is there.

There is another possibility that, unfortunately, has not been explored very thoroughly. Three quarters of this planet that we call our home is still unexplored. We have cities and neighboring villages that we can map. But there are also mountainous areas that have never been explored. There are huge chunks of Asia and Africa that have not even been mapped. Then there are our oceans: There has only been the tiniest bit of exploration of our ocean floors and they cover two thirds of our planet.

Is it possible that UFOs come from one of these places?

Before you put this thought down as pure imagination, read the recently released declassified documents from the Russian Navy. Like Project Bluebook, both the Brazilian and the Russian military have always classified and kept secret any/all UFO reports. In 2009, many of the Russian naval reports were declassified and published.

According to the Russian Naval reports, UFO's have been detected both in the skies *and beneath the surface of the oceans.* Russian Naval officers of no less rank than Admiral have reported being on ships that were followed beneath the sea by many UFOs. They have reported that when the UFO seems to get tired of tracking a ship on the surface, they accelerate to speeds believed to be impossible under water and disappear from the Sonar. The frequency of these reports has given a new name to the UFOs: "USOs" (Unidentified Submersible Objects). There have been more than a hundred claimed sightings of USOs off the east coast of Puerto Rico.

Numerous Russian Naval personnel have said they have seen UFOs burst out of the water, into the sky and speed-off into space at speeds far beyond our knowledge.

I'm not alleging these Russian Naval reports are wholly accurate, but it does open the door to other possibilities as to the source of UFOs.

If you think these possibilities are too far out, try matching any other explanations to the facts we have. When you have eliminated all other possibilities, whatever remains must be the truth, no matter how seemingly far out that truth may be.

There is nothing to support the theory that flying saucers are a secret weapon in some country's arsenal, although the military's X37B spacecraft could easily be taken for a UFO although it's kind of small (length 29 feet). It is cigar shaped, metallic and, unlike other aircraft, does not have a tail and fins. The problem with this thought is that there are only two of them in existence (at this writing) and there have been sightings of multiple UFOs.

There is nothing to support the theory that flying saucers come from outer space and that they are observing or preparing for an Earth invasion. There are far too many sightings to attribute them all to hallucinatory experiences. There are far too many similarities in sightings from around the world to believe that what people in Mongolia have seen is not the same thing as has been seen by people in the USA, Russia and Brazil. What other possibilities are there?

One possibility is that whoever and/or whatever the UFOs are, they are observing the Earth. As was said earlier, the Earth is a very warring planet…the kind of place you might want to observe, but not stay for a visit.

Whether or not they come from outer space (the most popular concept), the depths of our oceans (the Russian military concept) or from a crack in the time/space fabric of the world, they come from someplace we cannot perceive. By definition, that's another dimension. And from the descriptions of UFO observations given by trained, intelligent people, the facts seem to fit.

According to Project Blue Book, the Air Force's Bible on the subject of UFOs, there are numerous times these disc-like objects have been spotted on radar, or rather detected as UFOs on radar…only to disappear from the radar as quickly and unexpectedly as they appeared. The Air Force has given us the weak explanation that whatever it was, it was either a mistake on the radar, or an object moving too fast for the radar to track it, or a weather balloon which simply fell from the sky. None of these explanations makes much sense.

First try to understand how a radar screen works. It is a circular dial moving around a luminescent screen. The screen reflects a specific area of air space that it constantly scans. The space being scanned can vary, but generally it covers about a hundred mile radius. As the indicator passes a point, it leaves a clear impression of any object as a "blip" on the radar screen. Any objects which are in the scanned area appear as a dot or blip on the radar screen. The impression fades as the indicator moves clockwise. It takes approximately six seconds for the dial to make a complete circle and start again. So, an object appearing on the screen would logically still be on the screen in six seconds. If the object was moving at very high speeds, it would appear in a different location on the radar screen every six seconds. So an object which seems relatively stationary on the screen which disappears by the next six second rotation would either have to move extremely fast (in excess of 60,000 miles per hour) or perhaps explode in mid air. If an object exploded in mid-air, the wreckage would leave some trace on the radar screen. When no explosions are detected on the radar screen, we have to assume that the object disappeared by other means. As for mistakes made by a malfunctioning radar screen, UFOs have often been spotted by multiple radar scanners. It's not too likely that all radar screens in an area will malfunction at the same time. Slow moving weather balloons and birds are not worthy of consideration.

Assuming that the Naval Commander who spotted the UFOs from his ship was not one of these crazy UFO-nicks, his observations can be very meaningful to us. Whatever they were, they came from one of those dimensions that we cannot see, hear or feel, etc. They came from there, and that's where they went back to. So what are they?

I'm really not certain as to what they are, but I'm quite confident of what they are not: They are not intergalactic space craft from another planet or another solar system and they are not manned by some space beings who want to kidnap earthlings to see what they are made of. In fact, I am supremely confident that whatever or whoever they are, they are not dangerous to mankind nor do they present a threat of any kind. At worst, they are uninvited "observers".

Then there is the question of why no attempt has been made to contact us from these UFOs. There are several possibilities here: 1) If they are from a super-advanced society, perhaps their communication devices are too sophisticated to be detected by ours. 2) Possibly the sounds of their speech are in a range too high or too low to be detected by our receivers. 3) It could be, like some of the things were are discovering about our mysterious aura that whatever (or whoever) is inside these UFOs communicate by telepathy and not by vocal sounds. (4) Maybe whoever or whatever mans these UFOs (or USOs) they look at the Earth as being a very warring or dangerous planet and they don't want to communicate with us. Remember, there has never been a recorded time period on Earth when there were no wars or battles going on somewhere.

There are other possibilities including the concept that whoever or whatever is inside these UFOs may just not want to communicate with us. Certainly there are indications that UFOs have been observed for many years.

There was recently a report spread all over the internet that a cave drawing had been discovered in the jungles of India that was approximately 2,000 years old. It clearly showed a man in a space suit,what appears to be a flying saucer and what could be interpreted as a space wormhole.

This is just another example of how perverted people will try to deceive others.

The fact is that the drawing does exist, but it was not a recent discovery in India. It is a piece of a cave drawing in the Bradshaw Collection.

A little more thorough research revealed that the drawing was found on a cave wall in the northwestern part of Australia in 1891 by a team of archeologists working for the Joseph Bradshaw Foundation and the Society for the Vela; both societies have impeccable reputations and have uncovered many ancient cave drawings.

The foolishness of it all is that, although the newly published photograph showed only about half of the full cave drawing, the truth would have had far greater impact and is far stranger than the fiction: According to the Joseph Bradshaw Foundation, the drawing is more like 30,000 years old!

A BIBLICAL UFO

As mentioned earlier in this book, there are some stories in the Old Testament (also known as the Torah) that, if examined carefully, may raise an eyebrow. All thinking people will question the story of how Noah put two of every species of animal, bird and insects on his ark. Forgetting that many of these animals are natural enemies, and that many species did not live in the Middle East, the size of the ark would have been incredibly large and taken a lifetime to build without the aid of modern machinery. Yet the fact that there was a major flood is backed-up by a very similar story appearing the Mongolian Bible. It's important to remember that these are only tiny scraps of history as might be seen and interpreted by an extremely primitive man. If a Biblical character had seen an airplane in the sky, who knows how it might have been described: a giant bird… an angel…a God?

That's why a careful reading of Ezekial Chapter 001, Verse 001 through Chapter 2, Verse 002, may be quite revealing. The things that Ezekiel describes are what he has seen. The fact that a humanoid figure could fly meant to Ezekiel that he was an angel. A hovering platform in the sky could be nothing less than a God's throne. Most amazing from Ezekiel's descriptions are the outfits these angels he described were wearing. We have to recognize that language has changed over thousands of years. There was no way Ezekiel could describe things like ear-phones or helicopter blades in terms that we, who are familiar with such things, can describe them. Ezekiel had never seen a space helmet, but he describes "the firmament about their heads". In ancient terms, firmament was a round glass-like object.

There is a serious question posed by UFOlogists as to whether or not there were some space visitors to Earth in 593 BC. The Book of Ezekiel (in both the Old and New Testaments) describes "something". Remembering that Ezekiel was a slave and uneducated, the first chapter of his book opens the doors to a lot of questions. I've set it out for you, word for word. I put Ezekiel's wording on the left side and a more modern interpretation of the ancient terms he used on the right side. I think you will agree that it is nothing less than amazing:

1 ¶ Now it came to pass in the thirtieth year, in the fourth month, in the fifth day of the month, as I was among the captives by the river of Chebar, that the heavens were opened, and I saw visions of God. 2 ¶ In the fifth day of the month, which was the fifth year of king Jehoiachin's captivity. 3 ¶ The word of the LORD came expressly unto Ezekiel the priest, the son of Buzi, in the land of the Chaldeans by the river Chebar; and the hand of the LORD was there upon him.	1 – 3 - Reference to the thirtieth year was likely Ezekiel's age. The year was approximately 593 BC.
4 ¶ And I looked, and, behold, a whirlwind came out of the north, a great cloud, and a fire infolding itself, and a brightness was about it, and out of the midst thereof as the colour of amber, out of the midst of the fire.	4 - Is Ezekiel describing the cloud of dust a helicopter or other aircraft might make with fire coming out of its exhaust?
5 ¶ Also out of the midst thereof came the likeness of four living creatures. And this was their appearance; they had the likeness of a man. 6 ¶ And every one had four faces, and every one had four wings. 7 ¶ And their feet were straight feet; and the sole of their feet was like the sole of a calf's foot: and they sparkled like the colour of burnished brass. 8 ¶ And they had the hands of a man under their wings on their four sides; and they four had their faces and their wings. 9 ¶ Their wings were joined one to another; they turned not when they went; they went every one straight forward.	5 – Ezekiel is describing the landing on Earth of four men. 6 – Is Ezekiel referring to two earphones, a man's face and a speaker mask? Might the four wings be helicopter-type blades? See 10¶ for details. 7 – Is the calf's foot Ezekiel's way of describing metallic and leather boots? 8 - Hands of a man – Is Ezekiel stating that they had the appearance of men? 9 – A primitive man could not describe helicopter blades above a body any better than this.

10 ¶ As for the likeness of their faces, they four had the face of a man, and the face of a lion, on the right side: and they four had the face of an ox on the left side; they four also had the face of an eagle.
11 ¶ Thus were their faces: and their wings were stretched upward; two wings of every one were joined one to another, and two covered their bodies.
12 ¶ And they went every one straight forward: whither the spirit was to go, they went; and they turned not when they went.
13 ¶ As for the likeness of the living creatures, their appearance was like burning coals of fire, and like the appearance of lamps: it went up and down among the living creatures; and the fire was bright, and out of the fire went forth lightning.
14 ¶ And the living creatures ran and returned as the appearance of a flash of lightning.

10 - Is Ezekiel describing two ear-phones and a speaker mask inside a clear helmet? See22¶ for details on the helmets the men wore.
11-14 - Is Ezekiel describing how a person moving with helicopter blades might move? The blades rotated, but the bodies moved straight forward.

15 ¶ Now as I beheld the living creatures, behold one wheel upon the earth by the living creatures, with his four faces.
16 ¶ The appearance of the wheels and their work was like unto the colour of a beryl: and they four had one likeness: and their appearance and their work was as it were a wheel in the middle of a wheel.
17 ¶ When they went, they went upon their four sides: and they turned not when they went.

15 – Whatever Ezekiel saw, they appeared to be living (human) creatures.
16 – 17 – Ezekiel is clearly describing the circular image whirling helicopter blades create and how that might appear to a primitive man.

18 ¶ As for their rings, they were so high that they were dreadful; and their rings were full of eyes round about them four.

19 ¶ And when the living creatures went, the wheels went by them: and when the living creatures were lifted up from the earth, the wheels were lifted up.

20 ¶ Whithersoever the spirit was to go, they went, thither was their spirit to go; and the wheels were lifted up over against them: for the spirit of the living creature was in the wheels.

21 ¶ When those went, these went; and when those stood, these stood; and when those were lifted up from the earth, the wheels were lifted up over against them: for the spirit of the living creature was in the wheels.

18 – Again, is Ezekiel describing the round image created by rotating blades above the heads of the visitors.

19 – 21 - Could a primitive man describe a helicopter-type "lift-off" any better than this?

22 ¶ And the likeness of the firmament upon the heads of the living creature was as the colour of the terrible crystal, stretched forth over their heads above.

23 ¶ And under the firmament were their wings straight, the one toward the other: every one had two, which covered on this side, and every one had two, which covered on that side, their bodies.

24 ¶ And when they went, I heard the noise of their wings, like the noise of great waters, as the voice of the Almighty, the voice of speech, as the noise of an host: when they stood, they let down their wings.

25 ¶ And there was a voice from the firmament that was over their heads, when they stood, and had let down their wings.

22 – The term "firmament" is an ancient term for a clear globe-shaped object "…upon the heads…"…like a space helmet. The term "terrible" can best be equated with the modern term "awesome".

23 – Is Ezekiel referring to the reflection of helicopter blades on the "firmament" or crystal-appearing helmet?

24 - Is Ezekiel referring to the noise made by helicopter blades increasing their speed for lift-off?

25 Apparently, the visitors tried to communicate with Ezekiel.

26 ¶ And above the firmament that was over their heads was the likeness of a throne, as the appearance of a sapphire stone: and upon the likeness of the throne was the likeness as the appearance of a man above upon it.

27 ¶ And I saw as the colour of amber, as the appearance of fire round about within it, from the appearance of his loins even upward, and from the appearance of his loins even downward, I saw as it were the appearance of fire, and it had brightness round about.

26 – Is this a primitive man's way of describing a space shuttle, an aircraft or a mother ship hovering in the sky? Could Ezekiel see another man at the controls of the mother ship?

27 – Is Ezekiel trying to describe the return of the visitors to a space shuttle? Is Ezekiel describing the exhaust of the mother ship as it moved off?

28 ¶ As the appearance of the bow that is in the cloud in the day of rain, so was the appearance of the brightness round about. This was the appearance of the likeness of the glory of the LORD. And when I saw it, I fell upon my face, and I heard a voice of one that spake.

28 – It is completely understandable for a man who had never seen or even imagined a space craft to believe it was a God and the people that came from it were angels.

Considering that this was in approximately 593 BC, and Ezekiel had never seen...or even imagined...an aircraft of any sort, Ezekiel's description of people in space suits with crystal-type helmets with individual helicopter blades and a mother ship in the sky is pretty dramatic.

IS THIS WHAT EZEKIEL SAW?
ALMOST 3,000 YEARS AGO?

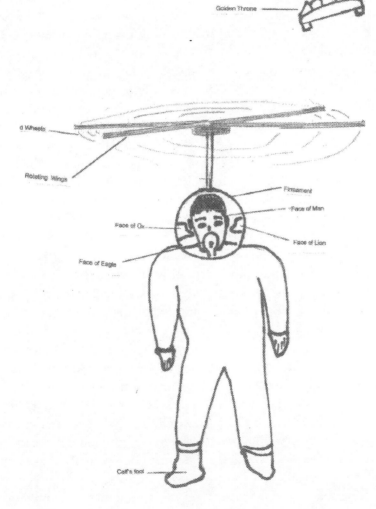

Now let's face mankind's biggest fear head-on: Are UFOs dangerous? Are they simply the precursor to an invasion fleet preparing to conquer the Earth and enslave or kill its inhabitants?

Just as when we spoke about ghosts, I've never heard of a ghost harming anyone. Lots of people are afraid of them, but that fear comes from a lack of understanding of what they are. The same thing is true about UFOs: I have never heard one single, credible report about a UFO harming anyone. I have read a couple of so-called reports about military aircraft from some country chasing a UFO and the aircraft being destroyed… but the reports I've read are clearly not believable. First of all, there seems to be little question that UFOs can move and maneuver at much greater speeds than anything we know of here on Earth. If a UFO was being chased by a military aircraft, it would simply outrun it; it would have no need to destroy the aircraft. To me, it is far more likely that the pilot of the pursuing aircraft made a pilot error and crashed. Then, too, if UFOs are from another dimension, they cannot bridge the dimension gap in a physical way. Of course, I'm not a military man, but I would wager that if any weapon was ever shot at one of these so-called saucers, the missile would go through it without harming it…because like a ghost…sometimes we can see it, but if we try to touch it…it won't be there. If there is a way to bridge the dimension gap, physically, it has not, as yet, been found.

We've already discussed the reasons why we cannot bridge a dimension physically, but what about the concept of being able to travel at such great speeds in order to, physically, reach other worlds: I will grant that Captain James Kirk and the Enterprise (of Star Trek fame) were able to travel at multiples of light speed (Warp Drive) on TV, but in practice, that type of travel is not very likely. Even at the speed of light (roughly 186,0000 miles per second) it would take years for any spaceship heading for another solar system to reach it, and even then, if the ship returned to its planet of origin, so many years would have passed that all the people the Captain and the crew knew on Earth would likely have died of old age. Even at "Warp 10", it would take 100,000 years to reach a star a million light years away. Travelling at speed we now travel at in outer space (roughly 25,000 mph), it would take many lifetimes to travel from our solar system to our closest neighboring solar system. Space travel is a very romantic thought, but a highly impractical one. It makes for good reading and good TV.

One interesting anomaly of Star trek: The Enterprise seems to be able to communicate with the Earth (or other star basis) on an instant basis although the source of the communication may be light years away. Even if the Enterprise could travel at multiples of the speed of light, the vocal and visual communications could not. It might take hundreds of Earth years for a Star Ship to communicate with the Earth.

Another anomaly is the concept of teleportation ("Scotty, beam me up!"). The ability to move your body, physically (broken into molecules), from one place to another in an instant. If you think about it, this could still not work in intergalactic travel, because a teleporter cannot move you any faster than its teleporting beam. Even attempting to teleport on a laser-type beam would play havoc with time. Put science-fiction aside and take a dose of reality. Galaxies, stars, planets, etc. in space are moving at billions if not trillions of miles per hour. How could a beam of any sort be fixed on an object moving at that speed, and then hold that beam there long enough to transport someone? Even the thought of doing so boggles the mind.

But, what about Teleportation from dimension to dimension? The concept is not entirely new. If one could figure out how to create a teleporter beam from one dimension to another… Thought travels instantaneously. If one could figure out how to travel via a thought wave, the problem could be solved. But it will take more than just a simple manner of accelerating or decelerating a thought wave. How could a person get their thoughts to move out of one dimension into another? Once again, we come to those magic words "portal" and "wormhole".

There are many possible portals here on Earth, in outer space, etc. The cold spot I felt in the haunted castle may have been one. Wormholes in space may be portals. A portal is, basically, a warp in time and space through which things can travel. I've never visited a black hole or a wormhole in space (nor has anyone else I've ever heard of), but there are thousands of questions that scientists have about them…with almost no answers other than they seems to suck-up everything around it.

But where does it suck them to? Black holesand wormholes have no center. Scientists tell us that black holes have an enormous "gravitational" pull. That's because everything near them seems to be sucked up by them.

But what happens when something is sucked into the hole? Does it just disappear? Or, does the black hole, like a whirlpool, suck you in only to cast you out someplace else? Some astronomers tell us they can actually see things sucked into black holes...but they never talk about seeing anything come out of them.

Visualizing black holes or wormholes as portals from dimension to dimension might actually create sensible answers to many of those questions. Of course, it would create a lot of additional questions that may reshape our world's thinking about time and space. These questions may not be answerable for thousands of years to come. But it makes a lot more sense than the way science now looks at them. A characteristic of portals is that they open and close. Therefore travel through a portal would be possible only when that portal is open...which may tend to explain why there appear to be fleets of UFOs at times, and then none for several months.

Another valid question might be "What could travel through a portal?" Certainly, I do not believe anything physical could travel through it. Logically, anything physical would have its molecules torn apart and scattered into a billion directions. But thought waves or "auras" might work nicely.

Einstein had another pet theory: That space itself was round and had its limits. Einstein said that if you could travel in one direction in space long enough and far enough, you'd wind up right back where you started... kind of like Columbus' theory that the world was round.

If Einstein was correct, and it is doubtful that anyone will ever prove or disprove his theory for many years to come, travel through the dimension we call space, if it were possible, would really get you nowhere...except back to where you started...and it would take you forever to get there. Thus, the concept of portals that will allow you to leave this dimension and arrive at another in an instant begins to sound more reasonable if there is ever going to be interdimensional or inter-galaxy travel.

Putting some of the facts together that I have been able to discern from reading a lot of eyewitness accounts, I note that the heaviest influx of UFOs seems to be cyclical. By cyclical, I do not mean any exact periods of time as measured here on Earth. Cyclical, perhaps, to a variable time system. This leads me to believe that whatever these objects are, and whatever their purpose is in visiting us, they can only come at certain times when dimensional conditions are right.

In concluding this chapter, another question may have arisen in your mind: It may have occurred to you since this book discusses thought processes or auras that may come from another dimension, and that the aura is the thing that feeds our brains... Does that mean that we are nothing but puppets to these auras?

To that I bring an emphatic "No". These auras are what we hear our mind saying to us. They do not direct the actions we take.

The thoughts entering our minds have been filtered by buffers and are limited by the capacities of our brains. We think a lot of thoughts that we never would or could do: thoughts of killing and mayhem, thoughts of great sexual prowess; thoughts of fame, success and recognition, etc.

We actually do what we decide to do...or not do, despite our thoughts. When I see a beautiful woman walking down the street, my thoughts may be telling me to "jump her" because no one's looking. But I don't. Why? Because as human beings, we can take any thought entering our heads and either act on it or discard it. Certainly there are many stories of people who follow some wild idea in their imagination...but the actuality is that even if and when they do, the reality never lives up to the level of the thought. We are still our own master and we are responsible for everything we do.

HOW TO SPOT FAKE UFO AND GHOST PHOTOS

There are so very many fake pictures of UFOs and ghosts circulating around the world, that it becomes important how to separate the phonies from the genuine. Yes, there are many genuine photos of UFOs and ghosts, but these days, it's very difficult to distinguish which is which. With digital photographs and photo shops available to everyone, you really have to know what to look for:

When I see a UFO picture or a supposed photo of a ghost (usually someone who appears in a photo who wasn't there when the picture was taken), the first question I ask myself is "Why was the picture taken?"

UFOs and ghosts do not, normally, pose for the camera.

So, if I see a photo of a long, narrow hallway with someone or something at the end of it, I immediately discard it as a fake. Why would someone take a photo of a hallway...or a staircase...or a room?

On the other hand, when I see a photo of a groups of people of an individual, and someone or something else appears in the photo (usually a face or some indistinguishable body parts), I have to examine it more closely.

I give little credibility to spots of light, whether in an ostensibly haunted house or in night sky. It very uncommon for people to carry a camera with them at night and photograph something in the dark sky... although cell-phone cameras are now more popular than ever and most have cameras that can be used on an instant's notice. But most cell-phone cameras are not capable of photographing something in a night time sky or in an otherwise dark house.

Another thing I look for in ghost photos are clothing: If I see a ghost wearing robes or even a shirt, I immediately discard it as a phony. The aura that is your life is made up of pure electromagnetic energy. It does not wear clothes, robes or anything else. It normally appears in photos as a dark shadow or a light mist.

Faces are something else. Apparently the aura, even when it has left the body, carries the memories of the face that it was...and frequently that face will appear in a supposed ghost photo. The energy may take the shape of the body it once was, but not distinguishable clothing.

One exception: When someone's life has been abruptly cut short (an accident, a war casualty, etc.) for a brief period of time, the aura does seem to remember the clothing the dead person last wore. That clothing fades into mist as the aura becomes more accustomed to being without its former body.

Remember the ghost of a girl I saw in San Francisco? She was wearing a tan pantsuit...the clothes she was wearing when she was murdered. Probably not yet convinced that she was dead.

Whenever I see a clear photo of a UFO, I know it's got to be phony. As mentioned earlier, they do not pose for the camera. Additionally, they are usually moving at high speeds. Cell-phone cameras are not very good at getting clear pictures of rapidly moving objects.

Almost all UFO photos that I believe to be genuine were pictures taken of people or places that one would normally take a photo...and in the background there is a tiny speck in the sky

When the speck is blown-up, it frequently reveals a disc or blimp-type object. You can always distinguish a blimp from a UFO: blimps always have a large tail for stabilization.

This may not cover all the aspects of spotting the phonies, but it should tell you how to spot the blatant fakes.

Unfortunately for those of us who are serious about our research, photo shops can now accomplish almost anything...and there will always be those who think it is great fun to deceive others.

Chapter 6

Precognition

Now let's look at two of the most remarkable aspects of ESP. Precognition and Retrocognition.

Simply put, precognition means the foretelling of an event, in great detail, before it actually happens. I have read of numerous such accounts, and if I can believe the books I've read about it, there have been thousands of alleged and recorded cases of precognition.

History is rampant with some of the more famous claims of precognition such as Joseph (Abraham's grandson) while imprisoned as a slave to the Pharaoh foretelling of seven years of plenty followed by seven years of famine; Joan of Arc foretelling the battle at Orleans; Rasputin warning the Tsar of Russia of several events that actually happened; etc. The most interesting one I ever read about was a man who worked for the Times Picayune newspaper in New Orleans, who allegedly told his editor that he had a dream in which he saw a small, private plane crash in the snow on a mountain top. He felt it was worth talking about because the "N" number of the plane (which identifies the airplane) was clearly visible, so he wrote it down when he woke up. His editor thought it might be worth trying to locate that airplane and seeing if that particular "N" number even existed.

Although, with a computer, you can locate virtually any aircraft by its "N" number in a matter of minutes, in the 1960's, computers were not available on a large scale. The tracing of an "N" number had to go through the Federal Aviation Administration. Anything that had to go through the bureaucratic labyrinth of the FAA took lots of time.

Before the FAA responded, and about a week after the "dream" had been reported, a small private plane bearing that same "N" number crashed in the snow-covered Rocky Mountains, and the pilot and one passenger were killed.

As reports of precognition go, that story is quite uncommon. Most claims of precognition are little things, like the bus or a train being late. People often report having a premonition that they must not board a commercial airliner...that crashed on that flight. Parents often seem to get premonitions regarding their children or other close relatives.

Then too, there were more than sixty crew members on the Titanic that refused to go on the famous transatlantic crossing because of premonitions of disaster.

The biggest problem with most of these so-called precognition claims is that the ones not happening are, most often, not reported. So, if a parent has several premonitions regarding his/her child, and only one of them actually happens, the parent will talk about the one that actually happened, and never mention the ten that didn't happen. And in the case of Rasputin, perhaps he issued a hundred warnings of things he foresaw to his Tsar, and ten of them actually came to pass. Was Rasputin a man with genuine precognitive powers? Do we count the hits and not the misses? How many people refused to board an airliner because of a premonition of a crash that didn't occur?

Almost all alleged precognitive experiences happen while you're sleeping and in a dream. As explained throughout this book, that would put you in closer contact with your aura. But does your aura have the ability to see the future?

Most doubtful!

Auras are great for seeing the past; for storing memories; for feeding information and understanding to the brain...but I know of no way for an aura to peek into the future. There are so many, many things that can occur that may change the future, that to me, it would be frightening if I believed there was a prescribed, written future that could not be changed. Man can travel into the future, but he can never go into the past. It logically follows that if someone goes into the future, in order to get back to where he started, he would have to travel into the past...and that can't be done...at least with our present knowledge.

Many novel and science fiction writers have suggested that you can go into the future, see it, go back into the past and do something that will change the future. It simply cannot be done.

Seeing into the future has been the stock and trade of gypsy fortune tellers and their crystal balls, tarot cards, Ouija boards or tea leaf readings. Please do not equate that with genuine precognition.

Nor should you confuse precognition with a "likelihood" of something happening. It is not uncommon for people to get premonition or precognitive experiences concerning things that are likely to happen. Little Johnny is doing exceptionally well in school and his mother has a dream in which he won the "student of the year award". The following week it actually happens. The mother may feel this was a precognitive experience, but it does not meet the criteria of genuine precognition.

In order for a case of precognition to be deemed genuine precognition, it (a) must be a future event, unlikely to happen, reported and recorded before the event takes place, and (b) it must be reported in sufficient detail to eliminate the possibility of "chance". That having been said, there is still much to be said concerning precognitive experiences.

One of the largest problems with precognition is the number of frauds and tricksters that allege to have the power of precognition. Numerous magicians and hucksters have tried to prove they have this power via trickery (ostensibly guessing the exact popular vote in an election a week prior to that election), but these are the tricks of a magician. They are not to be confused with the supposed foretelling of events such as in the Book of Genesis, God warning Lot to take his family from Sodom and Gomorrah before he rained down on it with fire and brimstone. Of course, the biblical tales have nothing to validate them.

Another problem of precognitive claims is the claim of some so-called prophets to bolster their own ego and to gain monetary profit. Jean Dixon, who allegedly was the seer to President John F. Kennedy, has often boasted that she warned him not to go to Dallas…that something terrible would happen.

Again, this cannot be classified as true precognition, because it does not meet the two tests above. Dixon did not foretell, in detail, exactly what would happen to the President if he went to Dallas, nor were there any specifics as to how and where this would happen. To classify Dixon's claim would put it more in the "premonition" category than in the "precognition" category. Many people warned JFK about Dallas because there had been all kinds of rumors circulating about big trouble in Dallas and JFK chose not to heed the warnings.

But, Ms. Dixon capitalized on the event and became a seer for the Weekly Enquirer and started foretelling yearly happenings of events. Most of them were "likely to happen" events based on current news. Still, many did not come to pass, and none of them had the specificity required to be called true precognition.

There was an interesting tale I heard a few years ago: A man, I'll call "Gene", who went to Long Island University (Brooklyn campus) had a part-time job writing for a now defunct newspaper called the "Brooklyn Eagle". He was doing a series for the newspaper on Juvenile Delinquency in Brooklyn. On a lark, he and a few of his friends went to a "fortune teller" in the neighborhood. The fortune teller told Gene "that because of something Gene was writing, in less than a year he would receive a telephone call from someone he didn't know that would send him on a trip to a place he'd never been where he would get work of a kind he had never known, and the result would be enormous success."

In actuality, in less than a year, Gene did get a call from an independent "B" motion picture producer who was doing a film on Juvenile Delinquency, and he offered Gene a job as a consultant to that film...in Hollywood. Gene went to Hollywood and the film was a financial success. As a result, Gene was offered a job to become the story editor for a new TV series... that ran for eight years! Gene did realize financial success beyond his wildest dreams. If you ever meet Gene and talk to him, he will tell you that this fortune teller predicted his future with uncanny accuracy.

Was that genuine precognition? Absolutely not!

So-called fortune tellers or gypsies with crystal balls who can foretell the future for individuals are almost always good "cold readers" who can pick up on little things and generalize enough to get the individual to believe they are really reading the future.

That so-called fortune teller may have picked-up from Gene or one of his friends that Gene was a writer. The rest of it did not have enough detail or specificity to be called genuine precognition. It was just a glib gypsy telling Gene what he wanted to hear. I'm not suggesting that Jean Dixon or other so-called psychics may not be more sensitive to the auras of other people than most of us, but their ability to actually foretell the future with any degree of accuracy is, at best, problematic.

Genuine precognition can be downright scary: Think about it. If even one of the thousands of reported cases of precognition is actually true and not someone's idea of a joke to play on the world, it means that the event foretold, in detail, was bound to happen…in just the way it was foretold. Could the event have been changed or was the dye cast upon the waters? The Times Picayune story about the airplane crash, if true, would be a case of genuine precognition.

And let's think a little bit further: Who or what cast the dye in the water? I mean, if that event was bound to happen in that way, and someone foresaw it and documented it before the fact, that means that the event was prescribed to happen. And, if an event is "bound" to happen, then it would be logical to assume that someone or something pre-set that event to happen in just that way. We have a word for that: "Fate".

Genuine precognition, if it really exists, establishes beyond a doubt that our lives and futures are cast in stone, and that this illusion we have of free will is just that…an illusion. If one event in our future is cast in stone, then why not everything? Simply because an individual was able to foresee only one single event does not mean that all other events were not "bound" to happen merely because someone did not foresee them.

This I cannot accept. As I said at the outset, genuine precognition is scary!

Virtually all cases of seemingly genuine precognition can be explained away by facts that we already have in place: The so-called precognition of Peter Hurkos locating and predicting the spot where the dead seven-year-old girl's body would appear, on the surface, would seem to be genuine precognition for which there is no known explanation.

However, the basic premise of this book would offer a simple explanation: Far more likely and logically, the dead girl's aura was hovering over the spot where the girl died. It was still there because of the sudden and unexpected death of the girl. Unquestionably, Hurkos had an extreme sensitivity to auras and, as he crossed over the bridge on that canal, he picked up the aura of the girl. From the aura he sensed that she had drowned and that her body was becoming unstuck from the mud. I believe that all other cases of precognition can be similarly explained.

In the case of Joan of Arc, we know that some soldiers visited her village shortly before she had her first premonition as the "Maid of Orleans". Let's allow for the fact that her sensitivity to their auras may have been high, and she picked up the soldiers' thoughts of an impending battle in Orleans. Combining that with a premonition, she announced that she could see a great battle coming in Orleans. Again, if her sensitivity to auras was high, that may also explain her being able to identify the disguised Dauphine of France. One thing our history books never talk about is how many "premonitions" Joan of Arc had that did not come to pass. Anyone reading Joan's history could reasonably assume that she believed she would have all the armies of France waiting to join her when she reached the walls of Paris. History tells us this did not happen.

Getting back to the story about the alleged reporting of the plane crash in the snow, I really wonder if an overly-exuberant editor and co-worker did not varnish the story slightly for public consumption and publicity. The story did get significant publicity and it did help the circulation of the Times Picayune.

If we look carefully into all recorded and documented cases of precognition, it is my belief that we will find an alternate, valid explanation in keeping with the premise expounded in this book. I'm certain most of these so-called cases of precognition have been reported in good faith and with sincerity. Then, too, history has a way of varnishing these tales for public consumption. If we examine any/all clams of genuine precognition, I believe we will find that the true facts differ markedly from the stories published.

RETROCOGNITION

Now let's take a brief look at the opposite phenomenon: retrocognition: This is best defined as the ability, through your mind, to look into the past and see things, in great detail, that you would or should have no possible way of knowing.

Retrocognition is far more common than many people believe, and it is based on a much stronger foundation than is precognition. There is a personal experience I would like to relate:

The first time I went to Paris, France, my wife and I stayed at the Intercontinental Hotel. This is directly across the street from the Le Louvre Museum and about a block away from the Louis XIV palace. My first night there I had a very fitful sleep, because I kept dreaming that I was hearing a waltz played by a group of violinist musicians. To the best of my knowledge, I'd never heard that waltz before, and it kept playing over and over in my mind.

Then I must've started another dream because suddenly I was at a ball at the Louis XIV Palace (I had not yet gone to visit it)…only I was not me… in this dream I was a girl! I was dressed in a manner quite differently than the period movies I had seen, so I asked another girl for a "looking glass". A "looking glass"? That term wasn't even in my vocabulary. I often looked in a mirror…but a "looking glass"? I looked in the glass and saw a very pretty red-headed girl. I wanted to look at myself more closely, but several other girls pushed me to the edge of the dance floor where I saw what appeared to be very wealthy and beautifully dressed people dancing. The music was coming from a group of four ornately dressed violinists standing in an alcove about twenty feet above the ballroom floor, playing that same haunting waltz. I watched people dance…until I woke up. It seemed that the dream had been so very real.

I was drenched with perspiration.

Even after a cold shower, the dream was still vivid in my mind although the music was no longer that precise waltz I heard in my dream. As much as I tried, I could not keep that music from fading away.

The following day, my wife and I had scheduled a visit to the Louvre Museum and we scheduled a tour of the Louis XIV Palace for the day after that.

The tour of the Louis XIV palace was very interesting with the guide talking about Madame Pompadour and others out of the pages of history, but I had no déjà vu feelings…until we got to the ballroom. I was almost ready to swear this was the same room I had seen in my dreams…but something was missing. There was no orchestra alcove high above the floor…so I pointed to a spot on the wall and asked my guide if there wasn't usually someplace above the dance floor where the musicians played.

The tour guide said "Yes…there was one up there, but it was removed when the Nazi's occupied Paris and used a portion of this palace as military headquarters."

I felt a cold chill run through me.

Although this brief retrocognition I experienced was, to me, quite impressive, a study of the subject revealed that it was not uncommon for people to dream of people and events that occurred long before they were born. The most interesting facet of this retrocognition is that you see people and places, in detail, that no longer exist…but things you see and hear in these dreams, often prove to be uncannily accurate.

If, in fact, your aura has been someone else's aura before you, it should not be surprising that memories of these other people would come to you when your mind is in direct contact with your aura, and your brain is not blocking these thoughts. This will be discussed in greater detail in the chapter of Hypnotism and Reincarnation.

This may further help to explain déjà vu experiences such as visiting someplace you've never been, but knowing you've been there before…or meeting people for the first time and feeling you've known them before. Maybe you have been there before…in a dream…or in a prior life. Maybe you knew this person in the past.

There are many problems with this: Almost all retrocognition experiences occur when you are asleep…in dreams. Most of these dreams are not remembered when you waken, and the few that are remembered are quickly colored by the light of day, the everyday process of living, and the desire not to have your own mind boggled.

The retrocognition factor also seems to play a large part in our dreams. We will go into this in the chapter on dreams, but a few words should be said before we get there:

When we dream, we often see faces and places that we have never seen. Sometimes the faces appear with astounding detail together with distinct personalities. It is my belief that these faces originated in your past and that they are knocking at your recognative door trying to work their way through the maze of daily events that fill the memory banks of your brain. There have been occasions when such a face appeared that I, half asleep, tried to open the doors of my mind to them and I found myself seeing places, people and things that I know must have come from my past because I had never seen them when awake.

If any readers of this book have had any interesting precognitive or retrocognitive experiences, I would welcome your writing to me and telling me about them.

Chapter 7

Hypnotism: The Magic Key?

It may sound strange for a book on unexplained phenomena to include a section on Hypnotism. Hypnotism is recognized and used scientifically as well as for entertainment purposes. The interesting thing is that hypnotism may well be the missing link that links everything else together:

WHAT IS HYPNOSIS

What is hypnosis? In its simplest terms, hypnosis occurs when the brain goes into a semi-sleeping state and the mind reacts to external suggestion. Even that definition is pretty fancy: Try to think of it as if you were in a cradle and your mother was rocking you and singing you a lullaby. In a way, this is a form of hypnosis.

One of the most commonly used forms of hypnosis is self-hypnosis. This is often induced through the use of meditation. If you stop to think about it, almost all of the Asian religions that spend most of their time in meditation claim to have reached a much higher plane of existence. To them, reincarnation is a certainty, and astral projection is a common occurrence.

As an adult, it's simply someone putting you to sleep by suggesting that you are so sleepy you can't resist sleep. Or, more accurately, suggesting to you that you are very sleepy...so sleepy that all sounds, other than the voice of the hypnotist, are faded out and you have no desire to resist doing what the hypnotist tells you to do.

Hypnotism has the remarkable facility of putting the brain to sleep. And, when the brain sleeps, the mind or aura takes over; similar to when you sleep and dream. This means that the hypnotist has direct contact with the aura or mind.

Strange as it seems, very little is really known about hypnotism. We know what it is. We use it in many scientific ways. We use it for entertainment and medical purposes. But very little is known as to "why" it works. Once again, we bring common sense and logic to the rescue:

We can safely assume that the brain is sleeping. The brain tells us that when we touch something that is very hot, we instantly pull our hand away from it. Under hypnosis, we can burn a subject's hand telling them that they will feel no pain…and the subject will feel no pain. If the hand is burned, when the subject awakens, it may need to be treated for burns, but the pain…the signal that the brain uses to tell us something is too hot, is not there. The mind has told the subject that there will be no pain, and the mind has, effectively, overridden the natural, protective, signals the brain sends us. This is not merely with overriding the brain's normal response to fire. Hypnosis is used throughout the world for painless childbirth and painless dentistry as well as breaking smoking and nail-biting habits.

When an individual is in a hypnotic sleep (erroneously called a "trance"), other strange things appear to happen:

If a hypnotist tells a hypnotized person that he or she is in a movie theatre watching a very funny movie and can't help but laugh…the subject's eyes will remain closed, but he or she will start laughing…sometimes hysterically because…in their minds the subjects are watching a very funny movie. If you ask the subject what the name of the movie is, who it stars, to describe the scene being watched, etc., you will get a consistent answer to every question. Yet the subject's eyes are closed.

When you tell a hypnotized person that he cannot feel any pain, you can run a sword through his body (if you're careful enough not to hit any of the vital organs), and the subject will not even flinch as the sword pierces the body. Many times I have run a sterilized needle through the backs of the hands of hypnotized people, and they were completely unaware of any pain or any other sensation when I did it.

When you tell a hypnotized woman that she will feel nothing but pleasure while giving birth to a child…the woman will feel nothing but pleasure. In fact, many physicians use the assistance of a hypnotist to create painless childbirth without the use of anesthetics.

If you tell a hypnotized person that he or she has super-strength and can lift the end of a car so a tire can be changed…believe it or not, the subject will do it (extreme caution is mandatory here, because without proper medical supervision, the subject may lift the end of a car, but may give themselves a hernia…or worse). In other words, the commands given to a hypnotized person by a hypnotist will be fulfilled even when the command calls for strength or memory not normally available in the subject. Strength, far beyond normal strength can be developed instantaneously. The mind of a hypnotized person can multiply 9999 times 9999 in seconds...or create new, beautiful art...or make a student with ADD (Attention Deficit Disorder) into someone who can concentrate and focus on a subject...or many other things that seem to defy convention. And it works!

Why? Now let's put all the things we know together with a little common sense and logic:

We know that when a person is asleep, the mind functions at a much faster rate (note the rapidity of dreams). The body is resting and allowing the functions of the body to do their job. We know that the mind functions best when asleep. Almost all great, innovative ideas have come to people while they sleep. When you dream, you can live though months of detailed living in a very few seconds. In your dreams you can see people you've never seen before that you can detail down to the crows feet in the corners of their eyes.

When you sleep, your mind can function at hundreds (if not thousands) of times faster than when you are awake because when you sleep the brain is "resting" or "sleeping" and cannot interfere with the speed of the thoughts coming from your mind or aura. Accordingly, a dream is not the function of your brain, it is the exclusive function of your mind or aura.

When sleep is artificially induced by using an anesthetic, we have learned that there are innumerably more cases of mind/body separation (astral projection). The reason for this is that the artificial forcing of sleep upon the body puts the brain into a very deep sleep. Much deeper than normal. And, when sleep is artificially induced by hypnosis, we get the same result as sleep induced by anesthesia except that no foreign substance is brought into the body to create the sleep. It is created by the suggestions of the hypnotist. Because hypnosis is induced by the hypnotist's voice, the hypnotist is making a direct contact with the mind or aura of the hypnotized person! I make this statement with little trepidation as there is more than adequate evidence to back it up.

I've mentioned, a few times, that the mind influences the brain and the brain controls the body. When a suggestion is given to a hypnotized subject such as "You can feel no pain.", the mind tells the body, even when a sword is being passed though it or a subject's hand is held over a hot flame, that there is no pain…and the subject feels no pain. If the brain was awake and active, it would warn the body of the invasiveness of the sword or flame and would make the body feel pain so that it would pull away from the source of the pain. But, since the brain is sleeping…deeply…

The mind can't stop a flame from burning the tissues of the hand any more than it can miraculously repair the rupture of the skin and the inner linings of the body if a sword pierces it. But the pain, which should be associated with these acts, will not be felt.

The same principal works if I tell a 90-pound girl that her body has a rigid steel bar going through it from her toes to her head. I can lift her up, place her head on one chair and her feet on another with nothing but air beneath the rest of her body. Then, I can stand, with my full 190 lbs on the center of her body without her body bending or giving even an inch. I've done this many times with hypnotized subjects. I have read that other hypnotists have actually placed a concrete block on the unsupported section of a girl's body, and broken it with a sledgehammer …without the body giving an inch. I would not recommend doing this because there are internal organs that may be injured. Still, you must ask yourself, where does that little girl get that kind of strength? Clearly the brain would never tell her to do something like that because the brain protects the body and knows it might be damaging to the body. But if the hypnotist commands the mind to do it, the mind orders it because the brain sleeps.

Obviously, our bodies have more strength and resistance to pain than we realize, but it is only through hypnosis that extraordinary powers can be called upon.

CONTROLLING THE BODY'S FUNCTIONS

One of the strangest things I ever saw was an experiment in hypnosis conducted at NYU's medical school where, under a physician's supervision, both wrists of a hypnotized young man were cut. Naturally, both wrists began to bleed. At the suggestion of the hypnotist that his left wrist was healed, blood from that wrist stopped and flowed only from the right wrist. When the hypnotist suggested that he had made a mistake; that it was the right wrist that had been healed, blood stopped flowing from the right wrist and started flowing from the left wrist.

The physical powers of our body are severely limited by our brain. Our brain is there to protect our body. That's why, when some driver cuts in front of you, your foot automatically goes to the brake without thinking about it. Our brain tells us, when we try to lift a heavy object, whether that object is too heavy for us to lift…without injury to the body. Under hypnosis, the mind bypasses the brain:

When you are asleep in a normal mode of sleeping, the brain is set on a "minimal function" mode. It may awaken you to tell you that you need to use the bathroom, or such. Generally, the brain sleeps and recuperates from the day's activities while you sleep. The brain, being a physical part of the body, needs this rest in order to function properly.

In the same situation as mentioned above: when you're driving, a brain that has not rested adequately, may hear the mind say "hit the brakes", but the brain is too sluggish to make the body to react with sufficient speed to avoid an accident.[3]

When you are asleep, the mind or aura takes over. In effect, it bypasses the resting brain and completely takes over the body imbuing it with thoughts, dreams, memories and a world that most people think of as unreal.

When sleep is artificially induced through anesthesia, hypnosis or meditation, the brain, rather than just resting, is put into a deep sleep so that it cannot function except to a very minimal degree unless directed to do so. This is why a person whose body is being cut open with a scalpel

---

3   Alcohol does not put the brain to sleep, but it does tend to make it "rest", thus slowing normal bodily reactions. Performing an act, such as driving, while under the influence of alcohol, by necessity, will slow the driver's reactions. Performing an "unforgiving" act, such as flying a plane even having only one or two drinks is playing with fire.

(something that would normally hurt or be painful) is put under anesthesia. The brain is put to rest so that there is insufficient brain function to tell the body that something hurts.

The same is true when a person is hypnotized. The brain temporarily shuts down and the external voice of the hypnotist directs the actions of the mind. Hypnosis is effective to a greater extent than anesthesia because anesthetics are, effectively, drugs to the brain which, occasionally, leave their mark when the anesthesia wears off. The person may awaken with a headache or a hangover-type feeling. Reality may be slow in taking hold.

Hypnosis, on the other hand, is gaining the cooperation of the subjects to allow their brains to be shut down. When a hypnotized person awakens, the brain feels extraordinarily rested. When people are awakened from a hypnotic sleep, they normally feel wonderful and deeply refreshed; similar to the way they might feel if they had an exceptionally good night's rest.

One of the biggest shortcomings of hypnosis is that anyone can make a conscious effort to resist the hypnotist. By definition, a resisting person cannot be hypnotized. Even partial resistance can help block the subject from getting into that "deep" hypnotic sleep. That's why surgeons usually use anesthetics rather than hypnosis when performing surgery. Any given person can prove difficult to hypnotize, but almost all people will quickly succumb to chemical anesthesia.

Another noteworthy advantage of hypnotism over anesthesia is that, sometimes, physicians have a difficult time reviving a person from anesthesia. There is never a problem awakening a person who is hypnotized. If a person is hypnotized and the hypnotist decides to go away on a vacation before waking the hypnotized person, the hypnotized person will slowly slip into a normal sleep and wake up feeling refreshed. Stories about hypnotized people who could not be awakened belong in Grimm's Fairy Tales. It just does not happen!

One of the most interesting facets of people who are either hypnotized or put under an anesthetic is the ability of the person to both see and hear while the brain is totally asleep. Astral projection is not uncommon among people who are under anesthetic...and while their mind and body are separated, the mind can see…and project very accurate images, and the ears can hear…as was detailed in the Joe W. story.

Here's another example:

A twelve-year-old girl on a stage in front of a large audience was hypnotized by an entertainment hypnotist and told, "Open your eyes. Everyone in the audience is naked!" When she opened her eyes, not only could you see the sudden shock on the girl's face, but her cheeks turned a deep crimson with embarrassment. When, a few seconds later, the hypnotist told the girl that the audience was fully dressed, but that she was naked, the girl contorted herself in an effort to cover what she thought was her exposed body.

Obviously, her brain was not working in its normal fashion: Her eyes were open, but what she saw was what the hypnotist had suggested to her mind. Her mind was seeing something that defied the normal function of the brain and the optic nerves.

Another very interesting thing about hypnosis is that the subjects seldom have any recollection of having been hypnotized. Most subjects, when awakened, do not believe they were hypnotized. Nor do they have any memory of what they did while hypnotized.

Usually the subjects will, subsequently, gain vague recollections of what they said and did such as one might get in trying to remember a dream. For this reason, it is of the utmost importance that anyone wanting to be hypnotized must work with a hypnotist of high moral character and reputation. The hypnotist has enormous control over the hypnotized subject, and if unscrupulous, could have the subject doing things they might never allow themselves to do when they are awake.

There is an axiom that a person will never do anything while hypnotized that they would not do while awake. This is possibly true. But remember that, under hypnosis, the hypnotist is communicating directly with the mind and not the brain. It is the brain that has logged and filed the moral and religious teachings and the warnings of teachers and parents, etc. If the brain is, effectively, shut There is really very little people will not do in their minds. In their minds, they may be violent killers, wonton sexual predators, daring acrobats, can have super-human strength and remarkable abilities. Many mild-mannered people are calculating and destructive in their minds. And that's what we're talking about here…direct contact with the mind. So always be careful as to whom you allow to hypnotize you.

If you are trying to make an effort to communicate with your aura, or perhaps experiment with astral projection, self-hypnosis and meditation are two excellent and harmless methods to use:

Most people can accomplish this by lying down on a bed in room by yourself, and fixing your eyes on a single spot in your ceiling. Try to communicate with your aura as if you were directly speaking to yourself; not out loud…only in your mind. Many find it helpful to listen to a recording of ocean breakers reaching the shore or birds quietly chirping in nature. Don't be frightened. The worst thing that will happen is that you will fall asleep and wake up after a short nap. Then you might want to try again.

TIME REGRESSION

One of the most fascinating things that can be done through hypnosis is "time regression":

Do you remember the name of the boy who sat next to you in kindergarten? Do you remember the kids who attended your third birthday party? Under hypnosis, you do. Remembering that the brain is a computer, all the memories you have are stored in that computer, and when in a hypnotic state, a suggestion from the hypnotist will cause the mind to bring up those memories from your sleeping brain. One of the reasons for this is that, while the brain is sleeping, it is not clogged with current happenings and the mind can pull things from its memory banks without the constant clutter of new visions and sounds entering it.

Numerous times, I've hypnotized someone and regressed them back to childhood, even infancy. It was not uncommon for me to have a man in his fifties tell me the name of his first grade teacher, describe him/her, and tell about the activities in the first grade class.

Chapter 8

Reincarnation

We live in a world filled with mysteries. To me, one of the biggest mysteries is how normally intelligent people can deny the "possibility" of reincarnation. There are more than five hundred cases of past-life regression (PLR) that have been documented and verified in painfully intricate detail. It should be far beyond the ability of any intelligent person to completely deny the "possibility" of reincarnation especially since the proof is so overwhelming.

First, let's look at what reincarnation is: Reincarnation is the belief that you have lived before and that you will live again in a different physical body. On the surface, this may seem a little far-out, but when you factor-in past-life dreams, ghosts, déjà vu experiences and the like, the "possibility" of reincarnation cannot be denied by any thinking person. The real problem is how you prove it.

Reincarnation is exceptionally difficult to prove because the reincarnated person may have no connection to the previous life. The reincarnated person may be born many years after the death of the person they replaced. It can be exceedingly difficult to locate family members and friends who remember the person who died when those family members and friends, themselves, may have died. How can you go back and verify details of something that happened many years ago when birth, death and marriage records (other than in big cities) were kept in a family Bible? How can you prove that your mind is carrying the life of someone who you may not have known...or known anything about? How would you be able to verify the life and/or death of that person? Or, even more difficult, know the names of the dead person's friends or the intimate details of his "private" life?

Yet, there are hundreds of millions of people who not only believe it, but base their lives on it. Both the Hindu and Zoroastrian religions, with hundreds of millions of followers, believe in reincarnation. The Hindus believe that if you live a good life as a human, you will come back as an animal. Zoroastrians believe you will keep living as people, over and over again, until you become one with God.

Yet, most intelligent people will often use the technique called "sophistry" to try and belittle those who have experienced it and will tag or label those claiming it as frauds, or people seeking their fifteen minutes of fame.

In the previous chapter we discussed how, under hypnosis, memories become very clear: clear enough to remember details of when you were just an infant. In the past hundred or so years, hypnotists have gone a step further and attempted to regress their subjects back, past their infancy, to a time before they were born. Hypnotists have not been 100% successful, but they have been successful often enough to make even the most skeptical people pause and reflect on the possibility.

Please take the time to read about the case of six-year-old James Leininger of Lafayette, Louisiana (later in this chapter) or the story told by the hypnotherapist of Bruce Kelly and the experience Kelly related about being sunk on the US Submarine Shark during World War II: Any intelligent-thinking person would have to open their mind to the "possibility" of having lived before. The reason these two cases were among the ones selected for this book is that the "deaths" did not occur so long ago that the family and friends of these people could not verify many of the facts.

There were more than five hundred astounding tales of past lives that could have been reprinted, but when the original "deaths" took place, it was too many years ago for any living person to be able to verify the details in the story.

"Past Life Regression" (PLR) is very real. PLR is extremely similar to retrocognition discussed earlier with the exception that retrocognition is something that "just happens"; mostly when you are asleep. There is no particular control or impetus that causes the retrocognition.

PLR , on the other hand, is forcibly induced by the suggestion of the hypnotist or by some occurrence that snaps the memory to the forefront.

PLR is regressing the age of the subject to the time they were born (at which time, numerous subjects will assume a fetal position with no suggestion to do so by the hypnotist)…and then beyond that. I've tried this on when hypnotizing several subjects, and each of them has remembered a past life. Whether these are real or imaginary past lives is extremely difficult to ascertain. There are a sufficient number of clues to suggest that this may be a link to something we cannot explain unless we accept the theory of the auras as previously set forth in this book.

Again this tends to support the theory that auras go from one person to another after the death of a person. The problem with PLR, is that it is almost impossible to prove. Under PLR, people will remember past lives in fascinating detail including the places where they lived, the names of their friends and neighbors. Frequently, under PLR, people will speak using words no longer in common usage. If you are a believe in reincarnation, this is certainly your cup of tea.

The single most interesting case of PLR that happened under my personal guidance, was a sixteen year old girl who, when regressed to a past life, started speaking in perfect French. Fortunately, there was a person present who understood French fairly well, and translated some of what the girl was saying.

Unfortunately, the translator missed a lot of what she said because the girl rattled-on so rapidly, and many of the words she used were no longer in modern French usage. When we awakened her, the girl remembered nothing, and in fact, doubted that she had been hypnotized at all. When several of the witnesses told her of what transpired, the girl became very frightened.

When asked, the girl acknowledged that she did not speak French; that she was studying Spanish in High School. Her parents were not French, nor were any of the people she was close to. Her family once had a French maid, but that was only for a very brief period when she was a pre-school age girl.

I wanted to hypnotize the girl again and have someone very fluent in French present when I did it. But circumstances being what they were, I received a draft notice and was whisked off to war. When I returned from my stint in the army, the girl and her family had moved and I lost all contact with her. I did try, unsuccessfully, to locate her and her family, but in those days, without the Internet to help you, it was extremely difficult and expensive to do so.

THE CASE OF BRIDEY MURPHY

Probably the most publicized case of PLR was the 1952 case of Morey Bernstein, a businessman and amateur hypnotist, who hypnotized a Colorado housewife named Tighe and regressed her to PLR. She began to speak in a very heavy Irish brogue, and said that her name was Bridey Murphy and the year was approximately 1830. That she lived in a small rural area outside of Cork, Ireland. She proceeded to describe the house she lived in, the kitchen, the outhouse, the necessity of going outside to the pump to get water, the names of her husband, her friends, her children and family, and the fact that she had flaming red hair. Bernstein hypnotized her many times after that, each time, writing down more information and greater detail of his subject's alleged past life.

When awake, Tighe stated that she had never been to Ireland, and, in fact, didn't even know anyone who had been there. This is believable because, in 1952, world travel was not what it is today: an airplane ride from New York to Europe was an ordeal, and long distance air travel was just beginning to gain public acceptance. Going to and from Europe by an ocean liner was still a far more popular way to travel. There was no Internet that might allow someone to research Ireland without going there, and I have to believe, as Bernstein states, that Tighe had never read a book on Ireland.

Bernstein was so fascinated by this, that he took a trip to Cork, Ireland, and tried to search out anyone who might have known a family with a Bridey Murphy. What he found was published in his 1956 book "The Search for Bridey Murphy". Bernstein alleges that he did find the area where the house once stood. When he spoke to natives of the area, they confirmed that the description of the kitchen, the house and the area were accurate. Bernstein even states that he met an elderly man who says that, as a child, he remembered the Murphy family and he believes there was a grandmother (deceased) named Bridey Murphy in that family.

This started a "reincarnation" craze in publishing. Because the topic was so poignant, several magazine publishers sent reporters to Cork to see what they could find...and they reported that they found nothing. Still, they all acknowledged that finding evidence of a small family in a rural area of Ireland from approximately 125 years earlier was a very difficult task. Most of the reporters and writers returned from the area of Cork, Ireland not dissuaded from believing the story.

There were, of course, many skeptics who tried to follow the life of this Colorado housewife from her earliest days in Wisconsin to find any clue they could use to prove the recollections of the Colorado housewife were not what they appeared to be. The technique called "sophistry". One reporter from the Chicago American (a newspaper that closed its doors in 1962) alleged to have even found an Irish family in the same city where Tighe lived in Wisconsin in which there was a woman named Bridey Murphy Corken. The family allegedly lived several blocks from the subject, Tighe, when she was a small child.

It's time to reiterate the Einstein maxim: "For every human who has an original or different thought or comes up with a new idea, there will be a hundred people of mediocrity who will try to destroy that thought and the person from whom the thought originated".

Let's assume, for purposes of argument only, that Tighe as a young girl just a few months old was very close to this Irish family: On the surface, this might attack the veracity of her statements made while hypnotized. The fact is that the Bridey Murphy Corken family had never been to Ireland. Even if Tighe had been very close to them (something vehemently denied by Tighe and her family), did she know them so intimately that they sang lots of old Irish songs to her? Many of those songs are no longer remembered even in Ireland, but under hypnosis, Bridey Murphy knew the songs well. Did she learn words from the Corken family that are no longer in common use in Ireland? Did the Corkens teach this infant to speak with a heavy Irish brogue? Not very likely! It simply does not make sense.

As has often been said in this book, genuine scientific proof of unscientific explanations is elusive and hard to find. Even when empirical or circumstantial evidence is found, there will be enough voids that need to be filled in that you could drive a truck through the openings. Most often, the "proof" lies in using common sense and logic as to what is and what was.

I mentioned earlier that while hypnotized, a person can remember the names of the kids who came to their third birthday party, etc. When Tighe was hypnotized, and regressed back to her early childhood, she had no recollection of knowing the Corken family. Small incidents may be forgotten, even while hypnotized (although a concerted effort while under hypnosis will usually recall these incidents). It does not make sense that there would be no recollection of a family with whom she was close enough to have learned to speak with an Irish brogue, learned lots of Irish songs (many of the songs were old Irish folk songs that are now scarcely remembered), or learned a bunch of ancient Irish/Gaelic words that are no longer used today.

One of the things that Bridey Murphy remembered was a wagon trip along the Irish coastline from Cork to Belfast. She described the scenery in immaculate detail. This would be very difficult for a person who had never been to Ireland to describe.

Is this proof-positive of reincarnation? While there will always be significant numbers of people who fear the truth and who will decry the Bridey Murphy story as a fraud, I found it to be completely consistent with everything else I have studied, researched and brought forth in this book. Proving almost anything is never easy. Proving something that opens new vistas of thought is almost impossible because it is frightening to many people. People will naturally tend to resist that which frightens them.

The case of Bridey Murphy is not inconsistent with PLR experiences I have had with several people I hypnotized, and in its own way supports the dream I had when in Paris about the ball at the Louis XIV palace.

In the proper hands, hypnotism is a very valuable tool that can open new worlds to us. Inasmuch as it tends to break down the walls put up by our scientific and orthodox religious communities, advancement in techniques of hypnosis, experimentation with hypnosis, etc, will be strongly resisted. The few who have the courage to want to try and break these barriers down, will be savagely attacked by those whose religious beliefs do not permit or recognize reincarnation.

Hypnotism and my experiences with past-life regression (or, if you prefer "reincarnation") have totally convinced me that we have all lived before…and will live again. There are some people who feel that I am a "nut" for believing in reincarnation, and there are some who feel I am an expert on past lives.

THE CASE OF SHANTI DEVI

Perhaps the best documented and most verified case of having lived before is the case of Shanti Devi:

Of all the hundreds of past life cases that I have studied, the case of Shanti Devi stands out as the most documented, provable instance of having lived before. What makes this so, is that Shanti Devi never lost her memory of her past life. The details of this case have freaked-out a lot of non-believers. In most past-life cases, the subject only has flashes and/or very vague memories of his/her past life brought out through hypnosis. Not so with Shanti Devi:

People hear of many cases of reincarnation these days, but in the early 1930s, information about a girl born in a little-known locality of Delhi, who claimed to remember a past life, was considered great news indeed. The girl at first was known only to the local people, but gradually news of her spread all over the country and finally all over the world. It was natural that the world should wonder about the authenticity of her story.

On January 18, 1902, a daughter was born to a family named Chaturbhuj, residents of Mathura, India. Her name was Lugdi. When Lugdi reached the age of 10, she was married to Kedarnath Chaube, a shopkeeper of the same locality; a practice often followed in India in the early 1900s.

When Lugdi became pregnant for the first time, her child was stillborn following a Cesarean section. For her second pregnancy, the worried husband took her to the government hospital at Agra, where a son was born, again through a Cesarean on September 25, 1925. Nine days later, however on October 4, Lugdi's condition deteriorated and she died at 10 A.M.

One year ten months and seven days after Lugdi's death, on December 11, 1926, a daughter was born to Babu Rang Bahadur Mathur of Chirawala Mohulla, a small locality of Delhi. The girl was named Shanti Devi.

Shanti Devi spoke very little until she was four years old. When she did start talking, she alarmed everyone in her family by telling them, "This is not my real home! I have a husband and a son in Mathura! I must return to them!"

This was India in the 1930s, so instead of taking their daughter to a psychiatrist for a dose of Ritalin, her parents told her, "Forget your past life. You're with us now." But Shanti Devi wouldn't give up. She talked about her former family to anyone who would listen.

One of her teachers at school, out of curiosity, sent a letter to the address Shanti Devi had given to her teacher as her "real home" in Mathura, inquiring if here had been a young woman who had died there not too many years ago. To his astonishment, the teacher soon received a reply from Shanti Devi's previous husband, admitting that his young wife, Lugdi, had passed away some years previously, after giving birth to their son. The details Shanti Devi had given to her present family and teacher about her old house and members of her previous family were all confirmed in intricate detail.

This launched the most thoroughly researched investigation of a case of reincarnation in modern history. Everyone got into the act, including Mahatma Gandhi, several prominent members of the Indian government, and a team of skeptical scientific researchers.

The team of scientific researchers, working under stringent conditions to ensure that Shanti Devi couldn't possibly be getting her information from any other source, accompanied the little girl to Mathura.

Despite the accompanying scientists making efforts to misdirect Shanti Devi to the wrong part of Mathura, on her own, she was able to lead them to her previous home, and correctly described what it had looked like years earlier before its recent refurbishing. She was also able to relate extremely intimate information, such as the description of scars on the private parts of her former husband's body, described extramarital affairs of family members that no one, outside the family, could possibly have known.

In a further attempt to trip-her up, when Shanti made her first visit to her former home in Mathura, the research team hired an actor to pretend to be her former husband while her former husband pretended to be one of the onlookers in the crowd. Shanti immediately saw through the fraud and identified the man who had been her former husband recalling to him some intimate details of their personal life together that her former husband, in complete amazement, acknowledged.

The award-winning Swedish journalist, Sture Lonnerstrand, spent several weeks with Shanti Devi later in her life, recording her story and verifying information about the famous government investigation.

THE BEFORE MOMMY

Most cases of people having memories of a previous life are not publicized because the memories sometimes come in dreams or in unexplained phobias or on unpredictable occasions. One such person told me about an experience she had with her own daughter. What follows is exactly what she published in her Blogspot Blog "The Silken Touch":

"In about 1978, when Daughter was 3 years old, she was very verbal. She had been speaking in three and four word sentences at 9 months, and then when she realized no one but her Mommy could understand her ("yellow" was "eeoo", for example), she stopped. When she started up again at 2, she had a huge vocabulary, near perfect pronunciation, structure, and grammar.

I'd had three miscarriages and a stillbirth before her. I was afraid she'd be all I'd have (I was 31 when she was born), so she was a 100% natural birth, and I was very involved with her. She'd never at that point even been left with a sitter. She had never been exposed to anything that I wasn't aware of. She had been enrolled in a thrice-weekly program for exceptional children starting at 14 months, but even there I knew about everything she saw and did.

......And I know that she'd never seen or heard of most of the things she told me about having seen and experienced before coming to live with me.

I was a bit surprised when one day I was starting supper, and she asked what we were having, and when I said "sausage", she said,

"Oooo, I like sausage. My before-Mommy used to make that all the time."

Me: "Your before-Mommy? What before-Mommy?"

She: "The Mommy I had before I came to you."

Me: "You had a Mommy before me?"

She: (Impatiently) "Yes!" (Frustrated) "The Mommy I had before I died and came to you!"

Me: "Oh. You had a Mommy you lived with, and then you died, and then you came to me?"

She rolled her eyes, stamped her foot, and went off to play with the dog.

Now, keep in mind, she's three. This is the same kid who, more than a year later, burst into tears when she discovered I had once been a child - "But whooooo took care of meeeee when yoooooooou were a baby?" I told her Gramma took care of both of us, and that satisfied her. To a child of three, what is now... always was...and always will be. So the idea of a before, especially where Mommy is concerned, is beyond inconceivable.

The next time Before-Mommy came up I was putting something in the oven, and she said, "My before-Mommy would really like that oven."

Me: "She didn't have an oven?"

She: "Yes, she had one, but not like that."

Me: "What was hers like?"

She: "It wasn't iron. It was like clay, and it was shaped like this (arms swinging in a large high mound), and you put the bread in a hole here (shoving motion about chin high), and the fire goes in here (walking around to the other "side" and motioning low). Vegetables and stuff go in here (back around to the "front", motioning to a lower hole). No doors. Yours is a lot nicer. You don't have to build a fire."

Over the next year and a half we had many strange conversations. They were always initiated by her, always in quiet moments, usually when we were alone, but occasionally when her father was nearby and could hear. (Thank goodness, a witness!)

During these conversations, she looked and sounded older. Her voice was lower. Her whole aspect changed. She moved differently, tighter, commented on things a child her age wouldn't normally notice, drew conclusions beyond her age. Sat quietly and conversed.

I also quickly learned that when the conversation was over, it was over. Once she wandered away, if I went to her and asked about something she had just said, she didn't know what I was talking about. It was like she had "spells" when she remembered Before-Mommy, but outside those spells, when the spell ended, Before-Mommy not only didn't exist, Daughter had no memory of having talked about her! I pushed a bit once, and she burst into tears because she thought I was telling her she was adopted. I learned to move very gently, to get as much information as I could at her pace, on every occasion offered, before the spell ended.

I also learned that I couldn't ask a "wild duck" question. I could probe deeper into whatever she was talking about, could ask questions about whatever her chosen topic was, but if I tried to go beyond that, the discussion was over. For example, I never found out what her name was, and that was driving me nuts. Still does. But the moment to ask never came.

The following is what she told me, in bits and pieces, usually kicked off by something we were doing, over the next year plus. It was completely consistent, and the details were always the same no matter from what direction they were approached.

She, her mother, her older brother, and "Old-Pa" lived in a house in the mountains. It was all mountainy. Pointy. Lots of big wide fields, all around. (There was apparently no father? When I asked about a father, she looked like she didn't understand.) "Old-Pa" (the grandfather, I suspect) couldn't walk. He sat in a chair with wheels. (Like a wheelchair, like in the hospital?) No, a chair like in the kitchen, but with wheels on the bottom. Brother put the wheels on it. Brother took care of their "little camels" in the fields. (Little camels? I finally figured out from her descriptions that they were probably alpacas. That's very interesting, because llamas, alpacas, and vicunas are in fact related to camels, and in this life she had been exposed only to camels, so that's the word she used?) Her mother wore a man's big hat, and big skirts, "not pants, like you".

When Old-Pa died, the three of them moved into town. Their "house" was one large room, and all the houses were attached around in a square. The oven (which some ten years later I discovered was a perfect description of a clay beehive oven) was in the middle of the room. There was a door and a window with shutters in front of the house, and a door in the back that opened to a courtyard that all the houses used. She had been allowed to keep two little camels when they left the mountain (because she cried for them), and they were kept in the courtyard during the day (but they could go in and out), and in the house at night. Water came from a well down the street. That was her job, to go get water. Her mother didn't wear the man's hat any more.

There was something about her having injured her leg, and she had to use "crunches" for a little while, but I don't remember. She had a doll her mother had made for her.

Their house was really pretty, because it had painted vines and flowers and all kinds of stuff on the outside, all around the doors and the window. Her brother lived with them for a little while, then he went away to go to school to be a doctor. He bought an old car so he could come visit them a lot, but the car spent most of its time "in the car hoppital", so it wasn't much good.

She: "And then I got sick and died."

Me: "Do you know what made you sick?"

She: "No. I couldn't breathe, I think."

Me: "How old were you then?"

She: "Twelve. My brother came home, but he couldn't fix me. Then I died."

Me: (Treading very carefully) "And then what happened?"

She: (Nonchalantly) "I went to the waiting place."

Me: "Waiting place? What's it like there?"

She: "Oh, you know (No! I don't!), just a waiting place." (Waving her hand dismissively.)

Me: "What were you waiting for?"

She "Time to get born."

Me: "How long did you wait?"

She: (Rolling eyes, silly mommy) "There's no clocks there! I just waited 'til it was time, then I came to you.

Me: "How did you know when it was time?"
She: (Frustrated) "Because it was time to get borned!"

Me: "Why me?"

She: (Super frustrated) "Because that's when it was time!"

Spell over.

That was our last Before conversation. She remembers absolutely none of it, any of it.

I believe every word of it.

I think that's why she was able to tell me, because I listened and accepted, and didn't turn her off or tell her she was silly the first time she said something outrageous. I suspect many children with old souls come through with memories, but there's a small window when they are able to talk about them, that short period between *when they have the words* and *when the before fades*. And if they are discouraged, if the right now reality is imposed and insisted upon, the window slams closed."

Of course, I have no way of proving or disproving what she told me, but she swears that every word of it is true…and, knowing her, I have every reason to believe her. Silk is a very down-to-earth person and would never make up a story like this.

If you still have some doubts, there are more verified stories of reincarnation:

THE REINCARNATION OF JAMES MCCREADY

This article appeared on the internet without any author's credit. It also appeared in the Uniontown, Illinois newspaper:

James Leininger, 6, of Lafayette, La., loves airplanes.

"He has always been extraordinarily interested in airplanes," said James' mother, Andrea Leininger, by telephone from their Louisiana home.

Lots of kids love airplanes, but James' story is unique. He has memories of being a World War II fighter pilot from Uniontown -- Lt. James McCready Huston, shot down near Iwo Jima in 1945.

At 18 months old, his father, Bruce Leininger, took James to the Kavanaugh Flight Museum in Dallas, Texas, where the toddler remained transfixed by World War II aircraft.

A few months later, the nightmares began.

"They were terrible, terrible," Andrea said. "He would scream, 'airplane crash, on fire, little man can't get out!' He'd be kicking, with his hands pointing up at the ceiling."

When James was 2 1/2 years old, he and Andrea were shopping and he wanted a toy airplane. "I said to him, 'Look, it has a bomb on the bottom' and he told me, 'That's not a bomb, it's a drop tank.' I had no idea what a drop tank was."

Neither of the Leiningers have ever served in the military, nor are they involved with aviation. Until James began showing an interest in planes, they had nothing aviation-related in their home.

Andrea's mother sent her a book by Pennsylvania author Carol Bowman, called "Children's Past Lives." The Leiningers started using Bowman's techniques of affirming James' nightmares and assuring him that the experiences happened to a different person, not the person he was now. "It helped. The nightmares stopped almost immediately," Andrea said.

However, the memories did not stop, but they do not come up all the time.

"I was reading him a story and he got a faraway look," she recalled. "I asked what happened to your plane? 'Got shot,' he said. Where? 'Engine.' Where did it crash? 'Water.' When I asked him who shot the plane, he gave me a look like a teenager, rolling his eyes, 'the Japanese,' like who else could it have been?

"What little kid knows about the Japanese," she asked. "He said he knew it was a Japanese plane because of the red sun. My husband and I were shell-shocked."

James provided other information. He said his earlier name was James, he flew a Corsair and took off on a boat called the Natoma, and he remembered a fellow flyer named Jack Larson.

Foods can set James' memories off, too.

"I hadn't made meatloaf in 10 years, so James had never had it," Andrea said. "When he sat down, he said, 'Meatloaf! I haven't had that since I was on the Natoma.' When we were getting ice cream one day, he told me that they could have ice cream every day on the Natoma."

Bruce began researching his son's memories and discovered a small escort carrier called the Natoma Bay, which was present at the Battle of Iwo Jima. Twenty-one of its crew perished. Bruce also discovered that only one of the Natoma's flight crew was named James, James Huston.

James Huston's plane was hit in the engine by Japanese fire on March 3, 1945, went down in flames and sank immediately. Flyer Jack Larson witnessed the crash.

James Huston was born Oct. 22, 1923, in South Bend, Ind., and lived in Uniontown during the 1930s. His father was James McCready Huston Sr., of Brownsville, and Daryl Green Huston, who was born in New Geneva and grew up in Uniontown. James was the only son. According to Lt. Huston's cousin, Bob Huston of Flatwoods, the elder Huston started several newspapers and published 13 books. He was living in Brownsville when two Navy officers informed Huston of his son's death.

"I didn't know James," Bob Huston said. His parents were divorced, "but I knew his father. He stayed with us in Brownsville. James was on his 50th mission and would have come home if he'd lived another five minutes."

The Leiningers have been in touch with Bob Huston.

"I knew what happened to James (Huston)," he said. "I was excited to hear from them (the Leiningers). The boy's mother was flabbergasted when all this happened."

Andrea believes that her son is the reincarnation of Lt. James Huston. "There are so many little things. I believe in reincarnation now."

Her husband, Bruce, remains skeptical. "He started researching to disprove what James was telling us, and ended up proving it all," he said. "I think he believes that James Huston's spirit has manifested itself in our son somehow."

The Leiningers have been in touch with Natoma Bay veterans, too.

"We didn't tell the veterans for a long time," Andrea said, "but everyone has a story about having had a spirit visit them. James' sister, Anne Barron, was in California talking to him the day he was killed. Anne believes James' story, because he has provided so much information that only her brother could have known.

"Families of the 21 men who were killed are talking to each other," continued Andrea. "It's brought them together."

The Leiningers plan to attend this year's Natoma Bay reunion and bring their son, James.

Andrea doesn't know why this has happened.

"If he did come back, why? Maybe it was so my husband could write the book about the Natoma Bay," she said. "It helped turn the tide of the war in the Pacific and was one of the most highly decorated carriers, but it hasn't received much recognition."

She said her husband has been working on a chronology of what's happened to James and is researching the book. "He has flight plans from the missions and has spent a year and a half on research. In the introduction, he's writing about how he found out about the ship."

That discovery, through a toddler's fascination with airplanes and nightmares, has led to a segment on national television.

ABC contacted Carol Bowman about her work on children's past lives and James Leininger's experience was the most verifiable, Andrea said. "And we agreed to share his story."

The following account of psychological sessions was written by a hypnotherapist named Rick Brown. It was first published under the name "The Reincarnation of James, the Submarine Man" and appeared in the Journal of Regression Therapy in 1991.

It is included in this book because the occurrences were recent enough that some of the people referred to herein are still alive and have been interviewed, verifying the facts as given in hypnotherapy session by a man named Bruce Kelly.

THE REINCARNATION OF JAMES JOHNSTON

James Johnston   Bruce Kelly

Those who would challenge the validity of PLT (past life therapy) often point to the lack of information which can be empirically validated. Their cry is, "Give us data! Give us names, dates, places!" For this reason, this contribution, in which a careful and methodical follow-up was conducted to validate the data obtained during the regression, is an important study. We would be interested in hearing from other PLT practitioners who have done similar studies and validations.

On February 11, 1942, the U.S. Submarine Shark, on which James Edward Johnston was a crew member, was depth charged and sunk by the Japanese Destroyer Amatsukaze. All hands including James drowned. The spirit that occupied the body of James appears to have reincarnated again on January 19, 1953 in the body of Bruce Kelly.

In hypnosis, Kelly has a clear and vivid recall of a past life as James. Past life regressionists rarely have the opportunity to research data presented by a client, but James Johnston lived so recently that many of the memories recalled by Bruce Kelly have been authenticated.

Documents from the Civilian Conservation Corps, the United States Navy, and civilian records such as birth certificate and high school attendance records verify the life of James. In addition, several of James' friends and relatives are still alive and have substantiated information recalled by Bruce Kelly while in hypnosis.

I am a Certified Hypnotherapist, experienced in past life regression. Bruce phoned me initially to ask if I would answer some metaphysical questions. We discussed reincarnation and what effect it might have in his current life. I told him that regression into past lives is easy to accomplish and that anyone can do it.

Our first meeting was on November 17, 1987, at the Covina Counseling Center in Glendora, California. During that session, I went through the normal preliminaries, explaining to him what hypnosis is, how it works, and why people are able to use hypnosis for past life regressions.

Bruce, a sales representative for a men's furnishings concern, was required to travel extensively. Most of his territory was accessible by car. Occasionally, it was necessary for him to fly, which terrified him. It was all he could do to board an airplane. We determined that his fear was of being in a closed place where he had no control. When the airplane's door was closed, terror overwhelmed him.

Bruce suffered another phobia: fear of water, even the water in a bathtub. Bruce could stand under the spray in a shower if his back was to the spray, but he could not face it. He could drink from a glass or wash his car. He could be near a lake or the seashore without difficulty, and he could even wade in shallow puddles or dangle his feet in a swimming pool. However, whenever the water got up to around his knees or approached his trunk, such as when getting into a spa or a swimming pool, or even a bathtub, he became anxious. Actual immersion in water brought on irregular breathing, dizziness, nausea, trembling, and cramps.

Bruce had one other complaint, a chest pain that had bothered him for much of his adult life, a stabbing pain that started in his stomach and went into his chest, in the area of his left nipple. Several doctors, after examining him, had found no cause for the pain, and concluded it was idiopathic--it was all in his head.

During Bruce's first session, we discussed his symptoms, established a therapeutic objective, and I demonstrated past life regressive hypnosis. On the second visit, I transferred Bruce's recollection to his past lives. Bruce was instructed to recall the time and place where he was first affected by the terror he feels in an airplane.

Bruce said, "I'm in a submarine ... I'm dying."

I then asked him for the name of the submarine, its number and where the incident happened. Bruce answered easily, that the submarine was the Shark SS-174, and that it was part of the Asiatic Fleet, stationed in Manila Bay. He was a crewman aboard the submarine and his name was James Johnston. I asked for the time and date of James' death. He was able to answer immediately and without apparent effort. He was also able to recall where he was on the submarine and what was happening around him. As James, he had drowned in a submarine, an elongated, cylindrical pressure vessel which was similar to an airplane in form, fit, and function. Bruce observed the separation of the spirit from James' body. It has been my experience that if a subject recognizes and accepts separation, then the subject can and will abandon symptoms manifesting in their current lives.

The terror that had lived with James died with James. After the hypnotic past life regression, Bruce no longer felt afraid. He had left all of James' terror and anxiety in the submarine, and was relieved of the signs and symptoms of claustrophobia and hydrophobia.

Even though the therapeutic objective had been accomplished, Bruce and I agreed to investigate the life of James Johnston. In hypnosis, Bruce poured out information about his prior life as James.

I began writing letters, and the information which verified Bruce's past life recollections began to come in. A trickle at first, then more, then a flood.

The U.S. Navy Historical Center and Operational Archives at the U.S. Navy Yard in Washington, D.C. is open to the public. I was able to verify many of Bruce's recollections by searching through the mountains of documents there and at the Military Reference and Service Branches of the National archives in Washington, D.C.

I traveled to James' hometown in Alabama and interviewed several of James' boyhood friends and relatives. I ran an ad in the local newspaper, asking people who knew James to please contact me. I also distributed fliers to the local Senior Citizens lunch program, and to the organizer of James' 1937-1938 High School Reunion. Everywhere I turned, I received verification of the information Bruce had recalled while he was in hypnotic trance.

James' mother, Annie, was unmarried. During the 1930's she and James lived in the Profile Cotton Mill Village, a company-owned village, complete with a company store and a tract of company-owned houses, which were occupied only by employees of the mill. Life within depression era company-owned villages was a dismal existence. James and his mother lived together in one rented bedroom of a company-owned house. James' mother was a gentle woman whose death in March of 1936 was a surprise to many and a traumatic blow to her only son. Her death left him even more isolated and alone.

In July of 1938, James joined the Civilian Conservation Corps (CCC) and was immediately sent to Tule Lake in Northern California. He also served in CCC camps at Scottsboro, AL and Guntersville, AL. James resigned from the CCC and joined the Navy in July of 1940. After Naval Recruit Training School at Norfolk, VA, he was transferred to the South Pacific where he became a crewman aboard the Submarine Shark.

In the taped regression that follows, Bruce is recalling James' pre-war days on board the Shark. The transcript is not verbatim. Persons in trance do not communicate in the same manner as those who are in the normally aware state. They are lethargic and sometimes require many repetitions of the same questions. Sometimes the dialogue flows. Other times it is so clear and eloquent that one may question if the subject really is in hypnosis. Frequently a subject thinks a verbal response has been made when it has not. Many times, responses are not complete sentences. Occasionally, responses are too colorful to print. Bracketed material reflects my research and comments.

Rick: Where are you?

Bruce: Manila.

Rick: Is there a submarine base in Manila?

Bruce: I suppose there is, that's where the operations headquarters are. [Cavite, in Manila Bay, was the headquarters of the Sixteenth Naval District. Manila Bay was the home of the Asiatic Fleet. Several submarine squadrons were permanently stationed there.]

Rick: Do you have a particular friend? A crew member, someone you spend your time with?

Bruce: I don't see anyone really close. There is another person that works with me in the escape changer. He had the same training that I did. He was with me through training.

Rick: Let his name come to you.

Bruce: Robert Miller. [Robert Francis Miller, Fireman Second Class, is listed as a crew member on Shark. Miller was born in Evansville, Indiana, May 24, 1918. Miller was 22 years old on the date of his death.]

Rick: Did you and Robert Miller come together from school?

Bruce: I think we graduated together. [In order for a man to be assigned to regular duty on a submarine in 1941, he had to have received training in the use of the Momsen Lung, an underwater breathing device used to escape from a disabled submarine. Both men were probably trained and certified to use Momsen Lungs in Pearl Harbor. They probably graduated together.]

Rick: Are you accompanied by other ships or other submarines in your operations?

Bruce: Yeah, sometimes.

Rick: What are the ships that accompany you?

Bruce: I think there is Porpoise, maybe Spearfish, not all submarines have names. I get numbers, I think we may have been sent there with other submarines that are like 37 and 38. [Submarines 37 and 38 were Asiatic Fleet Boats on station in Manila Bay with Porpoise and Spearfish].

Rick: Does your submarine have a number?

Bruce: Not that we are referred to as, we're just referred to as Shark.

Rick: What is the nature of your (Shark's) activities in this area?

Bruce: Just reconnaissance. There is a reason we are here, but we are not aware of it.

Rick: How do you feel about not being aware of what is going on around you?

Bruce: We don't like it very much.

Rick: Do you talk about it?

Bruce: One-on-one, or a bitch session, but nobody is questioning any officers about it. We just do our duty. [A close boyhood friend of James, who most times called him "Red" because of his red hair, or "Ed", told me that he thought World War II saw the last of what he called "The Willing Warrior". Willing Warriors did not question. Most were farm people who went where they were told, and did what they were told.]

Rick: Do you ever encounter ships other than U.S. ships?

Bruce: Yes.

Rick: What do you do?

Bruce: We observe them, shadow them.

Rick: We are going forward in time now until after you are aware that Pearl Harbor has been attacked and after war has been declared. Is that OK with you?

Bruce: Yes. [A time focusing process].

Rick: What do you feel?

Rick: We are mad. We are so mad, that the Japanese would do this to us. We are also a little afraid because we know we are in danger.

Rick: Is there a feeling of closeness in the crew?

Bruce: More than there was before. Yes, now we realize that we have to depend on the other person for our life.

Rick: So now there is a unity?

Bruce: Yes, more than before.

Rick: Do you have a close friend, a close person you can share your thoughts with?

Bruce: No. Not really. I work with Robert Miller, but he is not a friend. [James has been described by a boyhood friend as a happy but lonely child. Bruce consistently reports James' loneliness].

Rick: What part of the submarine are you in?

Bruce: I'm in the crew quarters.

Rick: Is the submarine surfaced or submerged?

Bruce: Submerged.

Rick: Is it day or night?

Bruce: I think it's morning.

Rick: What is the date?

Bruce: I believe it's February eleventh. [1942]

Rick: Okay, let's continue on with the morning of the eleventh. This is the morning of the loss of the Shark. Is that correct?

Bruce: Yes.

Rick: What are you doing in the crew quarters?

Bruce: I'm just relaxing. I am not on duty.

Rick: What is that duty?

Bruce: It involves the compartment, the escape hatches. It's a compartment by the torpedo room. [One of the roles of a past-life regressionist is to be a psycho-detective. The subject perceives many more sights, sounds and feelings than the regressionist is aware of and the subject may not report those perceptions. The subject is not intentionally withholding the information, but is focused on other things. The regressionist must recognize a clue or a significant bit of information as it comes from the subject. That is not easy to do and often times is not possible. In this case, I completely missed the clue about "just relaxing". In later regressions, it was determined that James was confined to his bunk with rib injuries received in a depth charge attack on February 8, 1942].

Rick: Do you have another man you work with?

Bruce: Yes, Robert Miller.

Rick: Is he standing watch now?

Bruce: Yes.

Rick: Why is the submarine submerged now?

Bruce: Because it's daytime hours and our mission is reconnaissance and Japanese ships have been reported in the area. [Shark was on her second and last war patrol. On February 7, 1942, Lt. Commander Shane reported the presence of a Japanese cargo ship. On February 8, Shark was told by radio from Surabaya to proceed to Makassar via the Northern coast of Celebes].

Rick: I want you to go forward in time on this day to the point where you start to become engaged with whatever causes

*you to sink. Go forward in time now ... [A time focusing process].
... as an observer, you will feel nothing: you only observe, and as an observer,
you begin to understand. You know what you have engaged that causes you to
sink. What is it?*

Bruce: It's a Japanese destroyer.

Rick: Are you aware of the name of the destroyer, its class, its size?

*Bruce: No. [The Japanese destroyer was the Amatsukaze. She was a 2033
ton Kagero class fleet destroyer, carrying 16 depth charges. Amatsukaze was
sunk June 4, 1945].*

Rick: Are you on watch?

*Bruce: Not at this time I am not. [James was confined to his bunk with
rib injuries].*

Rick: What time is it?

Bruce: I think it's about 11:30.

Rick: Morning or evening?

Bruce: Morning.

Rick: Is it a single destroyer?

Bruce: I don't think so. I think there are more, but I'm not sure.

Rick: What is the nature of the attack?

*Bruce: It's a depth charge, and it happens in a hurry. I haven't gotten to
my post yet. I have just gotten out of the crew quarters and we're hit. I am in
a long hallway and trying to get to my post and we are hit. Pretty severely, the
ship is really shaking and rolling and momentarily goes black.*

*Rick: Are you uncomfortable? [My question was to Bruce who was showing
discomfort and anxiety. James answered.]*

*Bruce: I am scared. I was knocked off of my feet by the impact and I am
trying to scramble to my feet in the dark and find my way. I guess to find my
way to my post. I am scared and confused. I guess that's where I want to go.*

Rick: Do the lights come back on?

*Bruce: Yes, momentarily. I have gotten to my feet and I am just getting to
a hatch and I'm going through the hatch when we are hit again and the lights
go out again. This one was a lot more severe. This one is a direct hit. No doubt
that this is a direct hit and I am knocked off my feet again.*

Rick: Must have been a very severe hit.

*Bruce: There's water in the compartment. The ship is flooding. It's flooding
fast. The last hit definitely ripped a big hole in it. I get the impression it was
close to where I was, maybe back close to the midsection, behind the conning
tower. That's where it took the hit.*

Rick: On which side?

Bruce: Right on the top.

Rick: And so water is rushing in very fast?

Bruce: Very fast.

Rick: Do you hear sounds of shouting around you?

Bruce: Not that much in the hatch that I'm going through. I am still in the hallway. I still haven't gotten to my post. There is one other person there. He's in the same situation I am. A panic. He's not hurt at this time, but there is water rushing in and filling up real fast. My thought is to get to my post with the possibility of getting out of the ship. But at the same time I am aware of the impossibility of this. Just that everything had gone wrong in a hurry. We are definitely going down.

Rick: Uh-huh.

Bruce: The blast was so close to the conning tower that it may have ripped into it. There may have been two depth charges, the one that I felt and maybe the sensation of another. I was kinda in a twilight because the first one knocked me out.

Rick: Uh-huh.

Bruce: More like one and then very possibly another one right afterward.

Rick: How long does it take for the water to fill the compartment?

Bruce: Not long, a minute or so.

Rick: What are your thoughts as the water is rushing in?

Bruce: The realization that I am dying. There is no way out. There's definitely no way out. No way that I can go anywhere. The water's too strong, the current is coming in. I have the sensation, the feeling that everybody on board is going through the same thing that I am. We are all dying quickly.

Rick: Is there anyone nearby?

Bruce: Walter Pilgram.

Bruce: He is older than I am.

Rick: Considerably older?

Bruce: Maybe mid-thirties. He's someone I haven't been close to on the ship. Just know of him. I know him by name. [Pilgram was born December 21, 1909. He was 31 years old on the date of his death.]

Rick: What does he do on the ship?

Bruce: A mechanic or an engineer. [Walter Pilgram was a Chief Electrician's Mate].

Rick: Uh-huh.

Bruce: Something like that. Never have really taken the time to talk with him or to discuss what he does. I just believe that is what he does. [Firemen Second Class do not associate with Chiefs].

Rick: Do you in any way attempt to exit the submarine?

Bruce: There's no way. The compartment, the hallway we are in just filled up too fast with water, and there is no way out. We just can't get out of this compartment.

Rick: Is that the compartment with the escape hatch?

Bruce: No. That's where I am trying to get to. The submarine is filling up with water so fast and was hit so violently that I'm sure that there is no way anybody can get out.

Rick: Uh-huh. Were you dead before the submarine got to the bottom?

Bruce: Yes.

Rick: Was everyone dead before the submarine got to the bottom?

Bruce: Yes, I think so. [Pause]

Rick: I'm going to count from five to one. When I reach the number one, your spirit will have rejoined your body and the time will be early in the morning of February 11th. Long before the attack, long before any problems. A time when you were very relaxed and calm and very much at ease. Five, back to being in the body, being a part of the body, the spirit and the body are together. Four. Going back to the time and the place and to the morning when you were in your quarters, relaxing. There, you are ... [I terminated the hypnotic trance and brought Bruce into full physical and mental awareness.]

The memories of James' past life episodes which flow so easily from Bruce's subconscious mind have freed Bruce from his irrational fears and resolved his claustrophobia and hydrophobia. Just as his doctors concluded, the phantom pain in his chest was without any physical cause. It was all in his head. Now it is gone.

Extensive research indicates that Bruce Kelly's memories of James Edward Johnston's life and death are accurate. Still, there is no proof, only converging lines of evidence suggesting Bruce Kelly is the reincarnation of James.

Rick Brown is a graduate of the Hypnotism Training Institute of Los Angeles and a Certified Hypnotherapist in full-time private practice in Glendora, California since 1987. He specializes in Stress Management and Stop Smoking seminars, as well as in the development of self-help audio cassettes. His background also includes a career in engineering and he holds many U.S. and foreign patents.

The following commentary was written by Stephen S., a member of the Board of the Regression Therapy Journal.

The historical validations in this case are too specific to be due to chance. The only possible alternative explanations, other than reincarnation, are: 1) accessing some psychic pool of information, like the "akashic records" or the "collective unconscious" (unlikely because the subject experienced these memories in the first person, and because long-standing phobias were involved and were cured); or 2) fraud on the part of either the subject, or the therapist/ presenter.

This article was published in 1991, and thus the sessions took place somewhat earlier, before the internet was in common usage. It is technically possible that the subject, having a prior interest in metaphysics (hence the reason for the initial contact with the therapist, to ask questions about metaphysics), wanted to perpetrate a hoax. He could conceivably have researched all this information beforehand, and pretended to divulge it under hypnosis. While this can't be discounted as a possibility, it seems very unlikely. For one thing, the subject accurately portrayed the personality of the deceased person. Had he obtained this information from personal associates (as the therapist did), those associates would have mentioned that Bruce Kelly had asked them the same questions earlier. Likewise, a records clerk in at least one of the archive facilities probably would have commented to the therapist that someone had asked for those exact same records earlier.

If these alternative explanations are discounted, then this case provides extremely strong evidence that at least some hypnotic past-life regression sessions are retrieving historically real past-life memories, and that they are memories of the same person in a previous incarnation.

Note: I have added the photos as of 3/13/06. They are from the cover of Rick Brown's book by the same name as this article, which I just purchased used. I had not seen a comparison photograph before this time. The two faces are quite similar, though not identical; but the eyes, and my intuitive perception of the mind behind those two pairs of eyes, indicate to me that this is a match. There is something in the gaze, despite the fact that James seems to harbor a lot of resentment and anger, while Bruce seems to be free of it. Since publishing this article I have learned that author Rick Brown has passed on.

6/20/06: I am now reading the full version of the account in book form. In the book, author/therapist Rick Brown reproduces Bruce Kelly's diary verbatim, including his decision to be hypnotized and his meeting with the therapist. It is clear from this account that there is no fraud on the part of Mr. Kelly (interestingly, he was a "born again" Christian when he began his search). That eliminates any reasonable hypothesis of fraud on his part, in my opinion--leaving only the unlikely possibility that Mr. Brown made up both Mr. Kelly and the entire account as a fictional work. That means that beyond a reasonable doubt, this case proves (yet again) that past-life memory may correspond to actual historical persons and events in a way that precludes chance. Which proves that reincarnation is real. Which proves that as a whole, our entire Western civilization is in psychological denial. Which proves that our entire Western civilization suffers from what, in an individual, would be considered some form of neurosis. Which I am tired of saying while nobody is listening...but, if you are listening, there it is.

Stephen S.

The reincarnation accounts I have included here are only five of a possible five-hundred I have reviewed.

There is no possible way for me to attest that I have personally verified any of these cases, but facts are facts, and denying facts when they stare you in the face is as close to genuine foolhardiness as can exist.

This is not to suggest that there will not be some skeptics who will state that these stories were made-up and/or proven to be false. But just as in the case of Bridey Murphy, the skeptics will rant and rave and even go so far as to make-up stories to disprove what is written here. They do this because (a) it does not comport with their religious or social beliefs and (b) they have such tremendous fear of the unknown that they are unwilling to accept the truth staring them in the face. If they cannot disprove or put-down what I have written, in all probability they will revert to making a personal attack on me just as political candidates attack and smear their opponents when they have nothing positive to say about themselves. The empirical or circumstantial evidence is there. You be the jury.

Chapter 9

Unscrambling Human Behavior

Inasmuch as this is a book to explain the unexplained, it could not be complete unless we take a good hard look at strange or seemingly illogical human behavior. Much of human behavior is unexplained and poses almost innumerable questions: Why do two children from the same family become two totally different people? Why do some people become gay? Why do some people become brilliant doctors and lawyers and others, from the same background, become criminals?

As you will see, everything in this book that has preceded this chapter will play a large role in explaining the complexities of human behavior and, in fact, will explain the diversity of behavior using the same theory:

The mind/aura for all of its force, knowledge and experience, has not made puppets out of people. It should be self evident that our actions are not controlled by our thoughts.

A simple example: If you're driving along in your car, and another car makes a swift, dangerous, cut directly in front of you, you may feel like speeding up, blocking the other car's path, pulling the driver out from his car and beating him up. Those may be your thoughts.

But do you do that? I hope not! You may mutter a few expletives under your breath (or even out loud), or you may throw a dirty-look at the driver of the other vehicle and then continue on your way grateful that the idiot didn't hit your car. Those may be your actions.

Clearly, your thoughts do not control you. The above having been said, the mind does have an influence on that thing we so loosely call a personality, or human behavior. It does not control, but it *is* a significant influence:

Have you ever wondered why it is that two children from the same family can be so different? How it is that the son (or daughter) of a moral minister can turn out to be a bank robber or a prostitute?

Science will tell you that it's in their genes. To some extent, science may be right, but the way the term "genes" is used, it has become another one of those scientific "trashpots" into which a myriad of things they can't explain get thrown. There are many more as we shall see.

Is it in your genes to become a criminal...or a panderer? How about homosexuality? Or pedophilia? Is that also a matter of "genes"?

Medical science can tell you, with a degree of certainty, from an analysis of your genes how tall you will become; whether or not you have a tendency towards obesity; whether or not you have a proclivity for heart problems; Alzheimer's disease; stroke; osteoporosis, etc. But note that all of these things are physical things. What have they got to do with personality or a tendency for antisocial acts?

To explain the latter things, again, medical science comes up with another of their "trashpot" gems: "There is a chemical imbalance in the brain." Really?

In order for there to be a chemically "imbalanced" brain, we first have to know what a chemically "balanced" brain is, and medical science can't tell you that. In fact, the chemical balance of all brains is different (except, possibly, in the case of identical twins). And, inasmuch as all brains have different chemical balances, it doesn't make much sense to say that one person has a chemical imbalance and another does not because one's behavior is considered to be antisocial by the majority of people. Yet, this is what scientists would have you believe.

The whole idea of "chemical imbalance" in the brain or "bi-polar" activity is just the latest in a series of new medical "trashpots" into which they can throw a lot of things they find themselves incapable of explaining with any rationality.

Consistently, medical science will try and attribute things like depression, moods, hyperactivity and the like to a chemical imbalance... or their most recent trashpot "bi-polar disease". They will treat these symptoms with medication and chemicals that will dull the senses of the brain. Again, this doesn't make sense. Sometimes it appears to work on the symptoms because the "dulled" brain cannot process information from the mind or aura as thoroughly as a normal brain, but it will never affect a cure. As soon as the brain stops being "dulled", the same pattern of thoughts that caused the problem originally will return.

Remember how it works: The mind or aura feeds the computer/brain with information: far more information than the brain can disseminate. If the brain is "dulled" so that it can process less than normal amounts of information, there will be some behavioral changes, even if they are only temporary while under medication. But the cause? If the thing influencing the behavior is still the mind/aura, then what has the medication accomplished? We need to look further.

THE EVIL TWIN

Let's take a brief moment to examine the "genes theory". Actually, using twins, it's very easy to disprove the genes theory of medical science that behavioral differences are in the genes: How is it that identical twins can turn out so different? They were born in the same sac with, essentially, the same set of genes. Science loves to cover it by talking about dominant genes and recessive genes, but the truth of the matter is that science doesn't know and, despite all their ballyhoo, they don't have the slightest understanding of what causes these differences. I'm not trying to belittle the importance of genes: virtually everything physical about you is controlled by your genes: the size and capacity of your brain, the strength and durability of your heart, the foods that please you (or displease you), your tendency towards obesity, your ability in athletics, etc. All of these things are physical and are controlled by your genes. But your personality and/or behavioral patterns are not!

If you've done more than just flip through the pages of this book, by now, you understand: When two individuals (or three or four) are born, whether or not they are identical or fraternal, an aura immediately surrounds each one. These auras are usually quite different and may have no historical relationship to the other. One aura may have a historical background of royalty, and another may have a background filled with axe-murderers. Of course, I am certain there are many times that the aura of a deceased loved one surrounds a newborn of the same family and as the newborn grows older, he or she begins to display the traits of the deceased loved one. Think about this: How often have we seen a child take on many of the characteristics of a recently deceased parent or grandparent as they grow older. This is because the aura of the deceased has entered the body of the newborn. It is really quite common when the aura wants to find a new body that they search for one very close to the one they knew before, or where they enjoyed life.

As human beings, we have no choice in the aura that chooses us, but as we shall see, we can control the behavioral patterns.

When children are small, the differences in their auras are almost indiscernible because the auras are feeding brains which, as yet, are incapable of accepting and processing even the most basic information. Speech has not, as yet, been developed, so a baby has no tools with which to use its aura. The baby responds to sounds...sounds that are pleasing. The baby responds to warmth of its mother and father. The baby can feel the pain of hunger or discomfort; but not much else. Even infants feel the love of their parents. The parents of twins see two identical (or very similar) children growing up. As the children begin to get a little older, their brains are now able to comprehend a little more of what their auras are feeding their brain, primarily because the child has learned a language...and we tend to think in the language we are taught. The thought process of twins becomes slightly different, and one may start to do better in school than the other...or one may be showing signs of being a prodigy on the piano while the other prefers baseball.

Still, both are young children and their very existence depends on their family. Until the child reaches puberty, environment plays the most important part in their upbringing.

As the child begins to enter puberty, the brain starts making quantum leaps in its ability to comprehend the information being fed to it by the child's mind/aura and the pubescent child starts to seek his/her own identity. The family may be financially well fixed, but one of the twins has an irresistible urge to steal things from the local Wal-Mart. He/she may have more than enough money to buy whatever he wants, but he secrets a special pleasure from "taking" things. And, if they get away with it (as they often will) it reinforces their secret desire to take things...even things they don't need or want. There is an old axiom: "When the fishing is good, you go back and fish again." So it is with children learning to do things their parents forbid. If they steal something and get away with it, they will be back for more!

One twin may start to find the field of law of great interest while another may feel a compulsion and desire to teach others. The combination of the brain and the mind/aura are creating two completely different patterns of human behavior from twins whose genes may be almost identical.

One twin may be a happy, sprightly child while the other becomes moody and withdrawn.

By the time they are well into adolescence, both twins, usually, have probably developed two or three distinct and separate personalities: 1) The personality they have with each other, 2) the personality they have around their parents, and 3) the personality they have around their friends. When they are young or adolescent, much of their parents' teachings are being contradicted by their friends, their experiences and their own thinking. At this juncture, they need these different personalities to help develop the one personality they will have when they mature. Many parents are in complete denial when they find out that their sweet, church-going, son has been arrested for shop-lifting or has been truant from school.

These differing personalities that each of us has when we are young are a direct result of the conflict between the developing mind/aura and the greater information now being taken-in by the brain. The mind/aura may be encouraging a person's brain to devote time to studies and become a doctor or telling us that we need to smoke pot or tobacco in order to be accepted by our peers. Or, the situation could be reversed wherein the mind/aura gives someone great mental satisfaction when they steal something while the memory banks in the brain are registering that it is against the law and there is the very real danger of being caught or going to jail.

But the mind/aura does not control! It tends to create a pattern of desires within each individual. What the individual does with those desires will be the individual's choice as a result of circumstances or simply a refusal to live the kind of life the mind/aura prefers. The mind/aura must often compete with the knowledge of life and information constantly being fed to the brain. The twin with a proclivity for law may wind up being a doctor because his father was a doctor and encouraged him to go to medical school. The natural-born teacher may wind-up selling semi-conductors because of financial needs, etc.

Simply because the mind/aura does not control, let's not minimize its affect on human behavior. Who among us has not thought of finding a box or a bag with a million dollars in it and secreting it away without telling anyone? Your information stored in your brain will probably tell you that the money belongs to someone else…that it could be drug money that some mobsters will come looking for, etc. Whether you decide to return the money to its rightful owner or secret it away for your own future use will be the result of your mind/aura's conflict with the knowledge the brain has stored.

THE ONGOING CONFLICT

There is a constant conflict going on between the mind/aura and the brain. This is supported in the volumes of books written by Sigmund Freud and other leading psychologists better known as the founders of the pseudo-science "psychology". They were first to recognize that the mind was not, necessarily, a part of the brain and that the functions of each were totally different from each other. Freud called it the conflict between the "conscious" and "unconscious". The "unconscious" is the part of you that wants you to do anything and everything to gain personal satisfaction. The "conscious" is the part of you that tells you to use caution and to do the "right thing". It's very easy to substitute the term "unconscious" with "mind" or aura, and the term "conscious" with "brain". A simple example of this constant conflict: A man walking down the street sees a very attractive girl walking towards him. In his mind, he may visualize a romantic liaison with the girl. His brain tells him to look straight ahead and keep walking. As a result of this instantaneous conflict, he smiles as she passes, and keeps walking.

Adolescents feel this conflict more strongly as their mind/aura and brain work to help them to develop their personality: "I know I promised my parents I would be home by eleven, but all my friends are still here." "I know I'm not supposed to smoke pot, but if I don't do it, no one will like me."

The mind/aura influenced the decision made, but it was the combination of the mind and the brain that made the final decision. Although the mind/ aura did not control your actions, it left a definite wake behind it: You may feel a tension in your stomach and the mind may keep reminding you of what it believes you "should" have done. Thus feelings of guilt become strong in the formative adolescent.

What Freud and his disciples had to say became the basis of what we now call psychology: the study of the human mind and behavior. But what these psychologists had to say did not answer all the questions the study of psychology created. A study of what they began to call "abnormal psychology" did not approach the reasons why the actions of some people seemed to be "out of control".

Thus the theory of "Heredity vs. Environment" was born, and psychologists argued furiously as to which of the two was more important in developing an understanding of human behavior. As we have discussed, previously, neither one answered all the questions about personality. Twins arriving in the same sac with almost identical genes and living in the same environment could be the antithesis of each other.

A new theory called "Gestalt" was created and became the by-word of psychology: This theory correctly came to the conclusion that the mind had a lot more to it than the sum of a person's experiences in life. Still, psychologists could not understand how our minds could have had experiences that our bodies did not.

Then came the field of medical science claiming that certain brains have a chemical imbalance and that's why behavior of some people is unusual. Since physicians cannot tell you what a chemically-balanced-brain is, it doesn't work to try and balance a brain to a standard that doesn't exist, with drugs. Each brain has an individual chemical balance in it unlike any other brain. Drugs react differently with every body's chemistry...so the medical theory of chemical imbalance is simply another "trash pot" that does not hold water.

It should now start becoming evident to even most cynical of readers that the scholars in the field of psychology are inching closer and closer to the theories expressed in this book. I'm open to other theories, but I know of none that explain human behavior as well or as thoroughly as the concept of the mind/aura and the cumulative experiences from having lived before. We could be a hundred times more knowledgeable as people if our brains were capable of computing all the information and experience our mind/aura is capable of feeding it.

Let's take a hard look at some of the problems of human behavior:

Masculinity and femininity are a physical thing and can be traced to genes. Still, there are some people who are "more masculine" or "more feminine" than others. This is not the fault of the individual, and can be attributed to genes. Yet, although it is not the fault of the individual, the mind creates "envy" of others who are more masculine or more feminine. This often creates suggestions by the mind to do or act in a manner to compensate for this envy. Whether someone takes such steps will, finally, be the combined decision of the brain and the mind. The mind may influence that decision, but it is the combination of the mind/aura and the brain that usually has the final word.

The question as to whether heterosexuality or homosexuality is a matter of the degree of masculinity or femininity in a person is still debated and is much too argumentative for discussion here. There are many documented cases of a man being virtually trapped in a woman's body and vice-versa. Still, many effeminate men (including most cross-dressers) are quite heterosexual. The decision to lead a gay lifestyle is, again, a decision made by the mind/aura and the brain. It is a "conscious" decision. The mind/aura may push the person towards a decision but, again, the information stored in the brain will influence.

Put simply, preference of company of the same sex does not a homosexual make! Professional athletes, businessmen, and factory workers often prefer the company of the same sex for a number of reasons too numerous to detail. It is only when a man makes the conscious decision to lead a gay lifestyle that he can truly be called a homosexual. Many heterosexual people have homosexual tendencies and still lead what we call a "normal" life. Even if a decision is made by a man to abandon a gay lifestyle and act in a wholly heterosexual manner, his aura will never let him forget his fondness for other men, although he may never again leave the heterosexual lifestyle.

Psychological or medical treatment cannot afford a "cure" for a gay lifestyle, because it is not an illness. It is a conscious choice.

Criminal activity takes place when the mind/aura overwhelms the brain and makes the decisions of the brain subservient to the desires of the mind.

As I have already said, normally the mind/aura does not control. It "influences", but does not control. The thought of going to jail keeps most people from doing things like stealing, killing, raping…and, of course, child abuse. In each of these cases, the brain has brought its memory banks to the surface about being caught, interrogated and jailed, but the mind/aura has calculated the probabilities of being caught and decided that the reward is worth the chance. All humans have the option of doing or not doing something illegal. The decision will always be a combination of the brain and the mind/aura.

Common legal defenses of criminals on trial of having been abandoned as a child or being raised in a housing project are, to me, without any genuine substance. The environment may influence the thoughts a person has, but it is a combination of the brain's memories and the mind/aura's thoughts that has the final word. Just like the person who is cut-off in traffic by someone else and responds by taking out a gun and shooting the other driver. The road rage was so strong that the driver "lost control". When someone allows their mind to make the final decision and ignores the warnings of the brain, deviant behavior results.

Medical treatment of such people leaves much to be desired: Electro-shock therapy may destroy a few brain cells, but it cannot affect the way a mind works. A pre-frontal lobotomy kills the brain's ability to compute any information fed to it by the mind. A lobotomy usually results in a walking vegetable. Treatment with psychiatric drugs usually impairs the person's ability to function in a normal society. None of these treatments seems practical.

The case of the man who killed someone else as a result of road rage may be the result of an explosion in the mind…but if it happened once, it can happen again. Men who physically beat women may apologize and feel genuinely sorry for their behavior, but as court records will attest, the likelihood of it happening again is extremely high. It is the opinion of this writer that such people are, and will always be, a danger to others.

There are many other examples of "deviant" human behavior that can be explained by the aura. As a final example, let's talk about serial murderers and serial rapists. I specifically use the term "serial" because the individual who attacks someone else in the heat of passion or in a fit of rage has a very different behavior pattern than the person who plots killings or attacks on others with the intent to do harm. Criminally, our laws treat them both the same.

Let's take a moment to look at these two deviant behavior patterns:

Why would someone deliberately try to harm the life of another; a person who, in all probability, he does not know. Once again, we have to look at the mind/aura feeding the brain.

The minds of millions upon millions of people send violent messages to their brains: The driver who was suddenly cut-off by another unthinking driver; the anger and vengeance we feel when we read about Japanese soldiers in WWII in the Philippines throwing babies up in the air and catching them on the end of their bayonets; the way our blood boils when we hear about someone attacking and killing a child, or remembering the horrors of the Holocaust.

I could go on, but the fact is that the mind does send our brains many messages of violence. On some occasions that can be a good thing: to a soldier in battle it can mean his very survival. But many people whose auras have fed their brains with feelings of hatred would like nothing better than to cut out the hearts of people they feel have wronged them.

But we don't do those things, do we?

The reason we don't is that we are still in the driver's seat. We are always aware that any aggressive act on our part could be met with an even more aggressive reaction on someone else's part. Our brains have stored an incredible number of facts that we call upon to keep from becoming a vigilante. But some people allow and even encourage the mind to overwhelm the brain's protective mechanisms.

Let's not make the mind/aura out to be a bad or violent thing. It also provides our brains with solutions to everyday problems. It creates the feelings of love and desire that are so important in life. It provides us with an understanding and appreciation of others. However, as rich as it is in experience and knowledge, the aura also has a darker side: It wants the person to whom it is attached to have creature comforts as well as spiritual comforts. It not only allows for love, it also allows for jealousy and hate. All emotions take place in the mind, not the brain. Emotions can create beautiful…and sometimes violent…actions from the brain. And, as I have said, the brain often has the final word.

The person who acts violently towards another in a burst of emotion is quite different than the person who carefully plots out an attack on another. In the first case, the brain has allowed an explosive mind to override it. In the latter case, the brain has acquiesced to a plan of deviant behavior. Let's delve just a little deeper: What is it that someone is trying to prove by harming someone else? Whether it's a matter of vengeance or criminal intent makes little difference: If you haven't already guessed the answer, it's the serial criminal's way of proving himself more powerful than another person. Even the schizophrenic or psychopath that hears voices ordering him to do violent things is still out to prove his power over others. Serial criminals do not just harm; they like to fill their victim with fear and helpless rage…or alternatively, they want to fill others with that fear or helpless rage.

Examples: Most serial criminals will "capture" an unsuspecting person, make them helpless with handcuffs or ropes (or sometimes using anesthetic to knock them out) and then torture them before killing them. Serial criminals (such as snipers) will derive their pleasure from making an entire community fearful…of the shooter. What greater "power-trip" could you have than knowing you have made an entire community (or nation) frightened of "you"? Never knowing when you will strike again.

And this is what the serial criminal is looking for: "power". It would never do to have a victim fight back, because that would mean the victim does not respect your power over life and death. For that reason, most serial criminals choose women, children or the elderly as their victims; the victim is not be able to fight back strongly enough to disturb the criminal's fantasy. That's why people who are in a position of power rarely, if ever, become serial criminals: they already have enough power. Most serial criminals are people in more menial positions who are subject to taking orders from others.

One of the most unusual aspects of the serial criminal is that he usually believes he is doing good for mankind and society by getting rid of people that harm it. That's why almost all serial criminals seek out a specific class of person to attack, such as a prostitute or homeless people or hitchhikers. The overpowering mind/aura has convinced the brain that the world will be better off without this class of people ...whatever that class may be.

Why? Again, the force of the criminal's mind/aura overwhelms the defense mechanisms of the brain that has been (ostensibly) taught to respect law and order, the rights of others and the knowledge of eventually being caught.

I've heard it said that serial criminals all think they are too smart to be caught...until they are caught. That statement is not really true. Most serial criminals leave tracks a mile wide behind them, but the police and other law enforcement agencies have so many things to handle, they may know everything about the serial killer...except his name.

The truth is that the typical serial criminal is not even concerned about the traces he leaves behind him. He is so overwhelmed by his mind/aura seeking to prove his power that he virtually cannot help himself. His brain is functioning in low gear while his mind/aura is a supercharged turbo. He simply cannot stop! The momentary high he gets from killing someone needs to be repeated ...like a drug addict.

Again, people like this will never be cured. When they are apprehended, their brain which had been flashing all its warnings, suddenly comes to the forefront because now the criminal is in the victim's position. In court, while on trial, most serial criminals look and act like normal people. But they are not. Unfortunately, such people, once incarcerated, should never again be let out onto the streets. They may want to change, but they have demonstrated that their aura is too strong and easily overcomes the cautions of the brain. They cannot function in a normal society.

There is a major, significant difference between violent crime and non-violent crime: Violent criminals must always remain behind bars, while non-violent criminals may readily adjust to a normal society. Many people, who as teen-agers, robbed a store or a home may find more than sufficient satisfaction of their aura's demands when, as adults, they use some of the perfectly legal means to cheat others.

Many CEO's of major corporations who steal from their shareholders, etc., have simply adjusted to a mind/aura that offers great satisfaction to rob and steal. We could go on almost endlessly. There are virtually countless people who have these strong desires that can only be fulfilled by acts against the public interest.

There is an excellent chance that even in your own family, kids that have been brought up well… perhaps regular churchgoers…have minds seething with unsavory things involving sex, crimes and power. But these are thoughts that may never manifest themselves in any way.

I'm not suggesting that these people can't help themselves or that they shouldn't be punished if they do something against their fellow man. No matter how strong the desire, a person capable of functioning in our society can control it. When someone lets their desires take over their life, they are possibly making themselves into a menace to mankind. Millions upon millions of people, when they see a beautiful girl (or a sexy "hunk") walking down the street, have desires spring into their head. But, they don't do anything about it, for many reasons. To name a few: fear of physical pain, fear of imprisonment, fear of hurting their families, fear of failure, fear of rejection, fear of disease, etc. The desires may be strong, but the combination of the mind/aura and the brain make these desires consciously controlled.

Sigmund Freud (the Viennese Psychologist) created a sensation in the 1930s when he published his ideas concerning the mind. He, too, agreed that the mind and the brain were separate entities, but the concept of an aura was too far advanced for him. Actually, his beliefs regarding the human mind fall very close to the truth. Accepting and understanding that, for his day and time, his concepts were pretty "far-out".

Now let's take a moment and compare that with what we have learned: Freud was absolutely right about the conflict in his mind taking less than an instant. The mind functions hundreds if not thousands of times faster than the brain. But Freud was wrong to think that this conflict went on in the man's unconscious mind and he was not even aware of his thoughts. In fact, the man was probably very conscious of his thoughts although in Freud's day and age it would never have been socially acceptable to admit this.

It is interesting to note how theories of human behavior have moved slowly, but in the right direction over the course of time going back to Plato and Socrates, up through Freud and into the present.

We are not victims of our genes (except for physical things), we are not victims of a chemical brain imbalance and we are not merely physical puppets for our auras to control. It is important that any free thinker avoid the scientific trash pots into which science likes to dump things they cannot explain. We must always stand responsible for our own actions.

So it is, that even with the great power of the mind/aura, we do choose our own course of behavior.

Chapter 10

Dreams

SURPRESSED DESIRES? A GLIMPSE INTO THE PAST?

We all have a secret world. Our world of dreams.

No one knows what you have dreamed about or are dreaming about unless you tell them. In his dreams, a physician may be a fireman. In dreams a Nun may be a wanton prostitute.

Do our dreams have any genuine significance?

Let's go back to one of our more basis themes: The brain is our body's computer and controller. Our mind/aura is the thing that feeds the brain information. Put simply: the brain is our computer and our mind/aura is at the keyboard!

When we're awake, our brain is dominant. My brain controls every action of my body including telling my fingers to press on the keyboard in order to get the correct letters to appear on the computer screen. It tells me to sit down, stand up, etc. The mind can tell you that pressing your fingers on certain keys is the right thing to do, but it is the brain that orders it done.

The keys my fingers stroke on my computer, in order to come out with what I'm trying to say, is suggested by the mind/aura. Maybe an even better way to phrase it is that the physical motion of the body (controlled by the brain) is necessary to accomplish what the mind/aura would like it to accomplish. This is not to suggest that our mind/aura may not offer us several other possible routes to take…but once our mind/aura has made a decision, the physical action to perform that decision is controlled by the brain.

When I'm driving a car, my mind tells me to slow-down as I approach another vehicle or prepare to make a turn as I approach a corner. The brain orders my foot to the brake pedal. Every physical action we take is controlled by the brain. Take note: as we approach another vehicle, our foot instinctively moves to the brake pedal. We did not stop to think whether or not we should put our foot on the brake; we just did it. That's a perfect example of the brain commanding our body without any input from our mind.

It may sound confusing, but the point is simply that when you are awake, your body is active and controlled by your brain. But when you're asleep, your body is relatively inactive. I use the term "relatively", because although all the organs inside your body are working when you sleep, and are purging themselves of all the impurities they have garnered during the day, your physical body is not moving as it does during the waking hours. It follows that when the brain is not being called to control your physical movements that it, too, is resting.

Notice, however, that our mind/aura comes to life when our brain is resting.

You may wish to ask does our brain ever sleep? The answer is a resounding "yes". Every part of our body needs to rest or it will wear-out quickly. The brain is as much a physical part of our body as our arms, legs, vital organs, etc. During the day, we use all these parts of the body and they need to rest at night in order to be able to function tomorrow. Sometimes the brain will tell us to stop working by making us feel very sleepy.

As the brain goes to sleep, your body becomes controlled by your mind.

WHY DREAMS ARE HARD TO REMEMBER

Ever wonder why it is that the only dreams we can really remember is either when we're starting to go to sleep or just about to wake up? If you piece together some of the other parts of this book, the answer is simple: Because just before you go to sleep, your brain is still slightly active and can file your thoughts into its computer banks, often remembering the images in your mind that are there. The opposite is true as you approach a waking state. Sometimes, what's going on in our minds is so traumatic that it will awaken the brain and some of that traumatic dream may be remembered. Nightmares frequently awaken our brain and wake us up physically.

When our body sleeps, our minds become dominant. It casts images into our thoughts that require no physical action from our bodies. These are what we call dreams. In dreams, time is vastly accelerated. We may dream about an adventure in which we are involved that has taken a month, a year…or longer and awaken to find that only a few minutes has passed. One of the reasons for this is that your mind is not encumbered by the same clock or calendar that encumbers our brains. In our minds, time has no barriers. Life itself has no barriers because the mind/aura is eternal. When we think about or create an image of a dead person in our dreams, to us that person is very much alive. Our image of that dead person may not be precisely as we knew them when they were alive, but there is excellent reason for this as we will discover:

So, when we sleep, it is not our brain at work…it is our mind/aura. Let me repeat: When you are awake, your brain is active….When you are asleep, the mind/aura takes over. How do we prove this? Of course, there is no "scientific" proof, but if common sense and logic are any criteria we can prove this easily:

In a dream it's not uncommon to relive an adventure or experience we had during our waking hours…only in our dream we have corrected some of the mistakes we made when we were awake. In a dream it's not uncommon to have a sexual or other physically pleasing experience with someone you might never approach in a waking state. In a dream it's not uncommon for us to review the problems which have been plaguing us during the day…and come up with solutions to those problems.

Most noteworthy is that in our dreams we may meet people we have never seen or heard of and have experiences of a type we would avoid if we were awake. Yet the people we meet in our dreams, most often are so detailed in their images down to the tiny scars on their faces or the crow's feet around their eyes, we wonder if, upon awakening, we hadn't known these people sometime during our waking state. Our dreams can be very meaningful if we approach them as being from our mind and not from our brain.

We also dream about visits from dead people we loved or admired, although these dreams usually happen when we are in the deepest stages of sleep and we don't remember them when we awaken. There is good reason for this, too.

To offer a rational explanation for our dreams and perhaps gain insight into what they are actually telling us, we must first recognize that our mind/aura is actually living in a different dimension that the one we see when we're awake. Obviously, our mind is with us all the time, whether we are sleeping or waking, but if we use the criteria our scientists have set forth, we cannot detect our mind with any of our five senses: sight ,sound, smell, taste and touch...then, according to science...it does not exist. We can't "see" our mind or aura. We can't "hear" our mind or aura.[4] We certainly can't "smell" our mind or aura; we can't "taste" it and we can't "touch" it.

So, according to the study of science, it doesn't exist. But we know it exits. We can hear our own voices, seemingly inside our heads, thinking about everything from what to prepare for dinner to how to solve the problems of starvation in the world or how to make some money during difficult economic times.

So, if it exists but can't be detected by any of our five senses then, by definition, it must exist in another or different dimension. Although we can't sense the physical presence of our auras, infra-red film and cameras can. The infra-red film and cameras can pick up the energy emanating from our electromagnetic auras. Accordingly, we know that there is an electromagnetic aura surrounding the body of every living person. Although we can't really "sense" it, we know that it's there.

We also know that the electromagnetic field surrounding each person does not die when the body dies. It seems to stick-around for a while, and then it slowly moves off. To where? We can only guess, but we're starting to get some reasonable clues.

This electromagnetic field (or aura) around our bodies contains the life experiences of all the other people it has surrounded before attaching itself to our bodies. It contains an incredible amount of knowledge gained over thousands of years. That's why a dream may contain a solution to an "impossible" problem or suggest a new course of action for us to follow in our waking state. Your aura may have previously surrounded someone who speaks a different language...and in our dreams we can understand that

---

4   What we "hear" as our minds is our own voice filtering through our brains. It makes no sound(s) for others or even electronic devices to detect.

language. But, as soon as we wake-up, we have no recollection of this. Your aura may have learned to talk with a severe Irish brogue (Bridey Murphy) or have lived in France (the girl I hypnotized who spoke only an ancient dialect of French) or remembered the living conditions in a mountain cabin (the "Before Mommy") that no child of three or four could possibly have known or even imagined.

Your aura exits in the same dimension as other auras. Therefore the aura of your dead mother or grandfather has much better contact with your aura than you could possibly have when you're awake because your aura and the aura of a dead loved one exist in the same dimension. When you sleep and your aura is dominant, your mind can catch glimpses of the dead…and sometimes of previous lives. The only real problem is that when your aura is the most dominant, you are in the deepest stages of sleep… and when you awaken, you don't remember what it was you dreamed about because your brain was sleeping and could not file the images of your dreams in its computer banks.

That girl I saw in my new apartment in San Francisco: Most likely, her aura was still around the apartment not being able to accept the sudden and unexpected death she suffered. When I started to sleep, my aura contacted hers and created a visual image in my mind of a girl I had never seen who had been murdered there. As my brain started to wake-up, the communication between the two auras in my room started to diminish as the waking brain blocked the other aura. The image was no longer available to my mind. My five senses took over. Yet, the image I had gotten was sharp enough for me to recognize her in a photograph weeks later.

Because our auras have lived so many times before (and will live again) they have a tendency to be "critical" of your physical appearance. You may be an extremely handsome man or beautiful woman…but your mind or aura will find lots of little things to diminish your physical opinion of yourself. The same is true of your work and/or your relationships. Your mind/aura will always be your greatest critic because it has been around many others who were better-looking, smarter and more innovative than you are.

When you get an image in your mind, it's, somehow, different than when you see something with your eyes. Think about any dream you can remember...if you can remember one. Think particularly about the images you saw in that dream. They were distorted, weren't they? When your brain sees something through your optic nerve, it isn't distorted at all. It's exactly what you see. But, if you remember when we talked about astral projection, we concluded that the aura could also see and hear. But the eyes and ears of the aura see things slightly differently: probably because the aura does not have an optic nerve and a retina such as we do.

In an earlier chapter, we asked you to try this experiment: When you wake-up tomorrow morning, before you open your eyes, try and visualize your bedroom from the perspective of your bed. Then open your eyes. Things are not at all as they were in your mind, are they? This is because your mind is still holding on to the vision that your aura had. Your mind sees things the way your aura sees them...which, generally is different than you see them when your brain has fully awakened and your five senses are active.

The reason we go over this is because, if your mind/aura is controlling when you sleep, the dreams you dream are as your aura has seen them. We often dream about events that happened during the day...but we dream about them in a distorted fashion. People we know are usually recognizable, but as before...they look a little different. Even deceased loved ones are slightly different than we remember them. Of course, in our dreams we may have another adventure with our dead family members... completely different than we had with them when they were alive...because to our mind/aura, they are not dead at all. They are living entities that communicate with our auras. Often, the aura of a dead loved one may be trying to communicate a message to you. Try to remember as much as you can about such dreams because, contained therein, may be information that is very important to you.

What about when we dream of strange things? People we've never met and places we've never been. People we've met acting in an unusual manner?

Remember, our auras have lived before and will live again. It has memories and knowledge far beyond our capacity to understand. Sometimes it will be in contact with the aura of a deceased loved one, and the loved one will appear usually doing or saying things that we remember about them. But there will be something different about the way they look. They will appear as seen by your aura. Remember that your aura and the aura of your dead loved ones are in the same dimension, and they can contact and communicate with each other, but only your aura can get inside your head until you die and your aura is released.

Sometimes, in a dream, you may visit a place that you've never been. Then, when you actually go to that place, it appears different than it did in your dream. Your actual visit sees the place clogged by traffic and high-rise buildings that were not in your dream. But, in your dream, you may be seeing the place as it was when your aura visited it; many years ago.

Sometimes an event during the day can trigger your mind/aura to pull up memories of a previous existence such as happened to me when I went to Paris for the first time. The faces we see are complete in all details… it's just that our brain has never seen them before. Sometimes, when we awaken we will puzzle over the intricate details of a dream with faces and places we don't recall. Obviously, our aura has seen the places and the people or it could not have created a detailed image in our heads. If you make a special effort and encourage your dreams, sometimes a dream will reveal a big part of a previous life you lived.

Don't become confused. We are not our bodies…we are our minds! The bodies will, invariably, grow old and die. But our electromagnetic aura will never die. When our body dies, we return to the dimension from whence we came. Since I have no memory of this, I don't know much about that dimension, although I know it exists. All indications are that our mind/aura will seek, find and adopt another body. When the brain in that new body gets large enough or matures enough, information from the mind/aura will start to be absorbed into the brain.

If you think about it, that explains why identical twins with almost identical sets of genes can become two completely different personalities; seek different careers; act in totally different manner from each other. Not while they are young and their brains have not developed, but as their brains mature…two extremely close twins, with almost identical sets of genes, will start to develop distinct personalities. Science offers no explanation for this.

If we recognize that each child has its own aura, and its own set of experiences from which to draw, then we can readily understand how it is that, as they become mature, their likes and dislikes can grow so far apart. Science can't explain it, but we can. Once we recognize that our mind/aura is eternal and the aura attached to each person has lived different lives, a lot of the world's mysteries fall neatly into place.

Of course I can't prove it scientifically, but if you open your mind and think about it, it makes a lot of sense…a lot more sense than science's present theories. The empirical evidence is there…you just have to look at it.

There are lots of clues as to what you were in previous lives in your dreams. Your dreams deserve a lot of attention.

What about "special" dreams? Dreams where you find yourself in a situation that's uncomfortable. Either you solve the situation in your dream…or you wake up. Again, your mind is trying to tell you how to solve your dilemma, but if the solution it offers is too uncomfortable for you to accept it, you try to reject the solution and, by doing so, awaken your brain. That's what we commonly call a nightmare.

One of the wonderful things about life is that we can train our brains to get some rest whenever we want: through meditation and through self-hypnosis.

When someone is hypnotized, the hypnotist has, effectively, put the brain to sleep so that it does not have any decisions to make. The voice of the hypnotist will make those decisions. If the hypnotist says that you're sitting in a movie theatre watching the funniest movie you ever saw, you respond by starting to laugh…exactly as you would if, in fact, you were watching such a movie. If the hypnotist passes a needle through your hand or tells you that you will not feel any discomfort …or tells you, during childbirth, that there will be no pain…what the hypnotist says will be what you feel because your brain is sleeping and it doesn't know to warn you that you're supposed to be feeling pain and it won't send a signal to your body to react to the pain.

As humans, we have the ability hypnotize ourselves and, instead of taking commands from a hypnotist, we can command our own minds and garner the same effect as though we were hypnotized by an outsider. Under self-hypnosis or when practicing meditation we can command our minds to let us in on the secrets of previous lives or even of what our aura's dimension is like.

When we discussed astral projection, did you notice that the people who astrally project themselves are either under self-hypnosis, meditating or have had their brain put to sleep by an anesthesiologist?

The power of dreams to unfold many of life's mysteries is ever present. We do have to use some significant effort to have the signals our aura sends us become meaningful.

Remember, your aura communicates to you when you sleep and communicates in the language you speak. It does take significant effort, but you can train yourself to remember many of your dreams and, when awake, see what messages they are really sending you.

Chapter 11

Faith Healers

REIKI VERSUS HAND HEALING

No book on the unexplained would be complete without taking a good, hard look at the "Faith Healers". The group of people who, until recently, were referred to as witches, witch doctors, faith and spirit Healers. Please do not confuse this with the modern technique of "Reiki".

Reiki is a method through which the passing of the experts hands over another person's body allegedly passes the energy from their hands into the body of the person they are working on. Reiki practitioners will claim that this can relax a person and make them feel completely renewed and rejuvenated as a person. Reiki is noted for removing the tensions of the day from the body.

If you stop to think about it, Reiki appears to be an offshoot of hypnotism without actually putting the subject to sleep. It is, in all probability, the power of suggestion combined with body massage. Reiki practitioners, I am confident, will argue the point. But Reiki is something that can be learned. It is taught by alleged Reiki experts and the use of Reiki has become widespread throughout the world, having started only about fifty years ago in Japan.

One definite similarity between Reiki and Faith Healers is the passing of energy from one person into another.

The "Healers" I'm referring to appear to have some special power within their bodies that cannot be taught or learned. It's either there or it isn't. If it's there, it's among the most remarkable mysteries on Earth: The "Healer" will actually touch the other person's body and will, allegedly, draw the infirmities from their body and cast them away. Healers have been credited with curing people of smallpox, scoliosis, brain cancer, appendicitis and a myriad of ills that normally prove to be fatal unless treated medically. The theory behind Healers is that the special power in their body flows through their hands; it actually invades the body of another person and draws out the physical problems much like a character in the film "The Green Mile", or in a Star Trek episode called "The Empath".

I know it sounds like science-fiction, but there are thousands of cases where the physician said there is "no cure" that Healers have brought about a complete cure.

Some pseudo-scientific studies have been made concerning what makes a Healer different than any other person. Several of the proven faith-healers were examined medically and one thing they all have in common is an exceptionally high energy level. This energy level has been measured and found to be double to triple normal energy levels. Every one of these proven faith healers said that they can actually feel the energy flowing through their hands into the body of the person they are attempting to heal when they concentrate their efforts on the patient.

Please do not suggest that I am telling people to abandon their Chemo-Therapy or Radiation treatments and find a Healer. I do, however, suggest they consult with one while undergoing their medically-advised therapy.

It is noteworthy that most of the so-called "Healers" throughout history were women. Before the medical profession became the bastion of male prestige that it represents today, it was the women who would go and tend the sick, hold the dying in their arms, pray for the infirmed…and yes, even cure many people of whatever it was that ailed them.

History tells us that the women were always known as the Healers until the Spanish Inquisition decreed that no one was more destructive of Catholicism than the women Healers who would often perform abortions and try to nurse the sick children back to health. The Inquisition reasoned that these were acts against God's will and, therefore, against the Church. It became a practice of the Inquisition to seek these women out and have them burned at the stake…or worse.

The result, of course, was that the women Healers went into hiding. Spain passed a law (which became almost universally accepted) that anyone who practiced healing without having been properly educated was a witch and must be destroyed. Inasmuch as women were rarely allowed to attend school beyond the fourth or fifth grade, only the men (with extremely few exceptions) went on to study the art of healing. This gave rise to an all-male medical profession, and pushed women into more subservient roles.

The early Healers, the women, should be given credit for having discovered almost all the herbs that are now used in medicine and sold in pill or injectable form. They deserve a lot of credit that has never been given them.

Possibly the strangest thing about these uneducated women Healers are the vast numbers of cases of sick, infirmed and disabled persons who were completely cured; completely recovered from their medical problems… without the aid of any herbs or medicines. Even today, there is a significant percentage of the world's population that relies on Healers.

There are still many third-world countries where medicine is practiced through Voodoo, Witchcraft or Witch Doctors. In areas where pharmacies and medical doctors don't exist, there is an astounding rate of cures for things that still are believed to be "incurable" by modern medicine. There are cultish religious groups such as Jehovah's Witnesses and Seventh Day Adventists with members who believe in natural healing to the point where they will fight to prevent their sick from getting medical treatment.

Like everything else we've discussed, there are vast numbers of people who claim to be Healers who are only too happy to take your money and hope for the best. Yet, for all of the phonies and out-and-out Charlatans who allege the ability to heal people's infirmities, non-medical healing has some of the most prestigious list of supporters known anywhere.

Perhaps the very term "Faith Healing" connotes a negative image: You may think of some TV evangelist waving his hands over a woman who allegedly suffers from Dropsy and had to be carried to the stage by several helpers, suddenly standing up and kicking her heels high because she loudly proclaimed her faith in Jesus.

That's show business! Pure and simple, it's entertainment and has been used by literally thousands of TV and tent evangelists to gain very significant donations to their "Godly" cause. This type of thing has nothing, whatsoever, to do with the true Healers.

Perhaps a better name for the true Healers would be "Hand-Healers". I use the term "true Healers" without hesitation because, even today, in our educated society and in major cities, there have been any number of

Healers who have been tested scientifically, under laboratory conditions, who have shown a significant success rate that, seemingly, defies medical explanation.

Among those tested, none of the Hand Healers had a perfect record, or, in fact, had the kind of success ratio we can attribute to modern medicine. The highest cure rate for the tested Healers seems to be slightly less than thirty percent (30%) of those treated. In all fairness, however, we should note that the recorded ailments, infirmities and injuries treated by the Healers were of a kind and nature that modern medicine had failed to be able to cure and where, quite often, the undertaker had already been told to prepare for a new guest. Accordingly, a 30% success rate becomes phenomenally high and somewhat of an embarrassment to the medical profession.

Let's allow for a little "puffery" and attempts to gain publicity. Still, if even **one** of the Hand Healers had any degree of consistent success, whatsoever, it becomes very noteworthy. This is especially true because the types of "incurable" ailments and maladies cured, without limitation, include AIDS, brain cancer, blindness, glaucoma, stone deafness, Lou Gehrig's disease, skin cancer, lymphoma and any other number of diseases and infirmities that most physicians have given up on and practically ordered the hearse to be ready.

I am not referring to things such as "hysterical" paralysis or blindness. Hypnosis has been known to cure hysterical paralysis and blindness, but I've never heard of hypnosis curing a brain tumor. The recorded illnesses cured by the Hand Healers were both diagnosed and treated by one or more physicians before Healing was tried.

Then, too, one cannot help but be impressed by the quality of the names of people who, having been cured, swear by the Hand Healers. They include statesmen, celebrities and any number of people who would have no reason, whatsoever, to make false claims.

From my point of view there is one other thing that sets the true Healers apart from the charlatans: None of the true Healers, to the best of my knowledge, ever charge anyone for helping them or curing them. True

Healers usually recognize that they have a very special gift and are willing to share it with others.

It has been said that behind every crime there is a motive. In the vast majority of cases, the motive is money. But, if there is no motive, then the crime is very unlikely to occur. People, who help others without remuneration of any kind, are not likely to be phonies.

An actress of no less stature than Cindy Williams ("Laverne & Shirley") will swear that she was suffering from severe scoliosis, a medically incurable curvature of the spine often resulting in severe physical limitations, hunchback conditions, etc. She will also swear that her scoliosis was cured; that her curvature was corrected to the point where she stands and walks straight and has no significant physical limitations…by a Hand Healer… who did not use surgery, traction or any medically accepted treatments… and who charged her nothing!

Claims like this must be taken seriously or at the very least investigated carefully. Let's look at how the procedure seems to work:

The Healer is brought in and he (or she) moves his hands over the affected area, frequently not even touching the person but moving the hands around the affected area at an almost-touching distance. Several Healers feel that "almost" touching is not sufficient and they let their hands virtually massage the affected areas. The ratio of success seems to be higher with those who actually use their hands to "touch", based on publicized claims, but there are no accurate figures to support this.

Cures are seldom immediate and, in fact may take several weeks or months of treatment before the first signs of recovery appear, and may even take a year or more to affect a complete recovery. Frequency of the treatment varies, depending on the urgency of the case, but there does seem to be a correlation between frequency and speed of recovery. Remember, these Hand Healers are voluntary and you are taking a significant portion of their life from them when they treat you.

As for cost, as I previously said, none that I have heard of have ever charged a fee. There are other considerations: If the healer was to charge a fee, he/she could be arrested and charged with practicing medicine without a license in most States; a criminal charge that carries a jail sentence.

Many of the Healers actually work through physicians. Yes, strange as it may seem, there are a significant number of physicians who use Hand Healers on cases the physicians feel are hopeless. The physician may charge a fee, but I would assume that the physician's fee would be covered by most insurance policies. Whether or not the physician pays anything to the Healer is something I do not know.

Many tests have been made of Healers under laboratory conditions, and some infra-red photography may be quite revealing:

The tips of the fingers on almost all Healers tested, showed noticeably excessive heat flowing from them. It seems that energy from somewhere inside the Healer was passing through the fingertips into the person(s) being treated.

This is not the first time infra red photography has revealed things we cannot see. The electromagnetic aura that has been the heart of this book has been photographed with infra red photography and always seems to be surrounding the head and body of the human photographed. Because the infra-red manages to photograph this type of energy, it is not much of a stretch to assume that the additional heat and energy flowing through the fingertips emanates from the Healer's aura.

If so, it would tend to explain another of the so-called inexplicable things in life:

It has often been shown, that the human body is its own best healer. Cuts and scratches heal by themselves. Illnesses are frequently overcome without the use of medicine. Keep this in mind as we search for the reason and logic behind Healers.

Remember, from the outset of this book, we have assumed that the aura that surrounds our bodies is thousands (if not millions) of times more intelligent than we poor mortals. The aura does its best to feed the brain information, but is severely limited by the brain's capacity to compute or accept the vast amount of information being fed to it.

HOW HAND HEALING WORKS

Now let's put a few things already in evidence together, and see if we can't come up with a reasonable explanation for Hand Healers curing the incurable…even if only in a limited number of cases.

Almost all Healers have one characteristic in common. They talk to their patients and soothe them…much like a hypnotist. Remember, that when the action of the brain is slowed down or sleeps, the hypnotist, therapist or Healer is in direct contact with the aura.

It is not unreasonable to assume that the aura, with all its vast store of information, may have seen these diseases before and also…may know of cures for these diseases that worked in the past. While in direct contact with a person's aura, and touching the inflicted area of the person's body, the aura may well be able to impart important information to the brain about these areas being touched. But, you ask, isn't that a little too far fetched?

It isn't far-fetched at all. We've seen how, while under hypnosis, a person can be made to feel happy, sad, increase the power of their muscles, not feel things that should be causing pain and even control the flow of blood. Likewise, when under hypnosis, very real pain or crippling infirmities that don't really exist, can be made to exist…even if only temporarily. Addiction to such things as nicotine and coffee can be cured over the course of several treatments.

The hypnotist, communicating directly with the aura of his/her subject, issues a command to the subject's aura. That command is relayed to the subject's brain and the subject sees, hears, feels, etc. what their brain is telling them to see, hear and feel…even if it isn't really there.

It is not unreasonable to assume that Healers, over the course of many treatments, can cause the brain of the subject to accept and compute the things necessary to cause healing. The brain controls the body, and if it is fed the right information, it can probably, in many cases, cure the body of its infirmities or injuries.

Please do not view this as a cure-all or even a substitute for the practice of medicine. More often than not, if your physician diagnoses your case as being "incurable", then it is incurable. But if there is even a slim chance that the body can heal itself…or that there is a chance that some non-medical cure is possible, why not take it?

Many physicians, even though they still think of Healers as being witch-doctors or over zealous religious freaks, do know Healers and, when all else seems lost, might be willing to help supervise a Healer's attempts at a cure for that which he, as a physician, cannot cure. Although Healers are frowned upon in the USA, especially by the all-powerful American Medical Association, Healers are generally accepted almost everywhere else in the world.

Although it is difficult to believe in religious Healers or those who claim that your acceptance of their God will cure you, there is a lot to be said for "Faith" and the "Power of Positive Thinking". In my opinion, when you have Faith and belief in yourself and your body's ability to cure itself (one of the foundations of Christian Science) it can and does help. But you should never use Christian Science or Faith or anything else without first taking a careful look at what medical science has to offer.

Without meaning to put-down medical science, readers are cautioned that if you are diagnosed with a significant medical problem, it **always** pays to get one or two more medical opinions. Medicine is not an exact science, and sometimes the treatment is worse than the cure. Chemo-therapy, which has cured many terminal cancer patients is also a deadly poison that destroys the body's own natural "immune system". Properly used it can be a blessing to a terminally ill patient. Improperly used, it can kill a patient. Always get more than one opinion.

Chapter 12

Energy: The Force of Life

What is "life"? Is it just opening your eyes in the morning and breathing in the oxygen from the air? Is it just waking up, going to work, having a woman or man to love, having children, etc.? Or…does the word "life" have infinitely more meaning?

If you believe the former, then there is no purpose in existence. When you die, someone will replace you ad infinitum. If you believe the latter, then there are a lot of questions that should be asked and not all of them can be answered with any significant degree of certainty.

If we assume that life has more meaning than the daily routine, we have to start by asking ourselves "What is the purpose of our existence?" If everything we have spent our lives learning about dies when our body dies, then life has no meaning. But, if the lives we live can retain some of what was learned, and use it in another life, then life not only has a meaning, it has a definite purpose.

That's what this chapter on "energy" is about. There is an unseen form of energy that stays with all living people. It is the underlying force that enables us to see, hear, appreciate beauty, love and create. It is an underlying force that pushes us to learn…and learn…and learn. Not always in textbooks, but by experimentation and experience. It enables us to read books like "Gone With the Wind" and visualize ourselves as Rhett Butler or Scarlet O'Hara; to imagine ourselves as Harry Potter fighting the lifeless dimentors; to live in abject poverty and visualize ourselves living in a land of milk and honey. That underlying force is the thing that makes us want to live whether we live in a castle, a jungle or in a slum.

If all the colorful explanations of that driving force were boiled-down to one single word to describe the essence of life, that word would be **"energy"**.

We live on a planet that is hospitable to life because the energy from a nearby star, our Sun, warms the surface of our planet in an otherwise frigid outer space. It creates an atmosphere so we can breathe. It allows plants to grow to provide food for the creatures that live on this planet.

Our planet holds its place in the cosmos due to what is called gravitational energy. We move about on the surface of that planet by using what is called mechanical or kinetic energy. We have developed to ability to manufacture things because we have learned to isolate thermal and chemical energy. We can see the beautiful colors of our world due to optical energy. We can learn new things and are able to accomplish far more than just eating and procreating because, distinguishing ourselves from all other creatures on this planet, we have learned to use what is called mental or psychic energy…also called electro-magnetic energy.

There are many, many types of energy, but since this is not a course in physics, let's concentrate on the one type of energy that separates human beings from all other plants and animal living on the Earth: Mental or Psychic energy. The body we live in is controlled by the electro-magnetic energy that surrounds us and lives inside us. This is the same mental/psychic/electromagnetic energy that contains the answers to some of life's most unanswerable questions; explains inexplicable happenings and, generally, provides us with an understanding of things we identify as being "paranormal".

The human being is, clearly, a different creature from all other living organisms on this planet. Other living things can contain mental energy, but to a significantly lesser degree than humans. Dolphins and Orcas are very intelligent…but can they read or write? Can they invent and use vehicles to propel themselves over hostile surfaces? Dogs can be intelligent… but can they cook a meal on a stove for their dinner or compose a sonata for others to listen to and enjoy?

Some animals have physical strength far beyond human strength. The human, however has developed tools, weapons and other means to overcome the superior strength of animals. I've never heard of a tiger or a gorilla capturing a human to be put on display for other tigers or gorillas to see.

Only humans have learned to use their planet for their own benefit; to enjoy the multitude of colors that only they can see.[5]

---

5 Some animals can differentiate bright colors from drab colors, but no other living creature besides the human being can discern the various shades of color and re-create them for their own enjoyment.

There is one other form of energy that seems to come from within all animals: physical energy. Unlike mental or psychic energy, almost all living things have physical energy. But notice how physical energy levels in humans vary with age:

Ever notice how, as children, we seem to be made of physical energy. We play hard and, when we get tired, we sleep well and re-charge our energy batteries. As we get older, our physical energy levels start to decrease and our mental or psychic energy starts to increase. Even at a very young age, most people will probably have started to channel their natural electro-magnetic mental energy into specific fields. Our energy may become directed toward medicine, law, raising a family, sports, sexual activity, artistic pursuits, etc. Then, as we continue to get older and we pass our physical prime, our physical energy level starts to diminish. Notice how older people prefer to sit around socially with a drink or a deck of cards rather than do something that requires physical energy.

Even as physical energy wanes, our psychic energy can be running at full throttle. When our psychic energy begins to wear down because life has become too routine and new, creative thinking has become a thing of the past, mental energy slows down and no longer seems to play a significant part in our lives…and our bodies begin to die.

Of course that's a huge over-simplification, but it does bear the ring of truth. Still, all energy is not "physical" energy. In fact, the essence of an individual's energy emanates from the mind. Mental or psychic energy is the most controversial form of energy and the least understood by science: All creativity and original thought comes from a person's mental or psychic energy.

Apparently, the ancient Greeks understood this. In his concept of "actus et potentia" Aristotle is quoted as saying that mental or psychic energy is the thing powering the operation of the mind, soul or psyche. A recent publication out of Princeton University said that psychic or mental energy is the "actuating force of life itself".

Sigmund Freud, the great Austrian Psychologist, touched on the surface of it with his attempted clarification of the "unconscious" mind being divided into three parts: the id, the ego and the superego. Some of Freud's disciples like Karen Horney and Jung attempted to delve a little deeper into mental energy, but they all only skimmed the surface because they all followed what was a maxim of their day and age: that the mind is part of the brain. Even to this day, there are some scientists trying to locate a portion of the human brain that contains the mind. Their efforts have been in vain.

The truth about the mind being a part of the brain was exploded about fifty years ago when the field of medicine began to wonder why football players and boxers who had their brains damaged by numerous blows to the head were still able to think with the clarity of an uninjured person. The blows often resulted in physical handicaps and speech problems, but their thoughts were still clear and precise. People born with cerebral palsy that incapacitates them physically, are still able to author great books and comprehend intricate chemical formulas. The answer that had been staring science in the face for centuries was that the mind and the brain are two completely separate and distinct things. The brain, like a giant computer, controls the physical actions of the body and the mind is an independent "thing" composed of an electro-magnetic energy.

Many people are physically handicapped or simply cannot readily adapt to physical uses of energy. But all people have mental or psychic energy. Even people with damaged brains or missing limbs or suffering from terminal illness still have very strong mental energy. And, on an individual basis, that's what life is about.

Let's take a closer look at the word "energy". Almost all scientists will agree that life itself is created by energy. Most of those scientists will also agree that energy cannot be destroyed. It can change its form, but it cannot be destroyed. But, if life is energy…and energy cannot be destroyed…What happens to the energy within us and surrounding us when we die?

Scientists and physicists, generally, agree on very few things. It was the concept that energy cannot be created or destroyed that led Albert Einstein to his Theory of Relativity and to his subsequent Space/Time Quantum Theory. The fact is that energy exists everywhere. You can see it come down from the sky in the form of lightning bolts; you can feel it in the air as soon as you step out onto the streets of New York or Tel Aviv…and we can all feel it inside ourselves when we get excited about a new idea.

Energy can change its form (such as the chemical energy of fossil fuels changing from chemical energy to thermal energy when it is burned and may then change into electrical energy), but it cannot be destroyed.

The electro-magnetic energy inside the brains of each of us can and has been measured. Even a damaged brain is full of electrical energy as can be measured on an electroencephalograph. Brain damaged people may not be able to control their physical movements, but they can still think, create and adjust because the electro-magnetic, psychic energy is still there.

Just look at some of the people who were born after their mothers used the drug thalidomide: They were born without arms, legs, no fingers, etc. Yet, the psychic energy level of their brains has allowed them to live lives as full as possible with their physical limitations…and even rationalize their good fortune at being alive.

There is no question that every brain is full of electro-magnetic energy. Doctors measure it regularly using the electroencephalograph. Yet, very little is known about this energy other than the fact that it exists. For some reason, until very recently, medical science has chosen to ignore the fact that there is even a larger electro-magnetic energy field outside of the brain. It has taken many years for science to acknowledge that each of us is surrounded by an electro-magnetic aura that is distinct to every individual. It's almost impossible to measure the energy level of this aura. This electro-magnetic aura is actually outside of the body, so measuring devices that attach to the body are of little use.

Just a hundred years ago, people were amazed when they saw this electromagnetic aura via the use of infra red photography. Now, aura photography is becoming very popular. An aura appears to surround every individual body with a multitude of colors and/or shades of gray. The most colorful auras seem to surround the most colorful, energetic people and the shades of gray surround people who have allowed their psychic energy levels to grow stagnant. Colors can change, but are clearly separate and distinct from one individual to another. Religious pundits have been quick to seize on the concept that the aura is, actually, our immortal soul. If that's what you choose to believe, so be it.

The color of your aura can change from an almost faded gray when you are watching television to a myriad of bright colors when you are writing or drawing something creative or working on an exciting business deal for the future. To the best of my knowledge there has never been a study done to correlate the colors your electro-magnetic aura emanates with the creativity of your mind but it seems to be logical that as your mental energy levels increase, the energy of your aura will also increase and the colors will become more intense.

Where does this lead us? Following a path of common sense, we can reason that if the mind is an electro-magnetic force; if everyone's body is surrounded by an electromagnetic aura, if the mind can remain highly functional even when the brain is damaged...then, as said earlier in this book, we should be able to surmise that the mind is located in the aura... or that the aura and the mind are one and the same.

This is a book about paranormal phenomena. For people trying to understand such unexplained things such as ghosts, and life after death, etc., we can gain tremendous clues from the little that science seems to know about energy. Again, energy cannot die or be destroyed! Therefore, if we, as human beings, are really a manifestation of energy locked into a specific physical human body then, even when the body dies, the energy continues to live. It cannot be destroyed. If that energy or aura is what we call your "mind", then your mind can never be destroyed.

Our bodies can grow old, wither and die like a leaf on a tree. But even the energy within a tree that has lost its leaves continues to produce new leaves every year and reproduces to form new trees. This is nature's course. We see it every day but we don't stop to associate it with our own lives because, as humans, we have developed enormous egos and like to feel that we are above nature's course of life. It is certainly true that the electro-magnetic energy levels of a human far outweighs the psychic energy level of a plant...but we are all creatures of the natural process that surrounds us.

If we look closely at nature's process, we can see how the energy or "life" in a tree works. It continues to live even when the tree appears dead. And, when a tree actually dies because it can no longer sustain its physical body, the energy from that tree goes to its numerous offspring.

Life and life's energy is continuous: Things that are old and worn-out are always replaced with things that are young and new. We can see this everywhere we look; even in the business world.

Now let's look a little closer at the one thing that concerns us most: Human Life:

What happens to this electro-magnetic energy that surrounds the human body (the aura) when someone dies? The body is no longer physically functional. But what about the mind? Assuming that the mind is composed of electro-magnetic energy that cannot be destroyed, then, unlike the physical body, the energy that we call the mind will continue to live.

That simple conclusion, reached through common sense and logic, has been the basis of almost every major religion in history. It has been the primary topic of thousands of books, movies, lectures, etc. What happens to us when we die? Does our spirit really go to Heaven or Hell? Is death simply the "end" of everything? What about people who claim to have past-life memories? How do past lives figure into this equation? What about entire religions based on reincarnation or belief in an immortal soul?

Of course, no one can know "for sure" until they die. But there are clues…lots of them. To understand these clues and follow a path of reason and logic, we must first strip away the facade of religious dogmas and look more closely at the few facts we do have with an objective eye. To do this, you must set your religious beliefs aside for a moment and accept the evidence without chastising yourself for not adhering to the religious dogma you were taught from childhood. Then, you must also strip away the constantly changing theories of science that presume, "When the brain dies, there is nothing more." Just open your mind and let some common sense seep in. Neither religion nor science can tell you with any degree of certainty what happens when you die. So, put yourself in the position of a juror in a courtroom trial: Weigh the evidence presented to you and reach your own conclusion.

With our minds clear of everything we've ever read or heard…or been taught… let's start by looking at some of the things both science and religion agree on:

We do know (and it has been photographed with aura photography) that when a body dies, the electro-magnetic aura that surrounded the body during life stays with the dead body for a short period of time. We don't know the reason for this, but possibly, since the aura is living energy, it is trying to get used to the fact that the body it has surrounded no longer functions. Then the aura moves away. It does not scatter or dissipate, but remains as a single unit. It does not stay confined to the room where the body lies in state, but moves through walls, ceilings, etc. to someplace else. Where? I don't know for sure…but I'm confident that it's not Heaven or Hell; at least not the Heaven or Hell that have been characterized in Sunday School.

So, where does that electro-magnetic aura go? Many people who have alleged (under hypnosis or in psychotherapy) to having memories of "past-lives" often refer to going to the "waiting place" after their past-life body died. According to numerous hypnotherapists, the "waiting place" (purportedly) has been described as someplace where people go after they die and wait to be re-born.

It's very interesting how so many of those claiming past-lives seem to remember their past life's funeral, who attended it, who spoke at the funeral and what was said. For the most part, these past-life memories seem to be amazingly accurate descriptions of the life that (ostensibly) was formerly led. Under hypnosis people have recalled detailed descriptions of the living conditions, names, family members, friends, etc. from their past life.

The question naturally arises "How can we verify any of these past-life claims?" The surprising answer is that hundreds (if not thousands) of them have been verified…some even when challenged by disbelieving, skeptical scientists and news reporters.

Without retelling the story of Shanti Devi (detailed elsewhere in this book), even the most skeptical person would have to ask how an eight-year-old girl could possibly describe the scars on intimate parts of the body of a man she'd never met…but whom she claimed was her husband in a former life. How this same girl could go to a village (in India) where she had never been and lead a bunch of skeptical newspaper reporters and scientists to the house where she claims to have formerly lived with her husband despite the fact that the reporters and scientists accompanying her were intentionally trying to mislead and misdirect her.

The Shanti Devi story is fascinating, and was written about in all of India's newspapers. Had this been the "only" instance of something like this happening It would be easy to set it aside and say that there was some sort of collusion going on to deceive the public. But this is far from the only verified story of reincarnation.

There are hundreds (if not thousands) of similar stories that fulfill the maxim of being "beyond a reasonable doubt". But these stories seldom get the publicity and the notoriety of the Shanti Devi case.

One such case that did receive a lot of publicity was the case of Bridey Murphy. "The Search for Bridey Murphy" was a best-selling book about fifty years ago. Without re-telling the story (it appears elsewhere in this book) a woman living in Wisconsin, who had never been to Ireland, described a past life in Ireland where she said her name was Bridey Murphy. She described her life, her husband and her children in Ireland about 125 years earlier. Of course there was no possible way this could be verified because, 125 years ago, City Halls in Ireland did not keep birth records, marriage and death records for people who did not live in the principal cities. Such history was recorded in a family's Bible, many of which were lost, destroyed and misplaced.

Yet, this woman, who had never left Wisconsin, when recalling a past life, spoke with a heavy Irish brogue, used words long out-of-date and, most impressive, described a journey from Cork to Belfast in a family wagon in such intricate detail as to quash any skeptics.

But there were skeptics (as there will always be skeptics), one of whom actually created a fictitious Irish family in Wisconsin and claimed this family baby-sat for this woman when she was a few months old. The skeptic alleged that this family filled this child's mind with descriptions of old Ireland. My research indicated that this so-called Irish family living in Wisconsin was not real, that they never baby sat for this woman as a child, and was generally, an excuse to give a skeptical newspaper reporter some publicity…which he got.

Bear in mind that reincarnation goes strongly against the religious beliefs of many and some very powerful religious leaders will go to extreme lengths to quell any proof of past lives. It contradicts what their Bible preaches and may make their religious teachings seem dubious, at best. Quite likely, verification of reincarnation would lose many of these religions some of their most fanatic and wealthiest supporters.

So, for just one moment, let's assume that there may be some merit to a claim of living a past life: This instantly begs the question "Why don't we remember our past lives?"

There are many possible answers to this question including, but not limited to, the capacity of the brain, the energy that previous life exuded, the unwillingness of the living to accept that there was a past life, etc. One that seems to be the most logical is that we do remember in spurts and at times, often in strange ways.

When a child is born, its brain is just a mass of undeveloped cells unable to feel, think or store memories. All a baby can do is feel the comfort and warmth of someone near them and distinguish the pain they feel when they are hungry. It seems that as the baby is born, it is immediately surrounded by an electro-magnetic aura although I know of no studies to verify this. We do know that the brain of the baby is still too undeveloped to be able to absorb any communication, or more simply put: the baby cannot think for itself. Whether the aura surrounds the baby at birth or shortly thereafter when the brain cells have started to develop is not important. Aura photography has been done on babies as young as a few months old, and the aura is there.

As the baby starts to grow, the brain begins to accept messages and thoughts, although the ability of the toddler to communicate its thoughts is still not there. Yet toddlers will sometimes see a picture or an object that reminds the toddler of a past life and the toddler may become inexplicably attracted to it or inexplicably fear it. As the toddler grows into a child, it is now capable of limited communication and it is still too young to have the brain cluttered with the problems of life.

This is the time when past lives seem to be remembered the best. The child may discover a make-believe friend who may be described as a child from the past. A young child may have a phobia and fear about water for no seeming reason. Yet, as this child's past life is uncovered we learn that a past life had died by drowning or was on a ship in a war and that ship was sunk. Or, the young child develops an unexplained fear of flying or heights. Or the child has an unexplained fear of a person or a pet. As hypnotherapists and psychologists have discovered, these (and other) seemingly unexplained fears and phobias are most often created by the events of a past life.

The ideal age for remembering a past life is usually between 3 and 5 years of age. The clutter of things trying to fill the memory banks of your individual computer (your brain) has not yet blocked-out the memories of what may have happened before birth, but the memories are fading rapidly. The child is adjusting to its new life. Some memories cling…especially traumatic ones. Children seem to have inexplicable nightmares that are totally unrelated to the life they know.

By the time the child has reached eight or nine years, there is so much input of things they are learning as living people, any past life memories are crowded out of their thinking. But the seemingly inexplicable phobias and fears remain. We seem to remember past lives best when we are children. Those memories appear to become buried as our brains become crowded with the facts of living. Often those memories seem to burst onto the surface when we are meditating, under hypnosis and/or in a good psycho-therapy situation. Buried memories may help to explain why children from a well-to-do family will become thieves or murderers, or even why one identical twin will study law and the other become a music composer.

When the living adult has reached puberty, the constant input of new people, new ideas and new learning have (usually) completely blocked-out memories of past lives. If there was some trauma in a past life, a man may still fear the water, or a woman may still fear men, but the energy within that living person will normally allow them to adjust. They may have unexplained thoughts or dreams, but they can probably live a somewhat normal life.

Let's step back for a moment:

We can state, with reasonable certainty, that when you die, the energy that was you in your lifetime continues to exist. It would seem natural for someone to want to know what it's like to be energy without a body. As I've said before, no one will really know for sure until they die…but we do have a lot of clues.

I've met a significant number of people who have had "astral projection" or "out-of-body" experiences. Usually, these experiences most often happen at unexpected times: when a person is under anesthesia and in surgery; when meditating and/or when hypnotized. Without going into too much detail (there is an entire chapter on Astral Projection in this book) the experience is one where the energy or aura that surrounds a person leaves the body and moves around through walls, ceilings, over oceans, etc.

This, to the best of my knowledge, is what happens when our body dies. Your energy can see (although vision is distorted since you no longer have optic nerves) and it can hear (although you no longer have ear drums). You can communicate by telepathy (you no longer have vocal chords). You do visit and communicate with the energies or auras of loved ones who have died.

This suggestion of what it is like to be physically dead is based on two things:

a) Conversations and interviews with people who have experienced astral projection, and

b) Written reports by people who have died…and come back to life. There are actually medical records of people who were declared dead by their physicians, where the heart and brain levels were completely dead <u>for periods of time exceeding one hour</u> who suddenly came back to life…without any brain damage.

All of these incidents that I have read about said, essentially, the same thing: that they left their bodies and somehow knew that it was not time to do so...and they returned to their bodies. All, without exception, reported that they could see, hear and communicate telepathically.

Now let's take a look at a different question:

Again, assuming our electro-magnetic energy has lived before in another body, it begs the question, "How many previous lives has it had?" "If energy can't be destroyed, will this pattern just continue indefinitely?"

As I said before, no one will really know for sure until they die. To the best of my knowledge, there are no clues. I've had dreams of being another person who lived hundreds of years ago...but I'll never really know whether they were past-life memories or just a fantasy in my dreams. I strongly suspect that they might be snippets from a past life because the energy from my aura appears to be quite strong and the strangest incidents have instigated déjà vu experiences.

The electromagnetic energy that is "you" will always be there...and as long as it is there, it is "You".

Chapter 13

The Truth About Our Bibles

Before this book concludes, it's important that we take a look at some of the inexplicable things we find in the Bible. Unlike the rest of the book, explaining mysterious happenings in the Bible is not, necessarily, a matter of logic and common sense. It relies heavily on what history has survived the years.

The prime purpose of this book is to explain the unexplained, and there is no single place where there are more unexplained phenomena than in the Bible. "Who" or "What" was this invisible God who created the Heavens and the Earth. Did Methuselah really live 900+ years? Were Adam and Eve really the first people on Earth? Was Jonah really swallowed by and spewed up by a giant fish? Did Jesus really walk on water or feed thousands of people from one loaf of bread? This book could go on almost endlessly citing events in the Bible that challenge the rational thinking process of man. The Bible does not offer any logical or common-sense explanations of these and a myriad of other events. Instead, it asks the readers to accept what is written on blind faith; to accept things as unexplained…and that's what this book is about.

Obviously, I was not living when most versions of the Bible were written; I have no possible way of knowing what was going on in the minds of those who wrote the Bibles. Rather, when you look at some of the world's major religions from an historical perspective and apply a little common sense, some of the alleged "miracles" may become reasonable and understandable. Some "miracles", such as the parting of the Red Sea, or Noah's Ark are totally inexplicable except as an act of God or as something created in the imaginations of the Bibles' authors.

Despite references in all Bibles as to having been written by God, in fact all Bibles were written by man…not God. If you are among those who believe the Bibles were written by God…then God Bless you and keep you. You won't want to read how your religion got started.

Please note that the Bible, in all its forms, requires the readers to "believe" and "have faith". Realistically, that's simply another way of saying "We can't explain." This book will make no attempt to discuss "faith" or "belief", but will try to look for common-sense explanations through whatever historical documents have survived the years. Typically, when almost all Clerics, Priests, Rabbis or leaders of any religion are asked to explain things they can't really explain, they rely on the axiom, "God moves in mysterious ways."

We will try to explain as many of the unexplained events in the Bibles as time will allow, but first we must take a giant step: We must look at the Bibles, not as the word of God, but as historical documents. If you are a firm believer in any religion, the historical facts I have researched may offend you, and if you are offended, I apologize. But historical facts, or rather, history as it has survived throughout time, is a matter of record. I cannot change what has been written by those who lived it or recorded what happened. In every case, without exception, recorded history will not be the same as things we were taught in Sunday school. In trying to explain the unexplained, there are bound to be some who will take offense.

Even in this modern world, there are vast numbers of religious fundamentalists who firmly believe that God made the Earth in six days and on the seventh He rested. There are vast numbers of these fundamentalists of several religions who believe that if they strap a bomb on their back and blow themselves up killing several people who have other religious beliefs, that God will reward them in the afterlife.

I have mentioned a few times that the Earth is considered to be a "warring" planet. Most of the wars on this planet have a religious undertone.

For historical facts dating earlier than 500 BC we have no place to search other than the Old Testament, and the facts in the Old Testament hardly qualify as "facts". There was some sort of Biblical history that was written down starting at about 200 BC, but these writings have crumbled to dust with age, and the stories they tell have changed dramatically since their initial writing. Every major religion in the world has met in convention numerous times with its scholars and its most holy men and discussed revisions and changes to the Biblical stories previously written. It was not until the Guttenberg Bible was published in 1455 AD that a single set of Biblical stories was put into print and distributed around the world. After world-wide distribution, it became more difficult to change the characters and the stories in the Bibles, but there have still been hundreds of changes made to the world's Bibles since the fifteenth century.

It is not my intention, in this chapter, to put-down anyone's belief concerning religion. I'm not trying to convince anyone that what he or she believes is not right. In fact, after reading this chapter, if people maintain their unbending faith in their chosen religion....more power to them. It's certainly a mark of unyielding tenacity.

There was a saying when I was in military combat: "There are no atheists in fox-holes." That's a very true statement. I knew of no one in combat...regardless of his religious beliefs who did not look to God to save them...spare them...let them live through the battle...to see their sweetheart/wife again...their children...their parents... Accordingly, I have come to the conclusion that all people, everywhere, believe in God. The God they believe in may not be the same as the one you believe in... but "...a rose by any other name..."

The problem in almost every religion comes from one thing: If you love God differently than that religion tells you to love God...you become the enemy of that religion! Every religion believes that "their way" is the "only" way. Most fundamentalists are willing to kill to defend "their" way. Foolish, isn't it?

The purpose of this chapter is to offer an explanation of some of the inexplicable happenings as written. As I said earlier, the only way this can be done is to look at the formation of the religions through an historical eye. If that history conflicts with your beliefs, so be it. If it reinforces your beliefs, great!

There is a plethora of historical information that we should have, but that we don't have. Probably, the closest thing we have to a written history of primitive man is called The Old Testament. The Greek or Hellenic histories were not written until thousands of years after the events in the Old Testament ostensibly took place.

As a matter of clarification, the Old Testament consists of five books, and the New Testament consists of twenty seven books (actually, there were seventeen additional books called the Apocrypha which were declared unsanctified by the Roman Catholic Church in the mid 17th century and were omitted from the popular, accepted versions of the New Testament).

There are numerous versions of the New Testament available for purchase that include the Apocrypha if you are interested.

THE "TORAH"

All major religions emanate from Judaism. So let's first address Judaism's Bible, The Old Testament or "Torah". The Torah consists of five books, all ostensibly written by the prophet, Moses: "Genesis" "Exodus", "Leviticus", "Numbers" and "Deuteronomy". Moses, supposedly, lived for a hundred and twenty years and wrote these books during his lifetime. Historians tell us that many of the things written about in "Deuteronomy" occurred about four hundred years after Moses' alleged death. So, for openers, the numbers don't add up.

The Old Testament purportedly takes us from the beginnings of man (5,500-odd years ago) until just prior to the alleged arrival of the Messiah.

The problems with the Old Testament are rampant. For starters, we have reasonable estimates that man has been on the Earth for millions of years (Carbon 14 radioisotope dating only goes back about 50,000 years, and we can effectively prove that man has been around that long. The problem is that after about 100,000 years, even bones become nothing but powder.) Granted, without argument, that carbon dating is not precise, but it does give us a general idea of how old something is, and to date, it is the only somewhat reliable tool we've got. The best evidence is that carbon dating is accurate to within several hundred years. It certainly is not going to miss by tens of thousands of years. According to the Old Testament, man has only been on Earth for slightly more than 5,500 years. At the outset, the Old Testament is significantly inaccurate as an historical document.

According to the Old Testament, God created Adam from the dust; turned one of Adam's ribs into Eve, his mate. The Bible is quite clear that these were the only two people on Earth. They had two sons, Cain and Abel. Cain killed Able, leaving Adam and Eve with one son only. *Then the Bible says that Cain went to the land of Canaan where he found himself a wife and lived among other people.*

Where did this wife and other people come from? The Torah goes on and on. Let's simply say that the Book of Genesis leaves a lot to be desired when it comes to historical accuracy.

Yet that's all the historical information we have! While it does not meet my criteria of logic that Moses split the Red Sea apart with his staff, or that Esau had a fight with an Angel, or that King Solomon was the wisest man who ever lived…within the Book of Genesis, however wildly incorrect the time period may be, there must be the seeds of the truth, no matter how distorted in the present day version of the Bible.

Many of the characters in the Old Testament also appear in the Mongolian Bible, in the Dead Sea Scrolls, etc. While the events and time periods involved may have been tampered with significantly, somewhere buried in the embellishment of time, is the truth about our beginnings.

The first writings of any sort that mention biblical characters were called the Dead Sea Scrolls (written about 300-250 BC). They were called the Dead Sea Scrolls because they were discovered in mountain caves that overlook the northern end of the Dead Sea separating Israel and Jordan. There is very little about the Dead Sea Scrolls that is Biblical except that several characters written about in the Old Testament are also mentioned in the Dead Sea Scrolls. Other than some characters, the few stories from these Scrolls bear little resemblance to the stories in the Book of Genesis.

There really is nothing noteworthy that has been garnered from the Dead Sea Scrolls, notwithstanding the fact that the Dead Sea Scrolls are not scrolls at all…they are bits of animal skins and papyrus (one scroll was written on copper) that were originally scrolls, but which have crumbled with age. Putting together the words or even sentences has been a labor far more difficult than had been anticipated by the scholars working on the Dead Sea Scrolls. When two tiny bits of papyrus are stuck together, it is a major problem to separate them without them crumbling into dust. Using moisture of sorts to separate them makes the already barely readable symbols totally unreadable. Put into proper perspective, the Dead Sea Scrolls are not very informative. They are, at best, a lot of guesswork and imagination of those attempting to make sense of them; trying to put the crumbling bits of papyrus together to make whole sentences or thoughts.

Then, too, the scrolls were written in Hebrew, one of the first common languages accepted by humans in the Middle East. This ancient Hebrew only contained a couple of thousand words (Hebrew has since been significantly expanded) and the description of things and events were limited in detail by the ability of the ancient Hebrew words to describe a person and/or an event carefully. The limited numbers of words in the language left a lot unsaid and a lot left open to multiple interpretations.

The problems created by the limited ability of ancient Hebrew to describe things fully, are miniscule when compared to the fact that the Hebrew language has only been used since 1,000 to 600 BC. The Dead Sea Scrolls were written about 300 BC about kings and people that supposedly existed thousands of years before the Hebrew language was formed.

In any language, for at least three thousand years, the stories of the Biblical characters were committed to the memory of the local village historians who, upon request, would relate the facts committed to their memory to others…including their successor village historians who, in turn, would commit them to memory.

Have you ever played the game of "Telephone"? Where a group of ten people agrees to relay a message? You whisper a written message into the ear of the first person on line; he/she whispers it to the second, etc. The message that comes out at the end of line usually bears little resemblance to the initial, written message.

Now let's assume that every forty years, a village historian died and was replaced by a new historian (life spans were much shorter in those days). In a four thousand year period, that means that there were at least 100 historians. It doesn't take too much imagination to figure out what a written message would sound like if it had to be re-whispered through a chain of a hundred people. It would probably be totally unrecognizable as to the initially written message and, in all probability, would be unrecognizable to the first twenty or so people in the chain. Considering that historians were important people, and were duty-bound to remember their history word-for-word, the message would still be significantly different after a hundred exchanges.

Then, too, there is and was war and politics. Politics is not a twenty-first-century phenomenon. Kings, regional leaders, military leaders, religious zealots and politicians of their day had their own agendas that they wanted inserted into their village's history so that their names, their victorious battles and their great deeds would be preserved for posterity.

When one nation conquered another nation, the history was changed to match the victorious nation's history. That's why the biblical histories from even neighboring villages were dramatically different from each other. The biblical stories, generally, deal with many of the same characters although the situations may be quite different from area to area.

Sometimes, however, there is a common thread of a character or an event that we can assume must have been based on the same set of facts. Note that the story of Noah and the great flood is talked about in the Mongolian Bible as well as in the Old Testament. The story is different and the timing is thousands of years apart, but to a careful reader, there is little doubt but that they are talking about the same event.

Although the first scraps of Biblical writings were written about 300 BC (The Dead Sea Scrolls) the first time all the complete stories of the Old Testament were put into written form was in approximately 800 AD; some four thousand years after the fact. In or about 800 AD, for the first time, the characters and the stories could be compared and, for lack of a better term, "made uniform". Actually, four hundred years earlier (approximately 400 AD), some of the stories of the Old Testament were written down, but the first complete compilation of the Old Testament, as stated before, was around 800 AD.

But starting to write down the stories we now get taught in Sunday school, was just the beginning. The content of the stories still differed dramatically. Some stories told of Kings that were great warriors, while other stories, concerning the same Kings, told of how they avoided wars with their wisdom. Something had to be done to make the biblical stories consistent. Starting in about the late 4th century AD, there were numerous religious conferences of Rabbis and Jewish scholars who attempted through logic, belief and negotiation to resolve the major differences in different versions of the Old Testament.

The reason the Jewish leaders felt a compulsion to "get their act together" and have a unified version of their Torah was, primarily, because some of the books of the New Testament had already been reduced to writing, and Christianity, as a force was burgeoning. Jewish leaders became afraid that Judaism would be consumed by Christianity. It became important that the stories upon which the Jewish religion was built be consistent and its word spread throughout the land.

Notwithstanding the efforts of the religious leaders, every Torah (containing the five books of the Old Testament) had to be hand-written on parchment and the writers and scribes made changes and errors in transcribing one copy to another. So much so that by the year 1000 AD, there were several very different versions of the Old Testament written down. They all contained the same basic stories, but the reading of what happened within those stories still had numerous, markedly different, variations. These variations had to be unified because even a one-word change became a challenge for the Rabbis of the world prior to the fifteenth century AD.

That all changed in approximately 1455 AD. The famous Gutenberg Bible (the first printed edition of the Bible) was published. The real importance of this is that for the very first time, it gave a mass distribution to a single set of biblical stories. People everywhere could read the same stories in the Old Testament. There have been innumerable minor changes to the Bible since its initial printing. Nevertheless, the Gutenberg Bible gave the Old Testament its first consistent set of stories.

There may have been other, ancient writings which could have given more credence to the Old Testament or at the very least, filled us in on ancient history, but Fate stepped in and reared its cruel head:

Starting about 500 BC, there were many so-called historical writings by the Greeks and the Phonecians but most writings were really stories of heroic deeds such as Jason and the Argonauts, Hercules, etc. Ostensibly they told of great wars and war stories (Helen of Troy & The Trojan Horse). Tales of things like the great warriors Hector and Achilles, are not to be taken literally, but are strongly revealing of the society that was present between 500 BC and 400 BC. The Greeks had mastered the method of inscribing on metal and stone, and the Phonecians on papyrus and parchment. Assyrians and Sumarians, using cuneiform (an even more basic language than Assyrian), managed to inscribe stories of battles in stone and tell tales of great Kings. Unfortunately, none of these writings told us anything about the creation, and the characters and events that fill the Old Testament.

The importance of this is that by the time the Old Testament ends, the world had begun to recognize the need for historical fact to be documented. Thus the writing of the Dead Sea Scrolls.

It became a routine thing for all Greek and Roman governors to write about the areas they governed, the Kings and the politicians, and about some of the people who had a strong influence in the regions they were governing. Not only was this a way of assuring the governor's place in history, but it gave mankind a written record of the events that took place. Both the Greeks and Romans became firm believers in recording of events. Virtually all of the known historical information from 200 BC through the first few centuries AD came from the Greeks and Romans; the histories written by the governors and their historians; the literature written by Sophocles, Socrates, Homer, Plato, etc.

During the reign of Alexander the Great in Egypt (about 330 BC), Alexander realized the importance of preserving these documents for future generations, and so he built the great Library of Alexander in Alexandria, Egypt. This library housed the original manuscripts for the Old Testament as well as the histories of Rome, Greece and Egypt. It is said that at one time, the Library of Alexander contained more than 700,000 original papyrus and parchment manuscripts. The Greeks and the Romans left their original manuscripts in the Library, but they had copies made that they kept in Athens and Rome.

On or about 50 BC, when Julius Caesar and his Roman legions were conquering Egypt, the Egyptians surrounded a garrison in Alexandria where Caesar and his legions had settled in. It is said the Egyptian troops came by sea to Alexandria and outnumbered Caesar's troops by almost three to one. To counter the larger numbers of Egyptian soldiers, Caesar instructed his men to attack and burn the Egyptian fleet. Some tricky winds took the flames ashore and set Alexandria on fire. The fire completely devoured the Great Library of Alexander, reducing to ashes the history of man. Nothing in the Great Library survived the fire. Fortunately, most of the Greek and Roman manuscripts had been copied and survive today such as the works of Homer and Plato and the histories of Greece and Rome. But if there were any documented histories of the beginnings of civilization written by the Babylonians, Assyrians and the Phoenicians, they were lost forever, and we are now left with the few scraps of facts we can glean from the Old Testament.

Those who ascribe the Old Testament to being the exact word of God are either unaware or in denial as to the making, the formation and the numerous changes that went into the first five books of the Bible. My research indicates that up to the printing of the Gutenberg Bible, there were more than 1,000 changes made to the Old Testament. There have been more than a hundred changes since the first printing of the Old Testament, although most of the changes following the mass printing of the Bible were minor ones.

The Talmud Torah (the so-called Laws of God) consisting of the Mishna, the Hagada and other books of lesser import, is no better when it comes to accuracy or historical reliance: There is a significant portion of the Jewish population who, today, still insists that every word in the Talmud is the word of God. They overlook the fact the first Talmud (after centuries of having been related orally by the village historians) was first written down by hand in the third century AD. It was changed in sufficient extent so that the first consistent version of it (on or about the 10th century AD) had little or nothing in common with the so-called original writings. There were two separate and distinct versions of the Talmud that differed, dramatically, in content: One was written by the Palestinian Jews and there was another, different, Talmud written by the Babylonian Jews. The Babylonian Talmud became the more influential and (eventually) relegated the Palestinian Talmud to history because Babylon was a far wealthier country and, even in the 10th century AD, rank had its privilege. To those who believe the Talmud is the exact words of God, it's a matter of which Talmud or which words of God you accept.

The Talmud, in its strictest sense, is a book of laws, much like the codified laws we have in our current system of jurisprudence. The basic difference was that, because Judaism was a religion and not a government, the laws could not be legislated laws. Therefore to give them credence, the laws written in the Talmud had to be the laws of God. What is not talked about today is the fact that, to a large extent, the laws that appear in the Talmud were legislated by the rabbinical conferences where religious scholars met and decided what it was that God really wanted his people to do and how he wanted them to act. To a significant extent, the rabbinical conferences based their decisions on their interpretations of the stories in the Old Testament…and we know how reliable those stories were.

Creating a set of laws for people to live by is a good thing. Civilization would not be civilized without laws and the means to enforce them. But most laws change with the times: Every year the law makers of each nation and state meet and discuss the changes that are necessary to keep up with the changing times. Unfortunately, the laws of the Talmud, being the laws of God are not changed or updated. Every effort to modernize the Talmud has been met with religious zealots crying that you cannot change one word of the laws of God. Wars have been fought over this, each side believing that they are the true messengers of God. Sad, isn't it?

A couple of hundred years ago, a new Jewish sect was formed called Chasidim (the ultra-religious Jews) whose basic tenet was that the Talmud is the law of God and must be followed to the letter of that law. Remarkably, this sect has grown and is now almost twenty percent of all Jews in the world. The Chasidim are easy to recognize because they wear the same clothing and practice the same traditions that were practiced two hundred years ago when the sect first started. It seemed logical for me to ask a Chasidic Rabbi why they don't follow the dress and customs of 5,000 years ago instead of those they developed two hundred years ago. The response was an angry glare.

The Chasidim are very staunch in their belief that theirs is the only way that life should be lived. In the more religious neighborhoods, the Chasidim will not hesitate to use violence against people who do not accept their beliefs. The Talmud says that the Sabbath should be observed by not working; as it was said that on the seventh day God rested. To the Chasidim, the term "work" includes turning your electric lights on or off, or driving a car, watching TV, etc. In fact, in Chasidic neighborhoods in Jerusalem, if you drive your car through their neighborhood on a Sabbath day, Chasidim have been known to stone your car, block it, pull you out of the car and beat you up for violating the Sabbath. After hundreds of years of being persecuted and the victims of unreasonable bigotry, you would think that the Jews would be the most liberal and tolerant people in the world. But, ultra-religious Jews can barely tolerate those who do not believe as they do. Most Chasidim do not even recognize non-Chasidic Jews as being Jews at all.

In many respects, the actions of ultra religious Jews are little different than the actions of ultra religious Muslims. I believe this to be one of the major causes of our Middle East problems: Neither group seems to understand the meaning of the word "compromise" or the term "live and let live". As it has often been said, "More people have been killed in the name of God than from all other wars throughout history combined!"

It is a sad commentary that there are large groups of people who refuse to allow their brains and culture to advance into the modern world because of religious beliefs. But, as bad as are the Jewish fanatics, in some respects the fanatic followers of Islam and Christianity are even worse.

In the nation of Israel, the Chasidim refuse to pay taxes or serve in the Israeli military service because they claim that the Talmud Torah says the land of Israel may not exist until the Messiah has come. And since they do not accept that Jesus was the Messiah, they claim the Messiah has not yet come. Why does the government of Israel allow this? The name of the game always has been and always will be "politics". The ultra-religious in Israel make up a significant portion of the voting population.

The Middle East is now and always has been a hotbed of religious fanaticism.

THE NEW TESTAMENT

A sister religion to Judaism is Christianity. This religion (and its many, many related religions such as Protestant, Baptist, Catholic, Methodist, Presbyterian, Lutheran, Episcopal, Seventh Day Adventist, Jehovah's Witnesses, Pentecostal, etc., etc., etc.) is based on the belief that a Jewish child, born of Joseph and Mary of Nazareth, and named Yoshua was, in fact, the son of God who had come to this Earth to save the souls of all its people. The Messiah or Savior.

This belief is supported and perpetuated by a series of books called the New Testament. According to the New Testament, Yoshua was a religious leader of such magnitude that his apostles (followers) of which there were twelve principal ones, wrote about the miraculous acts that he performed, the things he said, and how he "moved the masses" of people.

Actually, the New Testament was supposed to be a continuation of the Old Testament. The Book of Malachi (written about 500 BC), concludes the Old Testament with the words "So sayeth the Lord". This was supposed to be the end of the Bible. However, in Isaiah (Chapter 7, verse 14), in the Old Testament, Isaiah states that a Messiah of the Lord will be born on Earth. That chapter specifically says "Behold, a young woman shall conceive and bear a son, and shall call his name Immanuel". Also the Book of Malachi states that the world will be saved on the day of the Lord.

This gave the hope and expectation to a very primitive world for the birth of a son of God on Earth.

The term "young woman" in the Book of Malachi (Old Testament) was, in the fourth century AD, changed into the Greek word "parthenos" which means "virgin". This gave birth to the Virgin Mary story and the story of the Immaculate Conception, which is foundational to all of Christianity. Almost all believe that the Immaculate Conception refers to implanting of the baby Jesus in the womb of Mary. This is totally incorrect!

When the Christian leaders met in Nicea in 326 AD and in three subsequent conventions, they came to the conclusion that in order for the Virgin Mary to bear God's child, she had to be born "without sin". In other words, she (Mary) had to be conceived immaculately in her mother's womb. Therefore the Immaculate Conception refers to the planting of the seed in Mary's mother's womb so that Mary herself, in order to be able to bear God's child, was born of an immaculate mother. Of course, one could argue that in order to bear Mary immaculately, Mary's mother should have been conceived immaculately...ad infinitum.

Kind of stretches credulity, doesn't it? But that's really only the beginning of what is called "The Greatest 'Story' Ever Told".

Don't misunderstand me. This book does not, in any manner whatsoever, mean to imply that the religious zealots of Judaism or Christianity were anything but well intentioned. Changes they made as they wrote the books of the New Testament were intended to strengthen what was then a scattered religion of Christianity, and not for personal gain. No harm or disrespect of anyone's personal beliefs is intended. It's just that being a man of common sense and logic, if the stories and discussions contained in the Old Testament and the New Testament do not comport with what we know of recorded history, then I must research them and find out "why".

The books of the New Testament are significantly less historical than those of the Old Testament and are primarily concerned with what the Savior (Messiah) said and did.

One of the apostles, Paul, had been a Rabbi in a synagogue located on the northern shore of the Sea of Galilee, and it is to Paul that most of the credit for the New Testament goes. The New Testament says that Paul wrote numerous letters extolling the events in Yoshua's brief life span and detailing the miracles performed.

Unfortunately, at that time, parchment was not yet readily available, and papyrus (made from the skin of plants) was quite expensive. Paul did not have the facility to inscribe on metal or stone, so he wrote his letters on that which was available: dried palm leaves and, sometimes, in ink on stones. The durability of both is quite limited, and thus, the original letters of Paul crumbled to dust or were washed away by the rain in a matter of twenty or thirty years. They were re-written, hundreds of years later, by religious scholars who alleged they knew the content of those original letters. This fact alone gives the New Testament a shaky start. On the plus side, there were many histories of the time that documented the travels of Paul, Peter and John and recognized them as significant religious leaders of their day.

Actually there was little, if anything, written about the Jesus Christ with whom we are all familiar until approximately 350 years following Jesus' alleged crucifixion. The stories of the wonderful things done by Jesus that we now read in the Books of Thomas, Matthew, Romans, etc. were re-written hundreds of years later by religious scholars claiming to know the content of the original writings. But there were no original writings remaining for them to have referenced.

The reason is that as Christianity grew with power and popularity about 350 AD, the leaders of Christianity felt they had to back-up the stories they had been telling each other into written form. It's kind of like working backwards, but that's what was done to establish a written recollection of the wonderful and miraculous acts of Yoshua of Nazareth.

The New Testament, before becoming a cannon of 27 books, contained numerous other books that were written and reviewed by the early leaders of the church and discarded. The church leaders preserved only those books they felt supported the claims of their church.

During the ostensible lifetime of Yoshua of Nazareth, there was one man who wrote a detailed history that has survived the centuries. A Roman Governor was sent to govern the region which had been known as Zion or Judea (from which we get the word "Jew"). This land was soon to be renamed Syria Palestina Jordana by the Roman Emperor, Hadrian. That Governor, Pontius Pilate, was an historian as well as being the Roman Governor of that region. Based on his writings, Pilate was a man who wanted to be certain his name would not be forgotten, so he wrote a very prolific, detailed history of his reign as Governor of the Palestina territory.

The interesting thing about the history written by Pilate is that he often speaks of strong religious movements of the time taking place in the region: the squabbling between the Pharisees and the Sadducees; the talk among the religious leaders in the region of the coming of a Messiah; Pilate tells of great religious leaders like John the Baptist, Paul the Rabbi, and Peter the Fisherman, King Herod, and even mentions Mary Magdalene… but not one single word about a Yoshua of Nazareth! Not one word about the Jesus we all know! Not one word about anyone claiming to be or being identified as being the Messiah! Not one word about the man who allegedly "moved the masses". Nor was there any record of an alleged trial concerning a criminal named Barabbas or a public decision to let Barabbas go free and let Yoshua of Nazareth be crucified! Most modern day Christians and all followers of the New Testament allege that Pontius Pilate gave a crowd of onlookers a choice to either have Barabbas or Jesus crucified and the crowd voted that Jesus be impaled on the cross. But Pilate's history mentions nothing about this at all.

In fact, the absence of the name of Jesus or Yoshua of Nazareth in Pilate's history is just the beginning: A search through the Roman and Greek histories reveals nothing of a man called Jesus or Yoshua. I'm not suggesting that, for political reasons, the name of Yoshua or Jesus may not have been removed and the histories altered. That happened a lot. But it does seem strange that no history, anywhere, makes any mention of him until more than 200 years after his death. The first appearance of the name "Jesus" appears in the Roman History of Capernicus (not to be confused with Capernicus the mathematician) dated about 220 AD. Most historians feel the name of Jesus was added more than a hundred years later to lend support to the rise of Christianity in the mid fourth century AD.

Yet of all the major religions of that day, and there were many, only two have survived: Judaism and Christianity. And Christianity is, by far, the more influential and larger of the two.

A natural question that follows is "Why is it that Christianity survived all these years when there seems to be so little from historical documents to give it credence?" There is excellent reason for this. To understand it, we must go back to the reign of the Roman Emperor, Constantine the Great:

Constantine was the child of a military leader and a very loving mother. He was raised by his father during a time when the Greek and Roman Gods were competing for world stature. Actually, the Gods of Greece and Rome were the same, but bore different names. The Greek God Zeus had his Roman equivalent of Jupiter. The Greek Goddess Aphrodite had her Roman equivalent of Venus, the Greek Apollo was the Roman Mercury, etc.

Being raised as a soldier, young Constantine took part in many of his father's battles and by the time he had become a teen-ager, Constantine had killed many men, women and children…which he did not like doing but did it because it was expected of him. Even as young as he was, Constantine was recognized as an outstanding soldier.

Then, as might be expected of a young man fighting in wars, Constantine was wounded and thought that he was going to die. Both Constantine and his father were Sun Worshipers, a religion highly popular in Rome about 300 AD. Constantine was not afraid to die, but he felt very guilty about having slain so many people. So, Constantine asked his father to try and find some religion that would accept him and forgive him for all his sins. His father brought back two people who called themselves Christians. The Christians told Constantine that if he would accept Jesus Christ as the son of God and the Messiah, Constantine's sins would be forgiven and he could go to eternal heaven and peace. This sounded great to young Constantine…but Constantine did not die. He recovered from his wounds. Constantine never forgot the beautiful promise and the gentility of the Christians.

We have to step aside briefly and understand where the name "Christians" came from: There were many religious leaders who had started their followings in the Palestina region. By 200 AD, those followings had now spread around the Mediterranean. The one thing they all had in common was that they believed their leader/originator was the promised Messiah. Greek historians, started referring to each of their leaders as "Jesus Christos"…a Greek term meaning "Holy Savior". Thus the small religious cults were known as "Christians" because they all believed their originator to be the Holy Savior. Accordingly, the leader they worshipped was called Jesus Christos.

When Constatine was young, times were not good for Christians: There were small bands of religious sects calling themselves Christians all throughout Rome and the Middle East. These bands of Christians were few and far between. As a weak minority, they were badly persecuted by the Romans for no other reason than that their religious beliefs were different than the popular religions in Rome.

It's very important to note that the groups of people called Christians were called that because they worshiped a "Jesus Christos". The problem was that the "Holy Savior" or "Jesus Christos" they worshiped was not the same in all cases: Some called Peter the Fisherman their Jesus Christos; some called John the Baptist their Jesus Christos, some called Paul, Thomas, Matthew and others their Jesus Christos. This becomes vitally important in the history of Christianity. More about this later.

Constantine's wounds healed, and he went back into battles. As a young man in his twenties, his leadership abilities as a warrior were recognized, and he was put in charge of several legions of Roman soldiers. As such, in Europe, Constantine won many important battles for the Roman Empire.

A few years later, in recognition of his great victories for Rome, the Roman Legislature awarded the title of "August" to Constantine. Constantine was given the rank of General, and he was given Roman territory to rule. His new title of "August" gave Constantine a lot of power, but it also made him enemies: The then primary emperor of Rome, Maximinus, became quite jealous that this very young Constantine was given the title of "August", and seemed to be rising in power. Maximinus viewed Constantine as a possible future threat for his leadership of Rome.

Rome, at that time was so large and vast that they had several Emperors for different regions of the Empire. The most important part of the empire was around the city of Rome, and Maximinus was the Emperor of that region. Maximinus started to do what he could to belittle Constantine to the Roman Legislature by spreading false stories about Constantine as a way of keeping his own stature high.

Maximinus was also one of the great debauchers of Christians and thought it was great sport to throw them into an arena with hungry lions "to watch the fun". At first, Constantine simply ignored the chiding of Maximinus and concentrated on building his own region on behalf of Rome. However, the berating of Constantine by Maximinus began to take its toll, and many important people in Rome were starting to believe the things Maximinus was saying about Constantine.

Constantine's demands that Maxinimus repudiate the false statements about him were ignored. Constantine was thoroughly revolted by Maximinus' treatment of the gentile and loving Christians. The problem was that Maximinus had the largest and most powerful army in Rome: fully twice as large as Constantine's army.

Constantine had become an excellent military strategist over the course of years. Constantine had no love for Maximinus because of the things Maximinus had said about him and the way Maximinus treated Christians. Constantine felt something had to be done and made the historical decision to lead his army against Maximinus.

To be certain Maximinus knew who he was fighting, and "why", Constantine had his army paint their shields with the symbol of Christianity taught to him by the two Christians he had met: A cross representing the crucifixion of St. Peter.

Constantine, marched on the armies of Maximinus…and soundly defeated them. The abuse of the Christians in Rome was stopped immediately, and Maximinus was exiled. Constantine became one of the two most powerful Emperors in the Roman Empire.

The only other remaining powerful Emperor of the Roman Empire, besides Constantine, was Lucinius. Lucinius had declared himself a pagan and led a life of complete debauchery. If you put the treatment of Christians by Maximinus, on a scale of one to ten (ten being the worst), the treatment of Christians by Lucinius would have been an 11 or 12. Although Lucinius, had a large and powerful army about the same size as Maximinus, he had great respect for the military power of Constantine and his armies. Lucinius promised Constantine that, as a gesture of friendliness and respect, he would stop the debauching and murdering of Christians.

Within a few short years, that would change: Word got back to Constantine that Lucinius was again using Christians for lion food; forcing Christian women and female children to copulate, in public, with horses, donkeys, pigs and other animals that Lucinius and his cohorts found amusing to watch.

Constantine sent messages…and then warnings to Lucinius that were ignored. Constantine made another historic decision:

Again, using the Christian symbols on his soldiers' shields, Constantine and his armies attacked the part of the Roman Empire ruled by Lucinius. Unlike the battle with Maximinus, the battles with Lucinius were long, hard, and extremely bloody…but Constantine emerged victorious, and about 320 AD become the sole important Emperor of the Roman Empire.

With that new power came new problems: Constantine became the target for every assassin and would-be Emperor of Rome. In 325 AD, his own son tried to assassinate Constantine and Constantine was forced to have his own son executed. Constantine decided that he needed to do something:

He came up with the idea that if he could elevate some non-violent group to great power in Rome, then the non-violent group would be "next in line" and attempts to assassinate him would stop. Constantine remembered the gentility of the Christians. Constantine had always been a Sun Worshiper, and had no interest in Christianity except as a way to make his reign more peaceful.

He ordered that the leaders of all groups calling themselves Christians be brought before him. Constantine was dismayed when he learned they each worshipped a different Jesus Christos (Holy Savior). Constantine ordered them to meet in conference in Nicaea and work-out their differences. If they did that, Constantine would make them an extremely powerful force in Rome. If they didn't, Constantine would stop protecting them.

At the 326 AD Nicaea Conference, the Christian leaders could not agree on which of their saviors would become the one and only Jesus Christos; none of them wanted their Jesus Christos to be of lesser stature than anyone else's Jesus Christos. They realized that the alternative to agreement was probable death. They knew their fate hinged upon reaching some sort of accord. So, they all agreed to "create" a new Jesus Christos and to make all of the other Holy Saviors his Apostles. It became vital for them to give this new Jesus Christos a background and a history. Thus was born Joseph, Mary and Yoshua of Nazareth.

At the subsequent conferences in Nicaea, the new Jesus Christ was given a more detailed background and stories of each of his Apostles were identified as witnesses to the holiness of the new Jesus Christ. They gave the new Jesus Christ a birth date that coincided with the Winter Solstice: when days started to grow longer and the world would be reborn for another year. Unfortunately, they based the date of the Winter Solstice on the Julian Calendar that was in common use at the time. But the Julian Calendar was "off" by three days, so the birth date of the new one-and-only savior became December 25th instead of December 22nd.

Numbering of the years was also a major problem since many Kings and Emperors decreed that the year they took the throne would be "Year One" In 1582 A.D., Pope Gregory made an effort to straighten things out:. The Gregorian calendar was more accurate than the Julian calendar. Pope Gregory decreed that "Year One" would be "Anno Domini" (A.D.)...the year of our lord... and everything before that would be "Before Christos" (B.C.) The Gregorian calendar has been accepted by most of the world.

The glorious things each group of Christians had attributed to their former savior, Jesus Christos, were now attributed to the new, one and only, Jesus. They began to write the New Testament. "The Greatest Story Ever Told" and the "Immaculate Conception" were parts of Christianity's new look together with the story of Barabbas and the crucifixion ordered by Pontius Pilate.

And it worked! Christian followers were given great positions in the schools throughout the Roman Empire. Only Christianity was taught and all other religions debunked. Priests of the new Christian Church were given high positions in Roman government. Constantine ordered that any non Christians in Rome would have their taxes trebled, and there was a mad rush of Romans to become Christians.

With all the newly found power, there were bound to be disagreements among the Christian leaders, and a large segment of the Christians broke-off with the others in the City of Rome and called themselves the Papacy. They created their own history of the new, one-and-only, Jesus and his Apostles designating their original Jesus Christos (holy savior) as their first leader: Peter the Fisherman.

Constantine lived a full life and died a natural death.

Please do not interpret what I write to say that Jesus was not the son of God. All I've done is present the historical facts to the best of their existence, in simplified, easy-to-understand form. When it comes to religious beliefs, you must make your own decisions.

THE KORAN

Another sister of Judaism is Islam: This is a religion that follows the teachings of the Prophet, Muhammad. The entire religion of Islam is based on the Koran (Qur'an), the holy book or Bible of Islam.

Born in approximately 571 AD, in Arabia, there was nothing particularly notable about the early life of Muhammad. He made his living as a religious leader preaching about Ishmael and the Kabba Stone. The Kabba Stone was, allegedly given to Abraham by the Archangel Gabriel and taken by Abraham's son, Ishmael to the land of Arabia where Ishmael became a great religious leader. The large black stone is used as the eastern cornerstone of an ancient building in Mecca called the Kabba. The stone, similar in appearance to millions of other black stones found in the neighboring deserts, was considered to be holy.

When Muhammad, an acknowledged user of hashish, was about forty, he allegedly had a vision of the Archangel Gabriel who talked to Muhammad while he slept. Muhammad, while sleeping, starting muttering as if he was talking to Gabriel. His wife felt that what Muhammad was saying was so important that she allegedly transcribed what he said onto some palm leaves.

When Muhammad awakened he confirmed to his wife that he had spoken to the Archangel, Gabriel. There is a great significance to the fact that Muhammad believed he had been spoken to by the Archangel Gabriel. Ever since Ishmael's visit to Arabia, the Archangel Gabriel was considered the holiest of angels.

His first wife (most historians claim Muhhamad had four wives), allegedly, ran to tell the neighbors that her husband had been speaking directly with Gabriel, and crowds started to form whenever Muhammad went to sleep to listen to his mutterings and neighbors would write down what Muhammad said. This became the basis for the Koran.

Clerics in Mecca will tell you (and show you) what they claim is the original Koran written in Muhammad's hand on papyrus.

There are several problems with this:

Most historians agree that both Muhammad and his first wife were illiterate. It would have been extremely difficult for her to write down what Muhammad was saying and even more difficult for him to write the Koran if, as historians claim, they both could not read and write.

Nowhere in any of the Old Testament or old history texts is there any indication of Abraham being given an "enchanted stone" by the Angel Gabriel.

If, however, you recall that in the Book of Genesis one of Abraham's sons (by Hagar) was Ishmael, and Ishmael and Hagar were cast off to the desert by a jealous Sarah (the first wife of Abraham)…and if you further assume that Ishmael learned how to form a religious cult from his father, Abraham, it makes sense that Ishmael could have been the founder of Islam and told people that a black stone he picked up in the desert was given to his father by the Archangel, Gabriel. It would fit that Ishmael may have carried something with him from Abraham's household which he told the simple people of the desert was a gift from the Archangel Gabriel.

It is important to remember that fifteen hundred years ago, the people of the desert were very primitive, mostly illiterate, and mostly nomadic. To be told that one of them talked in a hashish induced sleep may not have been that unusual, but when the talking was believed to be with the most holy Archangel Gabriel, people listened and many believed Muhammed to be a holy man.

Following his initial espousing of the words ostensibly told to him by Gabriel, Muhammad's life took a turn for the worse economically, and things did not go well for him. Muhammad went to the city of Medina where he told anyone who would listen that the Archangel Gabriel had spoken to him. The more he espoused this, the greater was the number of people who began to follow and listen to Muhammad.

Several years after the initial revelation, and while in a hashish induced sleep, Muhammad again began to speak as though he was speaking the words of the Archangel Gabriel. By this time, Muhammad had enough followers that his mutterings were seen as the words of God coming through his lips. Many came to witness and listen to the words he spoke while asleep or under the influence of hashish, and attempted to copy his words down on whatever they could: palm leaves, parchment, rocks, etc. A significant problem is that shorthand was unknown at that time, and attempting to copy down all the words of a person as rapidly as he spoke them was virtually impossible, especially by a people where literacy was the exception rather than the rule. What they did write down was copied and re-copied with the blank spaces being filled in by memory. Often, the words spoken by Muhammad did not make sense and were later rephrased into terms that flowed more smoothly. These writings of Muhammad's words were carved into what we now know as the Koran.

Like the Letters of Paul, palm leaves and cheap parchment do not have a long life. And when they crumbled, believers and followers would attempt to re-write them from memory...or rather, the memory of what they had been told inasmuch as most could not read or write.

In all, Muhammad allegedly had twenty revelations.

Several historians have alleged that Muhammad was a pedophile. It is extremely difficult to look back fifteen hundred years and say what the man's sexual preferences were, but in reading the history of Islam, this much can be confirmed: At the age of fifty, Muhammad married a girl seven years of age. She was eighteen when Muhammad died. It should be made clear that pursuant to Sharia (or Islamic) law, a man is allowed to have four wives. Why, at age fifty, he decided to marry a child may never be known.

Muhammad reportedly died in about 632 AD at age 61. But the first printed version of the Koran was not published until almost a thousand years later, in 1530 AD.

The first printed versions of the Koran differed sharply from each other. Leaders of Islam met in conference and discussed the differences until a negotiated, acceptable, version of the Koran was first published in 1696 AD. The claim of some of today's followers of Islam that the original Koran is preserved in Mecca has about a snowball's chance in Mecca of being true. The handwritten version of the Koran now in Mecca was written not less than five hundred years after the death of Muhammad.

The spread of Islam throughout the Arab world was nothing less than phenomenal, and now boasts over 700,000,000 followers. Unlike the prophets of other religions, the prophet Muhammad was one of their own and not some fanciful character out of Rome or out of the Old Testament. As his success and numbers of followers grew, Muhammad started gaining the support of wealthy Arabs and Arab military leaders. To the wealthy, Muhammad was someone they needed to watch. To the military, Muhammad gave them the reasons they had been seeking to form massive Arabian armies and push into other, more prosperous lands. The historic Arabian Wars were commenced while Muhammad was Arabia's most important leader.

Even today, the followers of Islam are probably the most rabid and fanatic of any major religion. Muslims are required, every day, to bow down towards Mecca and the Kabba Stone. Every year, millions of Muslims trek across the Saudi desert to come within range of the Kabba Stone.

Like in all major religions, there are several books of Islam: The Sumah (traditions), The Ljma (consensus), The Ljihad (individual thought) and The Hadith (collection of Muhammad's sayings).

The Hadith, like the Hebrew Talmud, had two distinct and different versions: The first is the Hadith of the Sunni (the majority) and the other is The Hadith of Shi'ab. Unlike the Hebrew Talmud, one version has never been accepted by Islam and the Sunnis and the Shias are still at war with each other over which version of the Hadith is the holy version.

When Muhammad died, there was a major battle over who should take his place as Arabia's leader. The first claimant was his widow (Muhammad's first wife) and Muhammad's son. The second claimant was a Captain of Muhammad's army. It was finally resolved when the military had Muhammad's widow killed, but the split in Islam between the Shia and the Sunni has lasted through the present.

One additional comment about Islam is worthy of note: Islam has, for centuries, been thought of as a very war-prone religion with little regard for human life. History would tend to bear this out. Few followers of a religion (even the Christian Crusades and the Spanish Inquisition) were ever more barbaric in their wars than those fighting under the banner of Islam. Witness the Mahdi and other Arabian warring factions.

If you read the Koran, the very poetic and beautifully written Koran would seem to preach the absolute opposite of this:

No Bible of any religion has ever preached a more peaceful existence and greater love for his fellow man than does the Koran...with one extremely important exception. The Koran gives people the right to destroy any "infidels". An "infidel" is someone who does not accept Allah as the only God and Muhammad as his only prophet. Muslims have used this exception to murder hundreds of thousands of non-believers. Recently, in Lebanon, Muslims killed approximately 75,000 Christians simply because they were Christian.

Islamic law (called Sharia Law) is interpreted more strictly than any other, and the punishments for violation of these laws are exceptionally severe. Some Islamic countries still believe in burying someone up to their neck in the ground and then stoning them to death for such crimes as adultery. The Jewish Talmud also has its share of violent punishments: A person not observing the Sabbath "shall be smitten", but the ultra religious Jews do not even approach the vengeful retaliation of Islam when it comes to punishment for not strictly adhering to religious Laws.

THE BOOK OF MORMON

A brief mention should be made of the Mormons (Church of Jesus Christ of the Latter Day Saints) because few religions are growing with the pace, the devotion and the wealth of the Mormon Church.

Essentially, the church is one of the many branches of Christianity. It differs from other branches of Christianity because the two primary books that are paramount to the religion (The Book of Mormon and the Book of Revelations) are much more significant than the books of the New or Old Testaments. Both Mormon books were written at a time history was being recorded somewhat accurately. The Mormon belief is that Joseph Smith, a young man from western New York State, was inspired by a Christian revival, where he lived in 1820, to pray to God for guidance as to which church was true. In answer to his prayers he was visited by God the Father and God the Son, two separate beings, who told him to join no church because all the churches at that time were false, and that he, Joseph, would bring forth the true church. This event is called "The First Vision."

In 1823 Joseph had another heavenly visitation, in which an angel named Moroni told him of a sacred history written by ancient Hebrews and other inhabitants of North and South America. Conveniently, Smith was told, the tablets were buried in a nearby hill. The tablets (made of gold) were inscribed in a very strange script that no one could interpret. (Now, Mormon Elders allege the tablets were inscribed in ancient Egyptian). Angels came to help Joseph Smith interpret the inscriptions. These angels became known as the Latter Day Saints (to be differentiated from the Saints in the New Testament). With their help, Smith was able to interpret the inscriptions on those tablets and from them wrote The Book of Mormon.

Allegedly, there were eleven witnesses to the existence and the interpretation of these tablets by Smith. No one knows if or where the tablets are today.

It is a beautiful story and has captivated the hearts and minds of millions. Unfortunately, it does not jibe with historical records:

The "First Vision" story, was unknown until 1838, eighteen years after its alleged occurrence and almost ten years after Smith had begun his missionary efforts. The oldest version of the First Vision is in Smith's own handwriting, dating from about 1832 (eleven years after the event allegedly occurred). It makes little or no sense that, if true, this fantastic "First Vision" would be concealed by a man trying to establish a new church.

In 1828, eight years after he says he had been told by God himself to join no church, Smith applied for membership in a local Methodist church. Other members of Smith's family had joined the Presbyterian Church.

The eleven persons who claimed to have actually seen the gold plates were all very close friends of Smith (many of them related to each other). Their testimonies are printed in the front of every copy of the *Book of Mormon*. But, no disinterested third party was ever allowed to examine or even view the gold plates. Most of those eleven witnesses later abandoned

Smith and left his movement claiming that the so-called gold tablets never existed. Smith then called them "liars."

Contemporaries of Smith consistently described him as something of a confidence man, whose chief source of income was hiring out to local farmers to help them find buried treasure on their farms via the use of folk magic and "seer stones"...the same magic and seer stones he later alleged enabled him to discover the gold tablets, read and interpret their strange language. Smith was actually arrested and tried in 1826 on a charge of "money digging".

Suffice it to say that the historical holes in the Mormon story are large enough to drive an eighteen-wheeler through.

Joseph Smith stood firmly behind his statement that God had pronounced the completed translation of the plates as published in 1830 as being "correct". Yet, many changes have been made in later editions. There were thousands of corrections of poor grammar and awkward wording in the 1830 edition. There have been numerous other changes to reflect subsequent revisions in some of the fundamental doctrines of the church. i.e. An early change in wording modified the 1830 edition's acceptance of the doctrine of the Trinity, thus allowing Smith to introduce his later doctrine of multiple gods. A 1981 change replaced the definition of allowable church members from "white" to "pure," apparently to reflect the change in the Mormon church's stance on the "curse" of the black race.

There are numerous other contradictions between the Book of Mormon and historical facts, as recorded; far too many to list here.

There are many other great religions of the world: Hindu, Confucianism, Buddhism, Zoroastrian, etc., each having its own set of beliefs and each set of beliefs conflicting with the beliefs of other religions. The persecution by the majority religions of the minority religions in every area of the world has been rampant throughout history and continues to this very day; each religion believing that theirs is the "only" right way.

The persecution of the Jews and Muslims by the Christians, the persecution of the Kurds and the Zoroastrians by the Muslims, the persecution of the Hindus by the Zoroastrians, etc. The story goes on endlessly.

But the stories behind each of these religions is much the same. Only the method of practice is different. Each religion was built on the theory and hope that the life we lead here on Earth is so difficult that we shall be granted a reward when life on Earth ends.

When I was just a boy living in New York, there was a man who operated the service elevator in the apartment house where my family lived. I really liked him a lot and he was a confidante and a friend to me. My father and mother were divorced, and it was nice to have an older man in whom I could confide. I once asked him if he believed in heaven and hell. His reply was, "Well, the way I see it, I'm betting two bucks on the nose that I'm going to heaven. It's a sure bet, because if I lose, I'll never know I lost."

If people will stop looking for rewards in the wrong place, they may find out that there *is* an afterlife of sorts (explained earlier in this book), but it is one that no Bible in any recognized religion will acknowledge. Religion has become very big business. Few institutions are wealthier than the Catholic Church in Rome. Almost all religions thrive on hypocrisy: they all seem to want their followers to give or share all their earthly belongings with the church while the people who do the church's work take vows of poverty.

There are more than one hundred different versions of the Bible available for purchase today, each one claiming to be the word of God. Some of these Bibles contradict each other in major ways and others contradict each other in minor ways. It just seems unlikely to me that a God would knowingly contradict Himself.

There are several major religions that I have not written about. The story of Hinduism, Shintoism, Zoroastrianism, Buddhism, and many, many more are basically the same as those I have detailed. All known religions have a very weak pedestal on which to stand. The only possible exception is Deism which alleges that there is a God or Creator, but not one who answers prayers. Make no mistake: I am not anti religion and I am neither an atheist nor an agnostic. I believe in a God…a Creator. It may not be the same God you believe in, but whatever you believe, far be it from me to tell you that you're wrong. I just state the documentable historical facts. You make your own decisions.

Chapter 14

Our World

Where we live is, in actuality, among the most astounding things imaginable. Despite the alleged wisdom of world-renown physicists and astronomers, if you look at the photographs of the Earth taken from outer space…or even the photographs taken of any of the other planets in our solar system, the fact is that we are living on a little ball suspended in the middle of nothingness. Our little ball revolves about a nucleus we call the Sun.

We are fortunate to have an atmosphere around us which not only enables us to breathe deeply and live, but also creates a profusion of colors which make the place absolutely beautiful. As stated elsewhere in this book, we are the only creatures on Earth who can perceive color, its shades and nuances.

If we look through the most powerful of telescopes, we can see billions of other ball-like bodies essentially doing the same thing. It is the "atmosphere" that surrounds the Earth that sets us apart from the other bodies in space. Of course there may be billions of other planets with atmospheres in outer space, but we are not yet capable of seeing them, even through our most powerful of space telescopes. The likelihood of our ever seeing them or even knowing, with any degree of certainty that they really exist is extremely remote. The distances in space are unimaginably vast.

If we look through a super-powered electro-microscope, we can see atoms acting in much the same way. Little electron balls spinning around a nucleus like our sun with a precision accuracy that can and has been measured. Again, nothing visible holds these spinning balls in place.

But whether we look through a microscope, a telescope or just some photographs taken from one of our satellites, everything in inner and outer space is little balls spinning around larger balls, suspended in the middle of nothingness. There is the occasional comet that seems to have no nucleus, but as we have recently discovered, our comets travel in much the same way as do the recently discovered particles called "leptons and quarks". Doesn't that seem at least a little curious?

Our scholarly astronomers and physicists have told you that everything in inner or outer space, including the Earth revolving about our sun… and the tiny electrons revolving about their nucleus…are held in place by "gravity". That's one of those things that scientists tell us that seems acceptable…on the surface. But let's look a little more closely at it:

It is not unreasonable to ask, "Just what is gravity…and how does it work?" The most scholarly of our scientists will tell you that gravity is a "force"; one of the two most powerful forces in the world. Just what it is that creates this force or why it is there will be difficult, if not impossible, for them to explain. Scientists know how gravity works….basically. And, they can anticipate gravity's effects on our daily life…or predict how we can overcome that force in certain instances…but they really don't know what it is…or why it is.

Yet it is an essential key to our very existence. How can we live on a little ball in the middle of nowhere? How come it keeps spinning with incredible precision? Why doesn't the spinning slow down like when you spin a top or a gyroscope? Science will tell you that spinning objects slow down because of friction, and that there is no friction in outer space. But then, science recently had to change its mind when it got into the business of putting up satellites. There is friction in outer space and it does slow down the motion of our satellites. That's why they sink back into our atmosphere and burn up or crash to Earth.

So, how come the spinning of the Earth doesn't slow down? How come its daily rotation is so precise? How come revolving about our sun is so regular that we can anticipate the hours and minutes of daylight or darkness on any given day on any given spot on this planet century after century? What kind of a force is this thing called gravity? And even more important: Why don't we understand it? Why don't our scientists understand it?

When we try and understand it by looking through a telescope, all we can see is that, in our own solar system, every other planet is doing the same thing…but at different rates of speed. When we look through a powerful microscope, we can see that atoms…or rather the electrons spinning about a nucleus, are much like our own solar system. They, too, are little balls, suspended in nothingness, spinning around a nucleus with amazing precision.

Scientists will tell you that it is very difficult to try and learn much about outer space and to see other solar systems even with the Hubble Telescope because everything is so large and vast in outer space. Conversely, scientists will tell you that it is extremely difficult to learn much about inner space because everything is so tiny. We have only recently learned how to visually see an atom because everything is so infinitesimally small. But the similarities of what goes on in inner space and outer space raise the question if the study of one isn't really the study of the other.

One of the most intelligent men I'd ever known, a man named Leo Youdelman, who never graduated high school, told me that through the telescope we are trying to learn about the cosmos….about everything that is everything….but as the Hubble Telescope has revealed, the more we learn about the cosmos, the more we realize that we know less and less about it. The vastness of outer space is incomprehensible.

On the other hand, through the microscope, scientists claim they are learning more and more about the invisible microscopic world…the "nothingness" of inner space. Things so small that a billion electrons can be spinning around their nuclei…on the head of a pin.

Leo Youdelman quickly came to the conclusion that in time, through the telescope, man will know less and less about everything until he knows nothing about everything….and through the microscope we will learn more and more about nothing until we know everything about nothing. Not bad thinking for a man who never graduated high school!

The above metaphor is a little sardonic in its context and should not be taken literally. Generally, the metaphor is true, because the more man learns about the world in which we live, the more we realize that we know less than we had previously thought we knew. Still, each time we learn that we were wrong about something, our knowledge is actually growing.

And so we get back to the fact that everything in inner and outer space is held together by gravity. For lack of an ability to really define what gravity is and how it works, the term "gravity" has become a trash-pot for scientists into which they can dump a lot of unexplained things. But even science's limited knowledge of gravity is frequently incorrect: Scientists tell us that gravitational pull is very predictable: Like a centrifuge, the gravitational pull of the sun (our nucleus) is supposed to keep the planets equidistant from the sun at all times. But as has been revealed in recent years, the orbit of the Earth around the sun…as well as the orbits of other planets…are slightly elliptical (they go further in one direction than in another direction)…not round. The path of comets that we see is extremely elliptical…yet quite predictable. So, even what the scientists think they know…ain't necessarily so!

O.K. We may not know how it is that everything stays in place…how the rotation of the Earth and revolutions about the sun stay so consistently accurate. But surely the great scientific minds of our Earth can tell us what caused it or how it all got started…can't they?

As a child in school, all students of my generation were taught the theory of creation in two separate forms: In religious school, they taught that the world was created in six days and that on the seventh day God rested.

In high school they taught us that our solar system was created when another, larger, star passed close to our own sun. The gravitational pull from the larger star was so strong that it pulled gasses from the Sun. These gases formed into round globules of gas and as they cooled, they became what we now call planets.

This ridiculous scientific theory was not just some passing fad: This was the considered opinion of almost all the world's leading astronomical societies about sixty years ago. The problem with this "scientific" theory was that it left innumerable questions unanswered. For example, if the gravitational pull of the two stars was so strong, why didn't they pull each other together and collide? Even as a high school student, that question was posed to my science teacher…and I was made to serve detention for being disrespectful.

The "passing star" theory was replaced by the "constant state" theory: In simple terms, this is the way things are, this is the way things were, things will never change. Although it didn't explain how it all got started, there is probably a lot of merit to this theory. But, since it didn't wash with what we were thought we learning about outer space, it was quickly abandoned.

Then came the "Big Bang" theory. This theory literally wiped-out the "Constant State" theory because it gave more logical answers to many physical problems and explained some of the newer things we were learning about space...that everything seemed to be moving away from everything else. This was endorsed by virtually all recognized scientists and astronomical societies...until a better theory came along...because there were still too many unanswered questions.

Right now, scientists are talking about the Innumerable Plains of Space Theory and the String Theory. The "Planes" theory, in simple terms, means is that space is on a plane...not a flat plane, but a wavering plane which is separate and distinct from other planes of space. This theory seems to explain many of the things learned through the use of the space telescope, but...you guessed it....it still leaves a lot of questions about space unanswered. The "String Theory" and the "Super String Theory" are so complex that very few highly trained physicists fully understand it. But it does offer good explanations for a lot of things the Big Bang theory could not explain, and opens the door to explaining many of the things we call "paranormal". For example: the String Theory recognizes that there are other dimensions in our universe that we cannot see or feel with our limit of five senses (sight, sound taste, touch and smell). The Super String Theory goes so far as to acknowledge the probability...not possibility...probability of parallel worlds even possibly containing other planets like Earth with life forms like ours. This is not some far-out science-fiction; this is a key part of the science of quantum mechanics!

I don't possess the scientific intelligence to explain the String or Super String Theories in terms people can understand (or that I understand), but what we have learned from the study of "quarks and leptons" (the basic material that makes up all matter) is that the two most important forces in the world are gravity and electromagnetism. The two forces should be about equal, but the gravitational force is significantly weaker than the electromagnetic force and the only explanation for that is if the gravitational force is being shared with one or more parallel universes.

Enough said. It's complicated even writing about it.

So where do we go from here? It should be obvious that our astronomers and physicists are not going to provide us with any real answers...at least not in the foreseeable future.

CREATION – A SCENARIO

So, let's make up our own scenario about how we got here: We'll call it the "Super World Theory". It may not fit the scientists' idea of how a theory should be formulated; it will never pass the test of being provable; most assuredly it will be dismissed by any student of astronomy. It might even gnaw at the roots of religions that accept the six-day concept.

In truth, I can't even say I believe this is the way it happened. It's as plausible as any other theory of creation out there, and strangely, if you think about it, the reasoning behind the "Super World Theory" will set forth some possible answers to a lot of questions that, to date, those same astronomers have not been able to answer.

What I'm going to do is paint a scenario; one that will require a lot of imagination and, in a strange way, make some sense. Remember, this is just a scenario. I'm not asking anyone to believe that things actually happened this way or that it is even possible. And yet....

Turn your imagination on full blast: We know that inner and outer space have extremely similar characteristics. So let's use our imaginations and try to picture what it would be like if it were possible to live on the surface of an electron spinning about a nucleus. Like our Earth, we would be living on a tiny ball circling a sun-type nucleus, suspended by nothing. What we would see in the daytime is the bright nucleus (like our sun) and at night we would see the billions of other atoms within our range of vision reflecting the light of their nuclei (much like the stars). So, effectively, the view you would get living on the surface of an electron would be very much like the view you get living on the surface of the Earth...except that an electron doesn't have an atmosphere. Most atoms have several electrons spinning about their nucleus, so, if someone could actually live on the surface of an electron, he/she would be living in their own miniature solar system...similar to ours. Remember: we are using our imagination.

Hold onto that picture for a moment. Now we will unfold a scenario that scientists will "pooh-pooh". But as the scenario unfolds, you may find certain things making a lot more sense than the constantly changing "certainties" expounded by science. As we go through it, it will answer a lot of questions, which, through this writing, remain unanswered. It won't answer "all" the questions, but it may provide more than a few answers we don't have right now.

Just imagine that you lived on a highly advanced planet, much like our Earth with its own solar system and galaxy, etc. Only in this world, science had advanced far beyond the science that we know today. Let's imagine that on this "superior" world which, in some respects like our own Earth, the world had its problems, its greed and its politics. Let's further suppose that some brilliant scientist felt he had the know-how to create a more perfect world...a miniature world...perhaps on an atom under his far superior microscope. Of course it would take a mind incomprehensibly more brilliant than any on earth to be able to select or create a world similar in many ways to the world in which this brilliant mind lived, and put it all on a microscopic atom.

There would be several problems that would have to be surmounted: When you look at the stars, the farther away an object is, the more slowly it appears to move although, in fact, it is moving at incredible speed. The stars seem to be in the same place night after night, year after year, century after century, although they may be moving at trillions of miles per hour.

The distances in space are incomprehensible; the movement is faster than anything we can measure...and yet, to the naked eye, they appear to stand still enough to be used for navigation.

The opposite is true when you look through the microscope: the smaller the object is, the faster it seems to move. For example, an electron may be moving around its nucleus at about 250 revolutions per second. Of course, if you happened to live on the surface of that electron it wouldn't seem that way: If someone could be living on the surface of that electron, to that person each rotation it would make would be like a full day and each revolution about the atom's nucleus (sun) would be a full year...just like it is here on Earth. In this example, since our electron makes 250 revolutions per second about its nucleus as viewed by someone looking at it through a microscope, to someone living on the surface of that electron, 250 years would pass in what the superior world would measure as one second of their time.

It sounds a little complicated, but it really makes logical sense. As Albert Einstein tried to explain, time is relative and can only be measured by where you are. On the superior world, the time was one second. On the microscopic electron, the time was 250 years.

This would create a major problem for our scientist on the superior world: For this brilliant scientist to do anything with an electron revolving about its nucleus at 250 revolutions per second, he would either have to figure out a way to slow down the speed of the microscopic world to match the speed of the superior world...or increase his own speed to match that of the microscopic world. That's about the only way, the brilliant mind on the larger world would be able to observe and perhaps work to make changes happen in the smaller world.

Is that possible? Certainly not on the basis of any science we know of. But again, I'm asking you only to "imagine"....to suppose that, in a world in which science was so superior to our own science, that this type of thing might be possible. Physically, it would be against every law of physics we know. But let's forget about the idea of this scientist being able to actually slow down the pace of this electron to match the time in his own world, or physically trying to accelerate himself to match the speed of the electron.

Instead, let's imagine that this super-intelligent scientist living in a highly advanced world had developed a way to increase the speed of his own thought process to a point where his thoughts could match the speed of that little electron...as if he were living on it. His thoughts could match the speed of that electron though, physically and in reality, the scientist was still living in his own world. Perhaps, as a slightly more plausible thought, he could "release" his own thoughts at a speed equal to that of the little electron. That way, he could see and think as if he was living on that electron. And he could actually visualize things as if he was living on the surface of that electron. Of course he couldn't possibly move his physical body to that atom...just his thoughts.

And so this super scientist accelerated or released his thoughts and visited that electron. In talking about his "thoughts", I mean a kind of free-floating aura of thought.

What he saw was nothingness…black and void. But he wanted to create a world much like his own…except he would make this new, miniature, world perfect. So his thoughts returned to his laboratory, and he isolated that atom and selected one of its electrons for his experiment. Using his vast scientific knowledge, he heated that electron so that its core would be molten and hot. Then, the next day he went back to visit his electron again to see what affect the heating of its core had done. Only one day had passed in this scientist's life, but in that day, millions of revolutions had taken place on that electron (revolving 250 times per second around its sun) so, on the surface of that electron, millions of years had passed.

What the scientist saw when he sent his thoughts or aura back to that electron was that the warmth he had given the electron formed into moisture and gasses and that an atmosphere was forming; that some of the moisture had vaporized and risen into a sky now becoming colored by the gasses. He was very pleased.

When he sent his thoughts/aura back to his electron the next day (millions of electron years later), he noted that the sky had become colored and marked with clouds of water vapor and the bright nucleus about which the electron revolved had brought some external light and warmth to the surface of this electron.

Of very important note was that he could see the beginnings of life… mostly in the areas filled by moisture.

Using his technique of thought-acceleration, visits to his special electron became more than routine to the scientist. He was creating a new world under his microscope…and he would make it a perfect world. But our scientist faced another problem: He could send his thoughts to the electron, but how could he make his thoughts known to the creatures that were beginning to inhabit that electron? Anything he did to the electron would have to be done in his world, because he could not physically take himself to the microscopic world. He would have to find a way of making his thoughts known on the electron in order to, perhaps, influence its development. But that would come later, first he had to observe the electron's growth and development.

Our scientist's thoughts/aura went back regularly to that electron. He watched as every few million years went by how life was progressing. How, because of the moisture created by the hot, molten center, cold Polar Regions had developed at the tips of the surface of the electron, but that the central portion of the electron was hot and steamy. He was becoming concerned, that the strongest growth of life was reptilian and not homosapien in nature. He could allow for creatures of all types to develop in his perfect world, but if he was going to make this into a perfect world, it would have to be inhabited with creatures like himself, in his own image, and the growth of the reptilian monsters would never allow a homosapien species to survive.

Our scientist concluded that to slow down the growth of the reptiles and promote the growth of homosapien life, he would have to cool down the surface of the electron at its warmest points. The hot, moist surface was just right for reptiles, but not for people in his own image. But how to do it?

Nature or evolution stepped in and took a hand. The Polar Regions had become so heavy with ice, that the electron began to tilt. Its axis shifted and the Polar Regions rotated into the warmer area and the warmer areas became the poles. Over a few hundred millenniums the reptilian population, which needed the warm, moist climate to survive would freeze, and the melting ice at the equator would cool down the equatorial regions …giving homosapien life a chance to develop.

A day later, our superior world scientist saw that the shifting of the axis of the electron was having a desired effect: The reptiles were dying out and homosapiens were developing. Even more, he noted that the melting ice at the equatorial regions was receding toward the poles and left beautiful mountains and lakes in its path as the ice retreated.

A day later, our super scientist returned and noted that the reptilian population had become virtually extinct and the homosapiens and other primates had become the leading creatures on the electron. They were still far too primitive for the scientist to attempt communication. They did have a larger brain than most of the other creatures on Earth, but like most other creatures, they lived by instinct alone. But the next time the scientist revisited his electron with his thoughts, he found that the homosapiens species had advanced significantly and was learning to communicate by speech…even though language was very limited, there was definite communication.

For our superior world scientist, the time was right. Our scientist tried another vastly new technology: Using a new, improved version of his thought-acceleration process, our scientist noted that the developing homosapiens had learned to communicate by using simple words and language. The language was very basic, and there was no single language used everywhere, but by observations, the scientist quickly figured out the simple language being spoken on one part of the surface of the electron. Now he could actually understand the growth of the brains in these creatures. Our scientist had to try and communicate with them. His ego demanded that he tell these developing homosapiens that he was their creator and that everything they had was his doing. The problem was that while he could bring his thought process or aura to the electron, he could never physically visit the electron. Using his improved thought-acceleration technique, he tried a new, idea: He would have his thought process or aura surround an individual in the area of that individual's brain, and he would try to feed thoughts…his thoughts…into it. He tried, unsuccessfully, numerous times…and then, because he was a brilliant super scientist, he finally succeeded! He found a way to allow his thoughts or aura to feed the undeveloped brain of a young, male homosapien who would hear, whatever the primitive brain could absorb, in his own voice…as if there was a voice inside his head. Not all of our super scientist's thoughts…because the super scientist's thoughts were far too complex and detailed for the homsapien's brain to comprehend everything. Just a few basic, simple thoughts which the undeveloped brain might be able to comprehend.

Our super scientist explained to the young man that he was a scientist in another world or dimension and had created this world from an electron that was black and void and that it had only taken him six days to do it; how he had created an atmosphere and let the light of the nucleus shine through; how he had selected a type of life similar to his own…more or less in his own image, etc. Of course, the brain of the young man into whom these thoughts were transmitted, was far too primitive to absorb everything the scientist was communicating to him. In fact the brain of this primitive man could only compute very few of the millions of thoughts being attempted by our superior world scientist. All the primitive man could comprehend was that some invisible being had visited him in his head and told him about the creation of the world. To a primitive man, that must be a God...a God powerful enough to have created the entire world in just six days.

Sound vaguely familiar?

O.K. All the foregoing was a make-believe scenario. A bit of wild imagination. Could it really be possible?

In the sense that "anything is possible", it could be possible. More important, although this was a story for your imagination, if there was even the slightest possibility of it being true it would tend to answer a lot more questions than do the ancient histories of the Old Testament or even our great scientific minds of today. Is it true? Probably not! But let's first look at some of the more outlandish things in that scenario and see if they are really so outlandish:

The first and the biggest single problem with the scenario is how can the thoughts of someone become so accelerated or released as to become in sync with an electron revolving about its nucleus at 250 revolutions per second? Solve that problem, and the rest of the scenario becomes much more plausible.

The fact is that we already know that thought process can be accelerated and become free-floating. We've seen lots of verified examples of this throughout the book. For the moment, let's offer a simple demonstration to show that thoughts can be accelerated far beyond what we probably imagined...and most human beings not only have this ability, but have experienced it!

How many times have you been asleep and had a dream: In that dream, days, weeks or even months may have passed with incredible detail of the adventure you may be having in that dream....the people in that dream can be seen with detailed clarity...then you awake to find that only a few seconds or a minute has gone by.

So thought acceleration, clearly, is possible. But can thoughts be accelerated to the point that they could get into sync with an atom? Obviously, even our rocket scientists can't answer that with any credibility.

Notwithstanding that, thought acceleration or, perhaps, a better term would be the "speed of thought" is possible, and is only limited by the capacity of our brains to transmit, receive and compute the data arriving in an accelerated form. How we harness or control this ability of thought acceleration is quite another problem, but it certainly is not beyond the realm of possibility. Nothing...not even light, can travel as rapidly as thought.

As humans our egos run rampant with the concept that our brains are the most highly developed and capable brains that exist. That's true, here on Earth. But in a superior world, people could have brains many times more developed and capable; capable enough to receive, transmit and compute millions of times faster than we, on Earth, can do.

Another, more complex, problem with the scenario is the ability to understand the relativity of time: For the moment, suffice it to say that our limited scientific capabilities here on Earth have demonstrated that, in accordance with Einstein's Theory of Relativity, the time/relativity factor in the scenario is not out of line at all. An electron revolving about its nucleus at 250 revolutions per second would make almost 22 million revolutions in a 24 hour day on our superior world...assuming our superior world had a twenty-four hour clock, which is highly doubtful. Conversely, approximately 22,000,000 years would pass on that electron to one day on a 24-hour superior world. We have no way of knowing how many hours it takes to complete one day on that superior world. For our scenario, however, we assumed the superior world also uses a 24-hour clock.

It is important to remember that in our scenario we are dealing with "thought process" and not actual physical process. While we know that thought process can be accelerated, there have been few, if any books (other than science fiction novels) about any experimentation that says we could physically move ourselves from one world to another. Perhaps a more descriptive phrase would be move from one "dimension" to another.

But there is some evidence that our minds can do so. I'm not saying that physical transportation is impossible, but merely, that as of yet, we have no way of doing it.

Let's take a moment to clarify what a "dimension" is. A dimension is another existence or world from which there is little or no possibility of contact. According to the Super String Theory, this other world is separated from us by an invisible fabric of space and time.

Thought process is a function of the "mind", not to be confused with the "brain" (which is physical process). As we have repeated throughout this book, the location of the mind is not, necessarily, in the brain.

This brings us to another page in our hypothetical creation scenario:

Let's imagine that our super world scientist actually did find a way to send his thoughts to an electron and observe its development. I'm not suggesting that this really happened, but only that I want you to imagine it happening.

Now take careful note of what he did with our hypothetical "Adam" when our super scientist surrounded Adam with his aura and told him that the world was created in six days:

Our super scientist was so successful with his thought acceleration, he likely told other scientists and all his friends about it. Like any new phenomenon, his friends wanted to try it…and they did!

Is this where our electromagnetic aura originates? Are each of us surrounded by the thought auras of someone from a super world? We know that our auras try to feed us information…and we also know the capabilities of our brains is far too inadequate to absorb even a fraction of it.

This concept is quite far-out, and I'm not saying that it is "so". But, if there were any factual basis for it, it would make far more sense than any of science's theories that are out there.

One final thought before we close this chapter:

Understanding the time and distance factors that were an important part of our scenario, may be a little difficult: No one can really explain Einstein's theory of relativity in a few paragraphs, but let's give it a shot. Granted it will be an over-simplification, but it is important that the reader have a basic understanding of it in order to further remove any lingering doubts about the creation scenario being a possibility, even an unlikely possibility. The fact is that it may be a lot closer to the truth than we would like to admit:

Albert Einstein, brilliant man that he was, conceived the idea that time is "relative". That is, time to someone living here on Earth is one thing. To someone living on another planet it might be totally different. To a space traveler or to someone in outer (or inner) space, time may be totally different than it would be to anyone living on Earth or another planet.

As a simple example: If you lived on the planet Jupiter, one year would be the same as 11.9 years on Earth because it takes Jupiter 11.9 Earth years to complete one revolution about the sun. A day on Jupiter (including night) would be measured as 9.9 hours on Earth because that's how long it takes for Jupiter to make one complete rotation. In other words, on Jupiter, a year is almost twelve times longer than a year on Earth, but a day on Jupiter is less than half of what a day would be on the Earth. If you were a space traveler going from Earth to Jupiter (or vice versa), your internal clock would have to adjust: hours, days, weeks months and years would be completely different on Jupiter than they are here on Earth.

Without going into the theories concerning $e=mc^2$ or the speed of light (which are not readily understood by many) the above gives a simple example of the relativity of time.

Einstein also said that distance is relative. Ask yourself: "How fast are you really moving when you drive down the freeway at 60 miles per hour?" Well, of course, as we measure it here on Earth, you're travelling at 60 miles per hour! But the Earth is rotating at approximately 1,000 miles per hour…and the Earth is revolving about our Sun at approximately 300,000 miles per hour…and our Sun is on one of the tails of a galaxy known as the Milky Way and is revolving about its nucleus at several billion miles per hour…and the nucleus of the galaxy is moving….Get the idea?

So, how fast are you really moving? You might try and add all the numbers (if we knew what they were), but the fact is that you may be travelling north on the freeway, the Earth may be rotating to the west, and revolving in a southeasterly direction, etc.

In fact, we must conclude that distance, as well as time, is relative.

The above having been said, we should take another moment to think about our little scenario. It is kind of a far-out theory. But if you really think about it, it's a lot less far-out than the theories that science has dictated to us. There may not be any proof that the scenario is really "the way it happened", but there is no proof for any of science's theories about the way things started, either.

In fact, the more we think about our little scenario, the more we have to admit that it *is* an interesting thought just pregnant with many possibilities.

The whole idea of this little scenario is not to conclude that we are just an atom in someone's microscope. It was merely to show that there are other possibilities as to how the Earth was created and to open up your imagination. If you've got some other ideas, I'll be glad to read about them.

I'd love to know what exists in other dimensions, and I believe my aura will still be around if we finally figure out a way to go from dimension to dimension. Remember, we have an incredible advantage: If we are just a speck in some superior world's microscope, every single day that passes for them is millions of years passing for us. We have reached a point of development where we can now conceive of the existence of that superior world. Certainly, the computer/brains with which we have been provided are far superior to those of a few million years ago.

Following this thought through to its logical conclusion, it is probable to assume that in a few million more years, our brains will have significantly greater capacity, function many times faster, and will have a better understanding of other dimensions. We will continue to learn and improve because only one day passes in the superior world to several million of our years. It is to be expected that if we were created in the image of the people on the superior world, we will equal and surpass their levels of intelligence, achievement and capacity. If they could figure out a way to visit our dimension, maybe we can figure out a way to visit theirs.

EPILOGUE

Well, that's the story and those are the answers. We have covered only a small percentage of the unexplained, but by now, you should know the formula, and it should be easier to apply it to any number of other unexplained phenomena.

Some readers may feel that the explanations given in this book are pretty "far- out"…but, in fact, they are significantly less "far-out" than most of the explanations science has offered us. If you take the time to really think about it, the theories and explanations offered in this book are quite logical and make a lot more sense.

This does not preclude you (or anyone else) from coming up with other ideas that may make sense. The thing that makes the theories offered here so strong is the fact that they can be applied to a myriad of unexplained things. See if you can come up with a better formula that can be applied so well to so many different unexplained things. I'm not suggesting that you can't come up with one…but I'll bet that if you do it will be a lot more "far-out" than the explanations I have provided.

As has been said throughout this book, coming up with explanations that explain the unexplained is extremely difficult, because there is no solid proof. Of course there is no solid proof for some of the explanations in school textbooks, either. And, in fact, some of those textbook explanations defy common sense and logic. i.e. another star coming close to our sun and pulled out gasses that cooled and became planets; the concept that a virgin mother gave birth to a daughter who, as a virgin, gave birth to the son of God; that millions of people are lying about having seen flying saucers.

When you come right down to it, although the theories expounded in this book may not be provable, they are certainly not irrational. Common sense and logic give this book's theories a solid foundation.

The reason should be self-evident:

This book has taken a common sense look at the unexplained experiences and phenomena that I, personally, have experienced and that millions of other people have experienced. I have tried to make sense of them. Hopefully the book did its job.

I am a firm believer that all people have a duty to help their fellow humans to understand the world in which they live. When something completely inexplicable happens, it becomes an obligation to seek a rational explanation for it…or, if you can't find an explanation, to think logically about what could have caused the phenomenon. Most of the time, given a chance, your aura will help you.

Many of you have had similar precognitive and retrocognative experiences of your own. Some of you may have seen flying saucers in a different way than I have written about. Some of you may have had experiences with ghosts. I'm certain many of you have brothers or sisters who are totally different than the environment in which they were raised. If so, I'd like you to tell me about it.

As for religious beliefs, I apologize to any of you who have been offended by my pointing out the inconsistencies between your Bible and recorded history, and hope you will continue on whatever path you have chosen. When history (what there is of it) conflicts with your beliefs, stick with what you believe.

To those of you who have taken the time to wade through this book, I hope this book has been enlightening. I'd like to hear from you if you have experienced any of the things talked about here because my research is far from being finished. Something you may have experienced may open new doors and vistas in explaining the unexplained.

If you've had some interesting experiences with the paranormal, please write to me via e-mail at stebrel@aol.com and share them with me.

Stephen Ellis

ABOUT THE AUTHOR

Stephen Ellis is currently serving his fourth four-year term of office as a Probate Referee for the Superior Court of California. He currently holds the following higher education degrees:

B.A. - Long Island University
M.A. - Long Island University
J.D. - Blackstone Law School

Ellis has written columns for numerous newspapers including, without limitation, The Daily News (Los Angeles) "One Teacher's Voice"; The Herald Tribune (Los Angeles) "The Ellis Commentary"; The Daily Observer (Los Angeles) "It Just Ain't So". His articles have appeared in newspapers in California, New York, Ft. Lauderdale and Miami. His writings appeared regularly in Air Fare Magazine.

For many years, Ellis was a teacher in the Los Angeles and Beverly Hills Unified School Districts where he taught mathematics, science and law.

As an adjunct to his primary profession, Ellis became an entrepreneur in the business of buying businesses. He would buy businesses in economic troubles, fix them up, and resell them. He has been successful in the real estate business building and owing such hotels as The Dream Inn in Santa Cruz, California, briefly owning the lease on San Francisco's Mark

Hopkins Hotel and being financially involved in hotels in Las Vegas and Honolulu.

In the early 1970s, Ellis formed Los Angeles Helicopter Airlines, one of the more financially successful commuter airlines in the USA. LAHA was a scheduled airline offering service to and from LAX to several points throughout the Los Angeles area.

In recognition of his financial accomplishments, Ellis was appointed to the California Economic Advisory Committee for President John F. Kennedy, and served as an economic advisor to Mayor Sam Yorty of Los Angeles. Ellis, presently, is the president of the Los Angeles Professional Club.

BIBLIOGRAPHY

ABC News
   Could a Little Boy be Proof of Reincarnation (James Leninger)
American Society for Psychical Research
   Interpreting Aura Colors
American Journal of Hypno Therapy
   The Reincarnation of James, The Submarine Man
The Aura Experts.com
   The Meaning of Aura Colors
Austin, James H.
   Zen and the Brain
Baker, G.P
   The Age of Constantine the Great
Battino, Rubin
   Ericksonian Approaches
Bernstein, Morey
   The Search for Bridey Murphy
Best Meditation Techniques.com
   Meditation Techniques
Binder, Betty
   Discovering Your Past Lives and Other Dimensions
Blair, Forbes Robbins
   Instant Self Hypnosis
Browning, Norma
   The Psychic World of Peter Hurkos

Chalko, Tom J.
Workshop Notes on the Human Aura
Duke University Office of News & Communications
Parapsychology Testing
Einstein, Albert
Special Theory of Relativity (1905),
Relativity (English translations, 1920 and 1950),
General Theory of Relativity (1916),
Investigations on Theory of Brownian Movement (1926),
The Evolution of Physics (1938).
Elman, Dave
Hypnotherapy
Encyclopedia Brittanica
The Immaculate Conception
The Birth of Christ
The Creation of Christianity
Constantine the Great
The 326 AD Conference in Naecea
The Guttenberg Bible
Changes to the Holy Scriptures
Encyclopedia Wikopedia.com
Constantine
Quer'an
Fox, Oliver
Astral Projection (a record of verified cases)
Freud, Sigmund
The Ego and the Id
Interpretation of Dreams
Introduction to Psychoanalysis
Garrett, Eileen
Adventures in the Super Normal
Awareness
Greer, John Michael
The UFO Phenoemnon
Hall, Edward T.
The Dance of Life (the dimensions of time)
Hamond, Dr. Cordon
Handbook of Hypnotic Suggestions and Metaphors

Higley, Dennis and Rauni
The Truth About Mormonism
Holzer, Hans
Ghosts
Horney, Karen
Theory of Neurosis
Neo Freudianism
Hothersall, David
A History of Psychology – The Gestalt Effect
Hurkos, Peter
Psychic
I Have Many Lives
Jung, Carl G.
Dreams
Memories-Dreams-Reflections
Kurtz, Paul
A Skeptics Handbook of Parapsychology
Leninger, Bruce
Soul Survivor
Lewis, Thomas M.
The Medicine Men
Lexorian.com
Lexorian Encyclopedia -Koran
Lindgren, C. E.
Capturing the Aura; Integrating Science, Technology & Metaphysics
Lipton, Bruce H.
The Biology of Belief
Lönnerstrand, Sture
I Have Lived Before (the true story of Shanti Devi)
McAfee, John
The Fabric of Self
Milligan, Ira
Understanding the Dreams You Dream
Mitchell, Edgar
Psychic Explorations (a challenge for science)
Mock, Geoffrey
Synchronicity at Duke
Monroc, Robert
Journeys Out of the Body

The Mormon Church
  Book of Mormon
  Book of Revelations
Morris, Mark
  The Ghost Next Door
Muldoon, Sylvan
  The Projection of the Astral Body
Naparstey, Bellerinth
  Your Sixth Sense
The New Testament
  Matthew
  Mark
  Luke
  1 &2 Peter
  Apocrypha
Newton, Michael
  Journey of Souls (The life between lives)
  Destiny of Souls (Case histories)
The Old Testament
  Book of Ezekiel
  Book of Malachi
  The Story of Abraham
Packham, Richard
  To Those Investigating Mormonism
Pilate, Pontius
  The Administration of Judaea
Plato
  Republic
  Sophist
Polchinsky, Joseph
  The String Theory
Powell, Diane H.
  The ESP Energies (the case for psychic phenomena)
Princeton University Press
  Super String Theory (several different dates)
The Quer'an
  The Holy Book of Islam

Radin, Dean A.
  Entangled Minds (Extra-sensory experience in a quantum reality)
  The Conscious Universe
Randi, James
  The Faith Healers
Roberts, Nancy
  Haunted Houses
St. James, Jewelle
  My Reincarnation from Auschwitz
Schmeidler, G. R.
  Separating the Sheep from the Goats (Am. Journal of Psychic Research)
Schmicker, Michael
  Best Evidence
Shroder, Thomas
  Scientific Evidence for Past Lives
TheSilkenTouch@blogspot.com
  Silken Touch Blog –The Before Mommy
Smith, Joseph
  Joseph Smith – History
Steiger, Brad
  Real Ghosts, Restless Spirits and Haunted Places
Tingsley, Katherine
  Psychometry, Clairvoyance and Thought Transference
Thibodeau, Laura
  Natural Born Intuition
USA Weekend
  I Never Believed in Ghosts Until…(a compilation by USA Today)
Vallee, Jacques
  Dimensions (a casebook)
Van Buren, Elizabeth
  Refuge of the Apocalypse (doorways to other dimensions)
Wilson, Clifford
  UFOs and Their Mission Impossible
Wolfson, Michael
  The Origin and Evolution of the Solar System
Zammit , Victor
  Book 24 (proof of reincarnation)